The Journey
Toward God

The Journey Toward God

IN THE FOOTSTEPS OF THE GREAT SPIRITUAL WRITERS—
CATHOLIC, PROTESTANT AND ORTHODOX

Fr. Benedict J. Groeschel, C.F.R.
with Kevin Perrotta

CHARIS

SERVANT PUBLICATIONS
ANN ARBOR, MICHIGAN

Charis Books is an imprint of Servant Publications especially designed to serve Roman Catholics.

All Scripture quotations in the author's text introducing each section are taken from the Revised Standard Version of the Bible, © 1946, 1952, 1971, by the Division of Christian Education of the National Council of Churches of Christ in the USA. Used by permission.

Servant Publications
P.O. Box 8617
Ann Arbor, MI 48107

Cover design: Michael Andaloro
Cover illustrations: "The Journey to Emmaus" from Scala/Art Resource, NY. Script background from PhotoDisc. Used by permission.

00 01 02 03 10 9 8 7 6 5 4 3 2 1

Printed in the United States of America
ISBN 1-56955-149-1

LIBRARY OF CONGRESS CATALOGING-IN-PUBLICATION DATA

Groeschel, Benedict J.
    The journey toward God : in the footsteps of the great spiritual writers : Catholic, Orthodox,
    and Protestant / Benedict J. Groeschel and Kevin Perrotta.
        p. cm.
    ISBN 1-56955-149-9 (alk. paper)
    1. Spiritual life—Christianity.   I. Perrotta, Kevin.   II. Title.
    BV4501.2.G7785   2000
    248—dc21   99-089254

Contents

The Spiritual Journey

PREFACE

The idea of an anthology of writings about the spiritual journey or the spiritual development of the individual is not new. The twentieth century saw several in the English language alone, and they were all very helpful. But strangely they were not well known, and most of them are unfortunately out of print. Many who would be interested are unaware that these collections ever existed. As a rule, Christian anthologies were produced along denominational lines—Orthodox, Catholic, or Protestant. Some were even more restricted to particular groups, such as religious orders.

It struck me that we needed an anthology that was more in line with the developmental psychology of the spiritual life. I have written in this area for almost two decades, and when Servant Publications asked me to do a book of general Christian interest, I thought of this anthology. If there is anything that truly binds Christians together, it is the experience of those who are struggling to follow the Gospel, to answer the summons of Christ: "Follow me." I was blessed to have the assistance of Kevin Perrotta, himself an author and skillful editor, in composing this anthology. He brought to the project the experience of a lay person and father of a family, as well as his own insights as a religious writer. I will ever be grateful to Kevin for his assistance. Without him a long standing goal of my life would not have been achieved.

I am also deeply grateful to my old friend Charles Pendergast who has edited much of my work and whose skillful help was essential with this book. I also remain ever indebted to the many writers whose words are included— in some instances writings that have guided my whole life. I need to particularly thank the well-known evangelical writer Rebecca Manley Pippert for the suggestions on Protestant spiritual writers, as well as Art and Mary Wiser of the Bruderhoff Community for the selections from the Anabaptist tradition. As ever I am appreciative of the staff of the Corrigan Library at St Joseph's Seminary in Yonkers, especially Sister Regina Melican and Sister Catherine Duffy. James Monti helped with researching a number of Catholic authors. St. Vladimir's Orthodox Theological Seminary and Press in Yonkers as always provided a gold mine of material on the whole Eastern Church tradition.

Anthologies are particularly appropriate for spiritual reading because most readers don't have a great library of religious classics available to them, nor do they have the time to plow through pages of difficult writing, ancient styles, and archaic translations. Sadly, many who could profit immensely from the teachings of spiritual masters or the experiences of sensitive and literate souls are deprived of a real source for getting these blessings.

Let me warn you that a great frustration awaits both the readers and the compilers of anthologies. There is such a volume of instructive and edifying literature in the library of spirituality that we feel as if we are bailing out the ocean. But this kind of literature, of which the Bible itself is the first model, is so helpful spiritually that one can develop a blessed addiction. True, the Bible is the Word of God, inspired by the Holy Spirit, whereas human authors are simply guided by His truth. In this the Sacred Scriptures are unique among all writings. But anthologies of the spiritual life reflect the experiences, trials, and triumphs of those seriously seeking to respond to the call of grace—a call given constantly by Christ to the individual by the Holy Spirit. A devout follower of the Gospel may be mistaken or at times misled, but these adventures will almost always be interesting and instructive so long as they are serious attempts to respond to grace. As long as we are well aware that spiritual writers are not infallible and have their own personal point of view and unique call from God, we can learn from them, even though they may belong to a different tradition and even when they make mistakes. As in most of life's worthwhile endeavors, frustration is an unavoidable experience. This is all the more true in spirituality, where the adage is often repeated that those who drink will thirst for more.

The informed reader of this or any other anthology is likely to want to ask the author, "Why did you leave this or that out?" or "Why did you put this in? It's not my experience." No wise anthologist of spiritual writings pretends to have included the best, but rather to have illustrated for spiritual travelers some of the things and places that the great masters of the spiritual life have experienced themselves. My hope is that some readers, perhaps frustrated with my selections, will begin to assemble their own anthologies. This is all the easier in these days of duplicating machines and the Internet. Don't complain to me. Make your own anthology, and maybe send me a copy. Better yet, publish it yourself.

I have tried to be honestly ecumenical in the Christian meaning of that much abused term. With few exceptions my selections are from well-accepted Christian sources, and when I have borrowed from other traditions and from the sciences, I have tried to be fair. I make no apologies for this, because God calls us all through the Holy Spirit, who, like the wind, blows where He wills (see Jn. 3:8). We have not used quotations from Islam, which uses the first five books of the Bible, or from Hinduism or Buddhism, because they would take us away from our theme, which is the Christian spiritual journey.

I have largely followed the outline of development called the teaching of the Three Ways, which I attempted to partially correlate with contemporary developmental psychology in my book *Spiritual Passages* (Crossroad, 1982). A number of modern writers still in print have attempted to do this. Special mention must be made of Evelyn Underhill's *Mysticism*, Reginald Garrigou-Lagrange's monumental work *The Three Ages of the Spiritual Life*, and the very popular work of general religious interest, *The Road Less Traveled*, by M. Scott Peck.

With the single exception of the present Pope, I have avoided using living authors. This is not in any way to disparage several excellent living authors who have written so well on the spiritual journey. Often anthologists let time filter out what is of lasting value from what may have been of value only at a particular time.

A final word. An anthology should be enjoyed. It is a perfect kind of book to keep close at hand. Skip around, look at what's interesting at the moment, find a suitable quotation for an occasion, or take it with you for meditation at a time of retreat. You can use an anthology for years and never read it all. Find your own level of development and see what tasks in the spiritual life have been left undone, and then read a bit ahead. Don't get frightened of the spiritual heights. If and when you get there, the Holy Spirit will assist and guide you. If you are not familiar with Christian spiritual writing or the three-fold journey as it is described, pray fervently to the Holy Spirit, take Christ by the hand, and keep your Bible nearby. You can have the greatest adventure of your life—what St. Augustine calls the longest journey, the journey to Mount Sinai at the center of your own being.

Fr. Benedict J. Groeschel, C.F.R.
St. Crispin's Friary
The Bronx, New York
Feast of the Epiphany, 2000

The Spiritual Journey

INTRODUCTION

I am the way, and the truth, and the life; no one comes to the Father, but by me (Jn. 14:6).

If you have been struggling for some time to be a loyal, dedicated follower of Jesus Christ, then you probably have encountered two very distinct experiences. The first is that the observance of the Gospel teaching, the practice of meditation on Scripture and writings associated with the Christian life, and personal prayer and devotion to Jesus have all become more consistent, easier in the sense that they define your life and give you an even clearer purpose. In a word, you have experienced growing in faith, hope, and love. On the other hand, you may be just as aware that the struggle is more demanding, the Gospel more challenging and more encompassing, your own responsibility for past and present behavior more painful, your prayer and meditation more distracted, and your love of Christ more arid and less rewarding. If you are familiar with the Christian spiritual journey and with the works of spiritual writers who have themselves been deeply dedicated disciples, you will know that you are in reality on the spiritual journey and, despite all the struggle, you are making progress.

If this paragraph describes you or if you are moved by an inner desire that is unexplained and has been uncharacteristic of your life up until the present time, you will find much helpful information in this book. You will learn not only that what you are experiencing has happened to many others, but you will learn something much more important. If you read carefully, especially if you read other solid spiritual writings that this anthology may lead you to, you will learn what steps you need to take next.

Life as a Journey

For Christians the idea that the religious aspects of our lives should be seen as a journey is firmly rooted in the teachings of our Savior in the Gospel. Not only does He refer to Himself as "the way" (Jn. 14:6) but He also challenges His disciples to "follow me" (Mt. 4:19). This journey is obviously not one through space, but through time—a journey of the soul. In more contemporary terms such a non-spatial journey is called a journey through growth, or a journey as a process of development. St. Paul, that spiritual psychologist, is very clear that we must grow in Christ and that we must put aside the things of childhood in order to arrive at our full stature in Christ (see 1 Cor. 13:11). What's more, he advises us to press on so as to win the prize (see 1 Cor. 9:24). No Christian should really have trouble with this concept of the journey of the soul, because as we seek to grow in Christ, we all know that we have a destination—our Father's house, of which it has been said that eye has not seen nor ear heard, nor has it entered into the heart of man to comprehend.

The idea that life is a journey has also found expression in modern psychology. In fact this idea has possibly been the most productive, helpful, and lasting contribution of the whole psychological enterprise of the last half of the twentieth century. Psychology has made other valuable contributions, but they have all been very mixed blessings. On the other hand, the basic principles of developmental psychology have proved to be more helpful because they have been drawn from real life and not from theoretical constructs that reflect the outlook of a very specific historical moment.

In recent decades Christians of most denominations have become interested in their own spiritual development or growth in discipleship. We often call this our own faith journey. To be genuinely Christian, such an interest must see spiritual development somewhat differently from human development, physical or psychological. Growth in the life of the Holy Spirit is a gift of God. It is a grace won by Christ as our Redeemer and Savior, and not something that is our due as a result of human nature. Quite the opposite. Growing in the life of grace is not by any means the same as personality development. But since both the gifts of nature and grace come from God and are inextricably bound together in a Christian worldview, it is obvious that there must be some relationship between spiritual and psychological development.

After more than three decades of work as both a spiritual director and a psychologist I can sum up this relationship rather simply in the following observation: if you are growing spiritually in the love of God and neighbor according to the Gospel and trying to follow the Beatitudes, it stands to reason that you ought to be growing psychologically more mature and have a more healthy and balanced way of life. On the other hand, if you are becoming more mature and solving some of the inner conflicts that everyone has, such as self-hate, self-destructiveness, self-centeredness, and irrational fears and anxiety, you are likely to be more open to accepting the grace of God and giving the Holy Spirit room to operate in your own being. Mental health and spiritual maturity are by no means the same thing, but they are related. They can be both described as a journey, but only in one case does the journey have no end. As Clement of Alexandria, a third-century Father of the Church, observed, "Jesus Christ, by coming into this world, has changed the sunsets of time into the sunrises of eternity."

What Does Spiritual Mean?

Christian writers from the earliest centuries, following St. Paul's lead, have used the word "spirit" or "spiritual" to describe the growth and struggles of the inner man. Of course, the word spiritual can be abused to mean the spooky, the occult, even the diabolical. It often has a gnostic connotation— the idea condemned by the early Church that we are saved by some kind of secret knowledge. But when used properly, the word spiritual has an important meaning quite distinct from the word "religious." Religion can be described as the outer, or sociological, aspect of belief. In fact, in the case of the pagan Romans, their religion was only an external phenomenon requiring no inner conviction at all, much less any moral conversion. Sadly, this can also be said of the religious practice of some in our own times. The call to continuing and ongoing conversion is strongly given in the first words of our Savior's public life, "The time is fulfilled, and the kingdom of God is at hand; repent, and believe in the gospel" (Mk. 1:15). All serious Christians, especially those who have grown up in strongly religious homes, know that at a certain point in life they must choose Christ as their Savior and King and follow Him. Without this choice, which usually happens more than once, as the truth of the Christian faith becomes more imperative in a person's life, religion becomes only external and atrophied, a religion of "little faith." For this reason Christ warned that not all those who called Him "Lord, Lord" would enter the Kingdom of heaven (see Mt. 7:21). To be authentically spiritual means to have one's beliefs integrated into one's personality and behavior at all times. Nothing could be more obvious when we read the Gospels reverently and personally, trying to apply their summons and the challenges of Christ to our own lives.

Pilgrims Along the Way

Since the days of Saints Peter, Paul, and James, Christians have been sharing their experiences and giving counsel to their fellow travelers along the way of Christ. Thus there has developed a gigantic library of spiritual counsel and insight, along with an equally impressive library of theological and moral teachings. Genuinely spiritual persons throughout the three large groups of Christians—Catholics, Protestants, and Orthodox—have agreed far more about the spiritual life than about theology or moral teaching. Unfortunately, for the most part, members of these three large groups have often been totally ignorant of the spiritual experience of believers in traditions other than their own. Prejudice, defensiveness, historical conflicts, and just plain self-love have kept Christians from one tradition from even considering the possibility of spiritual growth and personal holiness on the other side. In this they have unwillingly slighted the Holy Spirit, who, as Our Savior has told us, "blows where He wills" (Jn. 3:8). Better communication, religious tolerance, and ecumenism have all opened the windows so that we can learn from each other's tradition.

My own experience can illustrate this. I learned much in my youth from the spiritual writings of Evelyn Underhill, an Anglican, and from the book *Markings* by Dag Hammarskjöld, whose Lutheran roots included a boyhood friendship with the renowned Swedish Archbishop Nathan Söderblom of Uppsala. Like many Catholics, I have loved the spiritual writings of the Eastern Church, those from before and after the tragic break between the Eastern and Western portions of the Church. Orthodox books like the *Philokalia* and the contemporary writings of Archbishop Anthony Bloom are valued by both Catholics and Protestants. It is interesting and probably reassuring to readers dedicated to their own tradition to know that studying the writings of Christians from other traditions may help them appreciate and clarify their own, because we all come from the same roots. I hope to publish soon a study of personal devotion to Jesus Christ in Catholicism, Orthodoxy, and Protestantism—a work that will demonstrate the remarkable similarity of devotion in these three traditions. This similarity not only grows out of our common history, but is based on the certain reality that all Christians are responding to the same Jesus Christ who is in eternal glory, sitting at the right hand of the Father, and sending the Holy Spirit, who calls us all to the same pattern of discipleship and holiness.

In the first chapter, we will look at the first stage of the journey toward God, which is conversion, or "turning toward God." But first, as a kind of prelude, we will begin with a few selections that touch on the experience that precedes conversion. That experience is the realization that God exists, that He loves and calls us—and that we have been created to respond to His call.

St. Augustine, Bishop of Hippo

"I am the way, and the truth, and the life" (John 14:6). Every man desires truth and life, but not every man finds the way. That God is life eternal, immutable, intelligible, intelligent, wise, and bestowing His wisdom, even some philosophers of this world have seen. They saw, indeed, but from afar, the fixed, settled, unwavering truth in which are all the governing principles of all created things. They saw, but they were in error and hence did not find the way to reach so great and ineffable and beatific a possession....

But Christ, who is with the Father, is the truth and the life.... As we had no way to go to the truth, the Son of God, who is in the Father and ever the truth and the life, became the way for us by assuming man's nature. Walk by Him the man, and you will come to God. You go *by* Him, and you go *to*

Him. Do not look for any way to come to Him except by Himself. For if He had not deigned to be the way, we would have always gone astray. Therefore He became the way by which you could come to Him. I do not tell you, look for the way. The way itself has come to you. Arise and walk.

Sermon 141

Sir Arthur Eddington, eminent British scientist

We all know that there are regions of the human spirit untrammeled by the world of physics. In the mystic sense of the creation around us, in the expression of art, in a yearning towards God, the soul grows upward and finds fulfillment of something implanted in its nature. The sanction for this development is within us, a striving born of our consciousness of an inner light proceeding from a greater power than ours. Science can scarcely question this sanction, for the pursuit of science springs from a striving which the mind is impelled to follow, a questioning that will not be suppressed. Whether in the intellectual pursuits of science or in the mystical pursuits of the spirit, the light beckons ahead and the purpose surging in our natures responds.

The Nature of the Physical World

Rabbi Abraham Isaac Kook, Chief Rabbi of Palestine

So long as the world moves along accustomed paths, so long as there are no wild catastrophes, man can find sufficient substance for his life by contemplating surface events, theories, and movements of society. He can acquire his inner richnesses from this external kind of "property." But this is not the case when life encounters fiery forces of evil and chaos. Then the "revealed" world begins to totter. Then the man who tries to sustain himself only from the surface aspects of existence will suffer terrible impoverishment, begin to stagger ... then he will feel welling up within himself a burning thirst for that inner substance and vision which transcends the obvious surfaces of existence and remains unaffected by the world's catastrophes. From such inner sources he will seek the waters of joy which can quicken the dry outer skeleton of existence.

Quoted by Herbert Weiner in *9-1/2 Mystics*

William Law, 18th-century English spiritual writer

O man! consider yourself. Here you stand in the earnest, perpetual strife of good and evil. All nature is continually at work to bring about the great redemption. The whole creation is travailing in pain and laborious working to be delivered from the vanity of time. And will you be asleep?

Everything you hear or see says nothing, shows nothing to you but what either eternal light or eternal darkness has brought forth; for as day and night divide the whole of our time, so heaven and hell divide the whole of our thoughts, words, and actions. Stir which way you will, do or design what you will, you must be an agent with the one or the other.

You cannot stand still, because you live in the perpetual workings of temporal and eternal nature; if you work not with the good, the evil that is in nature carries you along with it. You have the height and depth of eternity in you, and therefore, be doing what you will, in either the closet, the field, the shop, or the church, you are sowing that which grows and must be reaped in eternity.

An Appeal to All Who Doubt

Theophan the Recluse, 19th-century Russian Orthodox bishop

It may seem strange that communion with God still has to be attained when it has already been given to us in the sacrament of baptism and renewed through the sacrament of confession, since it is said: "For as many of you as have been baptized into Christ have put on Christ" (Gal. 3:27); "Ye are dead [that is, dead to sin through baptism or confession], and your life is hid with Christ in God" (Col. 3:3). And we also know that God is everywhere, not far from each one of us, "... if haply they might feel after him" (Acts 17:27), and He is ready to dwell in everyone who is willing to accept Him. It is only unwillingness, carelessness, and sinfulness that separate us from Him. Now if a person has repented and repudiated everything, and so gives himself to God, what then is the obstacle to the coming of God to dwell in him?

In order to remove misunderstanding, it is necessary to discriminate between different kinds of communion with God. Communion begins from the moment when hope of it is stimulated, and it shows itself on man's side in a yearning and aspiration towards God, and on God's side in good will, help, and protection. But God is still outside man, and man is outside God; they do not penetrate nor enter into one another. In the sacraments of baptism and confession the Lord enters into man by His grace, vividly establishes communion with him, and gives him to taste of all the sweetness of the Divine, as abundantly and intensely as those who have achieved perfection experience it; but afterwards He again conceals this manifestation of His communion, renewing it only from time to time—and then but slightly, merely as a reflection, not as the original. This leaves man in ignorance about God, and about His dwelling in man, until a certain measure of maturity or education has been attained, according to the wisdom of His direction. After this the Lord perceptibly reveals His abode in a man's spirit, which then becomes a temple filled by the Three Persons of the Godhead.

There are, in fact, three kinds of communion with God: a first in thought and intention, which happens at the time of conversion; and two others which are actual, of which one is hidden, invisible to others and unknown to oneself, and the other is evident both to oneself and to others.

The whole of our spiritual life consists in the transition from the first kind of communion with God—in thought and intention—to the third kind—a real, living, and conscious communion.

Quoted in *The Art of Prayer*

Cardinal Nicholas of Cusa, 15th-century Tyrolian bishop

Lord, Thou hast given me my being, of such a nature that it can make itself continually more able to receive Thy grace and goodness. And this power, which I have of Thee, wherein I possess a living image of Thine almighty power, is free will. By this I can either enlarge or restrict my capacity for Thy grace. The enlarging is by conformity with Thee, when I strive to be good because Thou art good, to be just because Thou art just, to be merciful because Thou art merciful; when all my endeavor is turned toward Thee because all Thy endeavor is turned toward me; when I look unto Thee alone with all my attention, nor ever turn aside the eyes of my mind, because Thou dost enfold me with Thy constant regard; when I direct my love toward Thee alone because Thou, who art Love's self, hast turned Thee toward me alone.

And what, Lord, is my life, save that embrace wherein Thy delightsome sweetness doth so lovingly enfold me? I love my life supremely because Thou art my life's sweetness.

Now I behold as in a mirror, in an icon, in a riddle, life eternal, for that is naught other than that blessed regard wherewith Thou never ceasest most lovingly to behold me, yea, even the secret places of my soul. With Thee, to behold is to give life; it is unceasingly to impart sweetest love of Thee; it is to inflame me to love of Thee by love's imparting, and to feed me by inflaming, and by feeding to kindle my yearnings, and by kindling to make me drink of the dew of gladness, and by drinking to infuse in me a fountain of life, and by infusing to make it increase and endure. It is to cause me to share Thine immortality, to endow me with the glory imperishable of Thy heavenly and most high and most mighty kingdom, it is to make me partaker of that inheritance which is only of Thy Son, to establish me in possession of eternal bliss. There is the source of all delights that can be desired; not only can naught better be thought out by men and angels, but naught better can exist in any mode of being! For it is the absolute maximum of every desire, than which a greater cannot be.

Quoted in *Come, South Wind*

PART ONE

The Stages of the Journey

ONE

Conversion

The time is fulfilled, and the Kingdom of God is at hand; repent, and believe in the gospel (Mark 1:15).

The process of conversion to God, which may be sudden or gradual, always leads to a life of ongoing struggle to seek first the kingdom of God and His righteousness. The effects of original sin, apart from the loss of eternal salvation as a child of God, will always remain. They include the darkening of the intelligence, the weakening of the will, the plunging of the emotions into turmoil, and the disturbance of human relations. By Baptism and conversion the individual continues to struggle to be ever more open to grace, that is, to the call of Christ and to the inspiration and gifts of the Holy Spirit. The following accounts, all drawn from eminent religious personalities, reflect the same struggle, the same upward movement that caused St. Paul to encourage us to press on to the prize. Some of the following writings are autobiographical and reveal the effects of grace. Other selections, especially those from Garrigou-Lagrange and Kierkegaard, are more discursive and illustrate the experience and psychology of growth and decline in the life of the Spirit.

Whether you are pondering the experience of St. Teresa or Jonathan Edwards, try to find some similarities with your own struggles. When you pause to study in a more objective way what is happening to these pilgrims, keep in mind that you are learning only in order to know how to love.

God calls all His children and wishes all to be saved. In the first chapter of Romans, St. Paul makes it very clear that the invisible things of God can be known by the visible things of His creation and that all are thereby summoned to worship Him by acknowledging His almighty power and divinity. It is not difficult to find many in the secular world who experience the mysterious call of God. This is all the more true of the people whom God has chosen to be His own and to whom He revealed Himself in so many wonderful ways in the Old Testament. It is the people of Israel, called only in later times the Jews (from Judean), who have given us the Messiah, and it was to them that He almost exclusively preached. Those familiar with Jewish spiritual writings of our time can easily see the call of the Holy Spirit in the lives of those who belong to the very same people as Jesus Himself. Although all Christians know that salvation comes from the grace of Christ won by His Incarnation, His life, and especially His sacrificial death and glorious Resurrection, we can and should hope that this essential grace is extended by the Holy Spirit to those who through no fault of their own will say to Christ, "When did we see thee hungry and feed thee ... or a stranger and welcome thee?" (Mt. 25:37, 38).*

It is an interesting fact that all major religions of the world agree that growth in the spiritual life is a journey. For the most part this journey is seen to have two phases: the first phase involves conversion and purification, usually understood in moral and ascetical terms; the second phase is enlightenment, or the discovery of the divine light already within or given at a certain moment by God. Although the Christian journey begins with conversion and moves toward a life of the spirit or an illuminated life, Christian spiritual writers from ancient times have spoken of a third, or highest, way, that of a partial union with God even in this life. Paul writes, "It is no longer I who live, but Christ who lives in me" (Gal. 2:20). This phrase psychologically expresses the meaning of the prayer of Christ at the Last Supper, "that they may all be one; even as thou, Father, art in me, and I in thee, that they also may be in us" (Jn. 17:21).

Beginning in the fourth century, St. Gregory, bishop of Nyssa, in the East, and St. Augustine, in the West, began to see the journey of Christians fol-

---

* For a discussion of non-Christians at the Last Judgment, see Joachim Jeremias, *The Parables of Jesus* (New York: Charles Scribner's Sons, 1972, 2nd ed.), 209–10.

lowing a threefold way: purgation, or deep conversion; illumination, or a heartfelt awareness of the divine intimacy, with love of God and neighbor; and finally the experience of union with God, which some writers, such as St. Bonaventure, have called the vestibule of heaven.

It will be obvious that the profound idea of union with God as we understand it here is a specifically Christian idea. The Eastern religions generally see the highest level of the spiritual life as a kind of absorption into the divine reality, like a drop of water into the ocean. For Jews the idea of union with God is almost blasphemous because of the holiness and uniqueness of God: "As the heavens are higher than the earth, so are my ways higher than your ways and my thoughts than your thoughts" (Is. 55:9).*

The idea of the union of the soul with God is clearly a very specific and unique teaching of Christ: "When I go and prepare a place for you, I will come again and take you to myself, that where I am you may be also" (Jn. 14:3). It should be mentioned that Luther himself would have difficulty with the idea of union with God, but evidently his eminent musical follower Johann Sebastian Bach did not. The words of his popular hymn, *Jesu, Joy of Man's Desiring*, seem to acknowledge the traditional Christian idea easily. Louis Bouyer, a distinguished historian of spirituality, indicates that Calvin went beyond Luther in this matter and saw the Christian experience not merely as justification and salvation but as actual sanctification.** Bouyer also states that in the centuries following the Reformation, groups as diverse as High Church Anglicans and English Puritans returned to the notion of personal sanctification. Hence we can explain the popularity of the Catholic book of spirituality, *The Imitation of Christ*, with so many Protestants of different traditions. This classic work profoundly expresses the experience of union with God, and especially of union with Christ.

---

*Some Jewish spiritual writers, I am told, particularly those like the Hasidim, who were influenced by Christians among whom they lived for so long, also speak of union with God in a way similar to the Christian unitive way.

** *The Spirit and Forms of Protestantism*

A Most Important Fact: Order

If we accept the spiritual journey as it is described by noted authors, then we need to take the steps of this journey in order. These are developmental stages similar to childhood, adolescence, early adult life, and the rest. You can't be a mature adult without completing the work of childhood and adolescence. Some get stuck at an early stage of development, like adult adolescents, and never quite get beyond it. Although they superficially appear to have become mature, in fact, they have simply gotten older.

Some in the first stages of conversion think that they have made much more progress than they really have. Later on, the realization that they still have a long way to go to complete the first phase may cause them to become discouraged and give up. In all Christian denominations one can find those who, like the seed sown on the rocks, spring up quickly but have no roots and wither away (see Mark 4:16-17).

Christian Conversion

"The time is fulfilled, and the kingdom of God is at hand; repent, and believe in the gospel" (Mark 1:15). Conversion, or *metanoia,* as the Greek New Testament refers to it, is the first real experience of the Christian spiritual life. For some who have grown up in a devout home and have never deviated much from Christ's teaching, conversion takes on more the aspect of an awakening, like the call of Nathanael, who was asleep under a tree and whom our Lord called a man without guile. Others, who have never really been active disciples even though they were baptized, or who have simply had no relation to the Gospel at all and are unbaptized, may experience a conversion that affects every level of their lives. If their conversion is authentically spiritual, it will be experiential (affecting how they perceive things), theological (affecting what they believe), moral (affecting what they do), and even emotional (affecting what they feel). In the beginning of a conversion, the emotional and spiritual are so close to each other that they are experienced as the same thing. In time a wise person will come to see that they are not identical at all.

The following selections, drawn from writers over a period of almost eighteen hundred years in several Christian traditions, speak of conversion or awakening. They are taken largely from the autobiographical writings of great spiritual personalities often called mystics, because their lives are dominated by the unseen realities of grace. The word "mystic," which frightens many people, comes from the Greek word "to close your eyes." Understand its meaning, that is, the presence of unseen reality, and don't let this word frighten you.

As you read and meditate on the following works, you need to think of an anthology as a mosaic rather than a painting. The selections were written in various specific contexts and are related to each other only as parts of a general theme. They might easily have been arranged in a different order. The present arrangement is intended to give you a clearer understanding of conversion and of each successive topic. Don't forget to open yourself prayerfully to the Holy Spirit as you go along, or you will miss the value of this collection.

St. Paul

Saul, still breathing threats and murder against the disciples of the Lord, went to the high priest and asked him for letters to the synagogues at Damascus, so that if he found any belonging to the Way, men or women, he might bring them bound to Jerusalem. Now as he journeyed he approached Damascus, and suddenly a light from heaven flashed about him. And he fell to the ground and heard a voice saying to him, "Saul, Saul, why do you persecute me?" And he said, "Who are you, Lord?" And he said, "I am Jesus, whom you are persecuting; but rise and enter the city, and you will be told what you are to do."

Acts of the Apostles 9:1-6

St. Augustine
A Light in My Heart

Thus I was sick at heart and in torment, accusing myself with a new intensity of bitterness, twisting and turning in my chain in the hope that it might be utterly broken, for what held me was so small a thing! But it still held me. And You stood in the secret places of my soul, O Lord, in the harshness of Your mercy redoubling the scourges of fear and shame lest I should give way again and that small slight tie which remained should not be broken but should grow again to full strength and bind me closer even than before. For I kept saying within myself: "Let it be now, let it be now," and by the mere words I had begun to move towards the resolution. I almost made it, yet I did not quite make it. But I did not fall back into my original state, but as it were stood near to get my breath. I still shrank from dying unto death and living unto life.

Those trifles of all trifles, and vanities of vanities, my onetime mistress, held me back, plucking at my garment of flesh and murmuring softly: "Are you sending us away?" And "From this moment shall we not be with you, now or forever?" And "From this moment shall this or that not be allowed you now or forever?" What were they suggesting to me in the phrase I have written "this or that," what were they suggesting to me, O my God? Do you in Your mercy keep from the soul of Your servant the vileness and uncleanness they were suggesting. And now I began to hear them not half so loud; they no longer stood against me face to face, but were softly muttering behind my back and, as I tried to depart, plucking stealthily at me to make me look behind. Yet even that was enough, so hesitating was I, to keep me from snatching myself free, from shaking them off and leaping upwards on the way I was called: for the strong force of habit said to me: "Do you think you can live without them?"

When my most searching scrutiny had drawn up all my vileness from the secret depths of my soul and heaped it in my heart's sight, a mighty storm arose in me, bringing a mighty rain of tears. That I might give way to my tears and lamentations, I rose from Alypius: for it struck me that solitude was more suited to the business of weeping.... And much I said not in these words but to this effect: "And Thou, O Lord, how long? How long, Lord; wilt Thou be angry forever? Remember not our former iniquities." For I felt that I was still bound by them. And I continued my miserable complaining: "How long, how long shall I go on saying tomorrow and again tomorrow? Why not now, why not have an end to my uncleanness this very hour?"

Such things I said, weeping in the most bitter sorrow of my heart. And suddenly I heard a voice from some nearby house, a boy's voice or a girl's voice, I do not know: but it was a sort of sing-song repeated again and again, "Take and read, take and read." I ceased weeping and immediately began to search my mind most carefully as to whether children were accustomed to chant these words in any kind of game, and I could not remember that I had ever heard any such thing. Damming back the flood of my tears, I arose, interpreting the incident as quite certainly a divine command to open my book of Scripture and read the passage at which I should open. So I was moved to return to the place where Alypius was sitting, for I had put down the Apostle's book there when I arose. I snatched it up, opened it, and in silence read the passage upon which my eyes first fell: "Not in rioting and drunkenness, not in chambering and impurities, not in contention and envy, but put ye on the Lord Jesus Christ and make not provision for the flesh in its concupiscences" (Romans 13:13). I had no wish to read further, and no need. For in that instant, with the very ending of the sentence, it was as though a light of utter confidence shone in all my heart, and all the darkness of uncertainty vanished away. Then leaving my finger in the place or marking it by some other sign, I closed the book and in complete calm told the whole thing to Alypius and he similarly told me what had been going on in himself, of which I knew nothing. He asked to see what I had read. I showed him, and he looked further than I had read. I had not known what followed. And this is what followed: "Now him that is weak in faith, take unto you." He applied this to himself and told me so. And he was confirmed by this message, and with no troubled wavering gave himself to God's goodwill and purpose—a purpose indeed most suited to his character, for in these matters he had been immeasurably better than I.

Then we went in to my mother and told her, to her great joy. We related how it had come about: she was filled with triumphant exultation, and praised You who are mighty beyond what we ask or conceive: for she saw that You had given her more than with all her pitiful weeping she had ever asked. For You converted me to Yourself so that I no longer sought a wife nor any of this world's promises, but stood upon that same rule of faith in which You had shown me to her so many years before. Thus You changed her mourning into joy, a joy far richer than she had thought to wish, a joy much dearer and purer than she had thought to find in grandchildren of my flesh.

Confessions, Book 8

St. Cyprian, Bishop of Carthage
Born Again Through Baptism

Once I lay in darkness and in the depths of night and was tossed to and fro in the waves of the turbulent world, uncertain of the correct way to go, ignorant of my true life, and a stranger to the light of truth. At that time and on account of the life I then led, it seemed difficult to believe what divine mercy promised for my salvation, namely, that someone could be born again and to a new life by being immersed in the healing water of Baptism. It was difficult to believe that though I would remain the same man in bodily form, my heart and mind would be transformed.

How was it possible, I thought, that a change could be great enough to strip away in a single moment the innate hardness of our nature? How could the habits acquired over the course of many years disappear, since these are so deeply rooted within us? If someone is used to fine feasts and lavish banquets, how can they learn restraint? If someone is used to dressing conspicuously in gold and purple, how can they cast them aside for ordinary simple clothes? Someone who loves the trappings of public office cannot become an anonymous private person. Anyone who is attended by great crowds of supporters and is honored by a dense entourage of obsequious attendants would consider solitude a punishment. While temptation still holds us fast, we are seduced by wine, inflated with pride, inflamed by anger, troubled by greed, goaded by cruelty, enticed by ambition and cast headlong by lust.

These were my frequent thoughts. For I was held fast by the many sins of my life from which it seemed impossible for me to extricate myself. Thus I yielded to my sins which clung fast to me. Since I despaired of improvement I took an indulgent view of my faults and regarded them as if they were slaves born in my house.

But after the life-giving water of Baptism came to my rescue and washed away the stain of my former years and poured into my cleansed and purified heart the light which comes from above, and after I had drunk in the heavenly Spirit and was made a new man by a second birth, then amazingly what I had previously doubted became clear to me. What had been hidden was revealed. What had been dark became light. What previously had seemed impossible now seemed possible. What was in me of the guilty flesh now confessed it was earthly. What was made alive in me by the Holy Spirit was now quickened by God.

Born to New Life

St. Francis of Assisi
Lord, What Would You Have Me Do?

In the soul of this young man there dwelt, by the gift of God, a certain innate and natural love of the poor of Christ, which, growing up with him from his earliest childhood, filled his heart with such benignity that, in obedience to the words of the Gospel, he resolved within himself to give to every one who should ask of him, and especially if the petitions were made in the name of God. Now it happened one day, when Francis was wholly engrossed by the tumult of worldly business, that a poor man asked an alms of him; contrary to his usual custom, he passed him unheeded and went on his way. But speedily recollecting himself, he ran after the poor man, charitably relieved his wants, and made a solemn promise to God that from that day forth he would never refuse an alms to any that should ask it of him for the love of God. And this promise he faithfully kept till the day of his death, meriting thereby an abundant increase of the grace and love of God. So that he was wont to say, after he had perfectly put on Christ, that even while he still wore the secular habit, he could never hear words expressing the love of God without his heart being deeply moved and affected. And certain it is, that in the sweetness and mildness of his bearing, the gentleness of his manners, his patience and docility—far beyond the ordinary custom of men, the munificence of his bounty, exceeding even the extent of his means—in all these things shone forth the beauty of this young man's soul, clearly betokening the abundant outpouring of the divine blessing reserved for him in days to come....

But Francis as yet knew not, neither understood, the great purposes of God towards him; for being by the will of his father engrossed by external affairs, and also by reason of the original corruption of our nature drawn down and depressed by earthly things, he had not learned to contemplate heavenly mysteries, neither did he yet know the sweetness of divine consolation. And, forasmuch as the Lord is wont, by afflictions and tribulations, to open the ears of the spirit, so, by the right hand of the Most High, he was suddenly changed, his body being afflicted with long and severe sufferings, so that his soul might be prepared to receive the unction of the Holy Ghost. Now, when he had recovered his bodily health, going forth one day, as was his wont, in apparel suited to his state, he met a certain soldier of honor and courage, but poor and vilely clad; of whose poverty, feeling a tender and sorrowful compassion, he took off his new clothes and gave them to the poor man-at-arms, thus at once fulfilling two offices of piety, by covering the shame of a noble cavalier and relieving a poor man's penury.

On the following night, when he was asleep, the divine mercy showed him a spacious and beautiful palace filled with arms and military ensigns, all marked with the Cross of Christ, to make known to him that his charitable deed done to the poor soldier for the love of the great King of heaven should receive an unspeakable reward. And when he asked for whom all these things were reserved, a divine voice answered him that they were for him and for his soldiers.

When Francis awoke early in the morning, not being yet accustomed to understand and interpret divine mysteries, nor through visible signs to ascend to invisible truths, he thought that this strange vision betokened some great earthly prosperity. Therefore, being still ignorant of the Divine Will, he determined to go into Apulia, there to enter the household of a certain Count of great magnificence and liberality, who dwelt in that country, hoping in his service to acquire military honor and renown, according to what he supposed to be the meaning of the vision. When he had travelled for some days together, he came to a certain city, when the Lord spoke to him in the night with the familiar voice of a friend, saying, "Francis, who can do most for thee—the Lord or the servant, the rich man or the poor?" And when Francis replied that the Lord and the rich man could do more for him than the poor, "Wherefore, then," said the voice," dost thou leave the Lord for the servant, and the God of infinite riches for a poor mortal?" Then said Francis, "Lord, what wilt Thou have me to do?" And the Lord answered: "Return home; for the vision which thou hast seen prefigured a spiritual work which thou shalt bring to pass, not by human counsel, but by divine disposition."

So, when the day dawned, Francis set forth in great haste towards Assisi, full of joy and confidence; and from that time he awaited in obedience the revelation of the Will of God, and withdrawing from the tumult of worldly affairs, he most devoutly besought the divine clemency to make manifest to him all that he was to do. And so, by the practice of frequent prayer, the vehement flame of heavenly desires increased daily within him, and already, for the love of his celestial country, he despised all earthly things as if they existed not; for he knew that he had found the hidden treasure, and like a prudent merchant he considered within himself how to sell all that he had to make it his own....

Now, as he was riding one day over the plain of Assisi he met a leper, whose sudden appearance filled him with fear and horror; but forthwith calling to mind the resolution which he had made to follow after perfection, and remembering that if he would be a soldier of Christ he must first overcome himself, he dismounted from his horse and went to meet the leper, that he might embrace him: and when the poor man stretched out his hand to receive an alms, he kissed it and filled it with money. Having again mounted his horse, he looked around him over the wide and open plain, but nowhere could he see the leper; upon which, being filled with wonder and joy, he began devoutly to give thanks to God, purposing within himself to proceed to still greater things than this.

He sought continually for wild and solitary places, where with tears and unutterable groans he poured forth long and fervent prayers, until at last our Lord was pleased to hear him; for being one day engaged in fervent prayer, according to his custom, in a lonely place, he became wholly absorbed in God, when Jesus Christ appeared to him under the form of a Crucifix, at which sight his whole soul seemed to melt away; and so deeply was the memory of Christ's Passion impressed on his heart that it pierced even to the marrow of his bones. From that hour, whenever he thought upon the Passion of Christ, he could scarcely restrain his tears and sighs; for he then understood (as he made known to some of his familiar friends not long before his death) that these words of the Gospel were addressed to him: "If thou wilt come after Me, deny thyself, and take up thy cross and follow Me." And from that day forth he clothed himself with the spirit of poverty, the sense of humility, and the affection of interior piety. And inasmuch as heretofore he had greatly abhorred the company of lepers, and could not endure even the distant sight of them, now—for the love of Christ crucified, who, according to the Prophet's words, was despised as a leper—he, in contempt of himself, sought out and served lepers with great humility and piety, and aided them in all their necessities. For he often visited them in their houses, giving them bountiful alms, and with affectionate compassion he would kiss their hands and their faces; and he desired to bestow upon poor beggars not only his money but even himself, oftentimes taking off his own clothes to cover them, tearing or cutting them in pieces for them when he had nothing else to give.

St. Bonaventure, *The Life of St. Francis of Assisi*

Friedrich von Hügel
The Conversion of St. Catherine of Genoa

Although conversions of apparent suddenness and profound depth and perseverance are rightly taken to be very special and rare graces of God, it would be depreciating their true significance to make their suddenness the direct proof and measure of their own supernaturalness or the standard by which to appraise the altitude of the goodness of other lives. God is as truly the source of gradual purification as of sudden conversion, and as truly the strength which guards and moves us straight on, as that which regains and calls us back. Hence such acts as Catherine's should not be entirely separated from those acts of love, contrition, and self-dedication which occur, as so many free graces of God in and with the free acts of man in the secret lives of human beings throughout the world.

The Mystical Element of Religion

St. Teresa of Avila
The Conversion of a Lukewarm Nun

I voyaged on this tempestuous sea for almost twenty years with these fallings and risings and this evil—since I fell again—and in a life so beneath perfection that I paid almost no attention to venial sins. And mortal sins, although I feared them, I did not fear them as I should have, since I did not turn away from the dangers. I should say that it is one of the most painful lives, I think, that one can imagine; for neither did I enjoy God nor did I find happiness in the world. When I was experiencing the enjoyments of the world, I felt sorrow when I recalled what I owed to God. When I was with God, my attachments to the world disturbed me. This is a war so troublesome that I don't know how I was able to suffer it even a month, much less for so many years. However, I see clearly the great mercy the Lord bestowed on me; for though I continued to associate with the world, I had the courage to practice prayer....

So, save for the year I mentioned, for more than eighteen of the twenty-eight years since I began prayer, I suffered this battle and conflict between friendship with God and friendship with the world. During the remaining years of which I have yet to speak, the cause of the war changed, although the war was not a small one. But since it was, in my opinion, for the service of God and with knowledge of the vanity that the world is, everything went smoothly, as I shall say afterward.

I have recounted all this at length ... so that the mercy of God and my ingratitude might be seen; also, in order that one might understand the great good God does for a soul that willingly disposes itself for the practice of prayer, even though it is not as disposed as is necessary. I recount this also that one may understand how if the soul perseveres in prayer, in the midst of the sins, temptations, and failures of a thousand kinds that the devil places in its path, in the end, I hold as certain, the Lord will draw it forth to the harbor of salvation as—now it seems—He did for me. May it please His Majesty that I do not get lost again....

O infinite goodness of my God, for it seems to me I see that such is the way You are and the way I am! O delight of angels, when I see this I desire to be completely consumed in loving You! How certainly You do suffer the one who suffers to be with You! Oh, what a good friend You make, my Lord! How You proceed by favoring and enduring. You wait for the other to adapt to Your nature, and in the meanwhile You put up with his! You take into account, my Lord, the times when he loves You, and in one instant of repentance You forget his offenses....

Now, then, if the Lord put up with someone as miserable as myself for so long a time, and it seems clear that by this means all my evils were remedied, what person, no matter how bad he may be, has reason to fear? For no matter how bad he may be, he will not be bad for as many years as I was after having received so many favors from the Lord. Who can lose confidence? For the Lord endured so much with me only because I desired and strove to have some place and time in order that He might be with me. And this I often did without eagerness but through my own great struggles or through the strength the Lord Himself gave me. For if those who do not serve Him but offend Him derive so much good from prayer and find it so necessary—and no one can truly discover any harm that prayer can do, the greatest harm being not to practice it—why do those who serve God and desire to serve Him abandon it? I, indeed, cannot understand why, unless it is that they want to undergo the trials of life with greater trial and close the door on God so that He may not make them happy. I certainly pity those who serve the Lord at their own cost, because for those who practice prayer the Lord Himself pays the cost, since through their little labor He gives them delight so that with the help of this delight they might suffer trials.

Because much will be said about these delights that the Lord gives to those who persevere in prayer, I shall not say anything here. I say only that prayer is the door to favors as great as those He granted me. If this door is closed, I don't know how He will grant them. For even though He may desire to enter and take delight in a soul and favor it, there is no way of His doing this, for He wants it alone and clean and desirous of receiving His graces. If we place many stumbling blocks in His path and don't do a thing to remove them, how will He be able to come to us? And we desire God to grant us great favors!

To make known His mercy and the great good it did me not to abandon prayer and reading, I shall speak here—since it is so important to understand these things—about the heavy battery the devil uses against a soul in order to win it over, and about the skill and mercy with which the Lord endeavors to bring it back to Himself, and about how to be on guard against the dangers I was not on guard against. Above all, for love of our Lord and for the great love with which He wins us back to Himself, I beg souls to watch out for the occasions. For we have nothing to rely on for our defense when we are placed in these occasions where there are so many enemies against us and so many weaknesses of our own....

I wanted to live (for I well understood that I was not living but was struggling with a shadow of death), but I had no one to give me life, and I was unable to catch hold of it. He who had the power to give it to me was right in not helping me, for so often had He brought me back to Himself and so often had I abandoned Him.

Well, my soul now was tired; and, in spite of its desire, my wretched habits would not allow it rest. It happened to me that one day entering the oratory I saw a statue they had borrowed for a certain feast to be celebrated in the house. It represented the much wounded Christ and was very devotional, so that beholding it I was utterly distressed in seeing Him that way, for it well represented what He suffered for us. I felt so keenly aware of how poorly I thanked Him for those wounds that, it seems to me, my heart broke. Beseeching Him to strengthen me once and for all that I might not offend Him, I threw myself down before Him with the greatest outpouring of tears.

I was very devoted to the glorious Magdalene and frequently thought about her conversion, especially when I received Communion. For since I knew the Lord was certainly present there within me, I, thinking that He would not despise my tears, placed myself at His feet. And I didn't know what I was saying (He did a great deal who allowed me to shed them for Him, since I so quickly forgot that sentiment); and I commended myself to this glorious saint that she might obtain pardon for me....

This is the method of prayer I then used: since I could not reflect discursively with the intellect, I strove to picture Christ within me, and it did me greater good—in my opinion—to picture Him in those scenes where I saw Him more alone. It seemed to me that being alone and afflicted, as a person in need, He had to accept me. I had many simple thoughts like these.

The scene of His prayer in the garden, especially, was a comfort to me; I strove to be His companion there. If I could, I thought of the sweat and agony He had undergone in that place. I desired to wipe away the sweat He so painfully experienced, but I recall that I never dared to actually do it, since my sins appeared to me so serious. I remained with Him as long as my thoughts allowed me to, for there were many distractions that tormented me. Most nights, for many years before going to bed when I commended myself to God in preparation for sleep, I always pondered for a little while this episode of the prayer in the garden....

I had such little ability to represent things with my intellect that if I hadn't seen the things, my imagination was not of use to me, as it is to other persons who can imagine things and thus recollect themselves. I could only think about Christ as He was as man, but never in such a way that I could picture Him within myself, no matter how much I read about His beauty or how many images I saw of Him....

I found great consolation in sinners whom, after having been sinners, the Lord brought back to Himself. It seemed to me I could find help in them and that since the Lord had pardoned them He could pardon me. But there was one thing that left me inconsolable, as I have mentioned, and that was that the Lord called them only once, and they did not turn back and fall again; whereas in my case I had turned back so often that I was worn out from it. But by considering the love He bore me, I regained my courage, for I never lost confidence in His mercy; in myself, I lost it many times.

Oh, God help me, how it frustrates me, my soul's blindness despite so much assistance from God! It made me fearful to see how little I could do by myself and how bound I became so that I was unable to resolve to give myself entirely to God.

As I began to read the *Confessions* [of St. Augustine], it seemed to me I saw myself in them. I began to commend myself very much to this glorious saint. When I came to the passage where he speaks about his conversion and read how he heard that voice in the garden, it only seemed to me, according to what I felt in my heart, that it was I the Lord called. I remained for a long time totally dissolved in tears and feeling within myself utter distress and weariness. Oh, how a soul suffers, God help me, by losing the freedom it should have in being itself; and what torments it undergoes! I marvel now at how I could have lived in such great affliction. May God be praised who gave me the life to rise up from a death so deadly.

It seemed to me my soul gained great strength from the Divine Majesty and that He must have heard my cries and taken pity on so many tears. The inclination to spend more time with Him began to grow. I started to shun the occasions of sin, because when they were avoided, I then returned to loving His Majesty. In my opinion, I clearly understood that I loved Him; but I did not understand as I should have what true love of God consists in.

Life, chapters 8 and 9

John Wesley, Founder of the Methodists
A Heart Strangely Warmed

24 May 1738. In the evening I went very unwillingly to a society in Aldersgate-street, where one was reading Luther's preface to the Epistle to the Romans. About a quarter before nine, while he was describing the change which God works in the heart through faith in Christ, I felt my heart strangely warmed. I felt I did trust in Christ, Christ alone, for salvation; and an assurance was given me that He had taken away my sins, even mine, and saved me from the law of sin and death.

I began to pray with all my might for those who had in a more especial manner despitefully used me and persecuted me. I then testified openly to all there what I now first felt in my heart. But it was not long before the enemy suggested, "This cannot be faith; for where is thy joy?" Then was I taught that peace and victory over sin are essential to faith in the Captain of our salvation; but that, as to the transports of joy that usually attend the beginning of it, especially in those who had mourned deeply, God sometimes giveth, sometimes withholdeth them, according to the counsels of his own will.

After my return home I was much buffeted with temptations; but cried out, and they fled away. They returned again and again. I as often lifted up my eyes, and He "sent me help from his holy place." And herein I found the difference between this and my former state chiefly consisted. I was striving, yea, fighting with all my might under the law, as well as under grace. But then I was sometimes, if not often, conquered; now, I was always conqueror.

25 May. The moment I awaked, "Jesus, Master," was in my heart and in my mouth; and I found all my strength lay in keeping my eye fixed upon him, and my soul waiting on him continually. Being again at St. Paul's in the afternoon, I could taste the good word of God in the anthem, which began, "My song shall be always of the loving-kindness of the Lord: with my mouth will I ever be showing forth thy truth from one generation to another." Yet the enemy injected a fear, "If thou dost believe, why is there not a more sensible change?" I answered (yet not I), "That I know not. But this I know, I have 'now peace with God.' And I sin not to-day, and Jesus my Master has forbid me to take thought for the morrow."

The Journal

Søren Kierkegaard, Danish spiritual writer and philosopher
Remorse, Repentance, Confession: Eternity's Emissaries to Man
There is, then, something which should at all times be done. There is something which in no temporal sense shall have its time. Alas, and when this is not done, when it is omitted, or when just the opposite is done, then once again, there is something (or more correctly it is the same thing, that reappears, changed, but not changed in its essence) which should at all times be done. There is something which in no temporal sense shall have its time. There must be repentance and remorse....

But there is a concerned guide, a knowing one, who attracts the attention of the wanderer, who calls out to him that he should take care. That guide is remorse. He is not so quick of foot as the indulgent imagination, which is the servant of desire. He is not so strongly built as the victorious intention. He comes on slowly afterwards. He grieves. But he is a sincere and faithful friend.

If that guide's voice is never heard, then it is just because one is wandering along the way of perdition. For when the sick man who is wasting away from consumption believes himself to be in the best of health, his disease is at the most terrible point. If there were someone who early in life steeled his mind against all remorse and who actually carried it out, nevertheless remorse would come again if he were willing to repent even of this decision. So wonderful a power is remorse, so sincere is its friendship that to escape it entirely is the most terrible thing of all....

A Providence watches over each man's wandering through life. It provides him with two guides. The one calls him forward. The other calls him back. They are, however, not in opposition to each other, these two guides, nor do they leave the wanderer standing there in doubt, confused by the double call. Rather the two are in eternal understanding with each other. For the one beckons forward to the Good, the other calls man back from evil.... These two calls designate the place and show the way. Of these two, the call of remorse is perhaps the best. For the eager traveler who travels lightly along the way does not, in this fashion, learn to know it as well as a wayfarer with a heavy burden. The one who merely strives to get on does not learn to know the way as well as the remorseful man. The eager traveler hurries forward to the new, to the novel, and, indeed, away from experience. But the remorseful one, who comes behind, laboriously gathers up experience.

Purity of Heart Is to Will One Thing

Jonathan Edwards, Puritan minister and writer
First Conversion

I had a variety of concerns and exercises about my soul from childhood; but had two more remarkable seasons of awakening before I met with that change by which I was brought to those new dispositions, and that new sense of things that I have since had. The first time was when I was a boy, some years before I went to college, at a time of remarkable awakening in my father's congregation. I was then very much affected for many months, and concerned about the things of religion, and my soul's salvation, and was abundant in duties. I used to pray five times a day in secret, and to spend much time in religious talk with other boys, and used to meet with them to pray together. I experienced I know not what kind of delight in religion. My mind was much engaged in it, and had much self-righteous pleasure, and it was my delight to abound in religious duties. I, with some of my schoolmates joined together and built a booth in a swamp, in a very secret and retired place, for a place of prayer. And besides, I had particular secret places of my own in the woods, where I used to retire by myself and used to be from time to time much affected. My affections seemed to be lively and easily moved, and I seemed to be in my element when I engaged in religious duties. And I am ready to think, many are deceived with such affections, and such a kind of delight, as I then had in religion, and mistake it for grace.

But in process of time my convictions and affections wore off, and I entirely lost all those affections and delights, and left off secret prayer, at least as to any constant performance of it, and returned like a dog to his vomit, and went on in ways of sin....

But God would not suffer me to go on with any quietness, but I had great and violent inward struggles; until after many conflicts with wicked inclinations, and repeated resolutions, and bonds that I laid myself under by a kind of vows to God, I was brought wholly to break off all former wicked ways, and all ways of known outward sin, and to apply myself to seek my salvation, and practice the duties of religion; but without that kind of affection and delight that I had formerly experienced. My concern now wrought more by inward struggles and conflicts and self-reflections. I made seeking my salvation the main business of my life. But yet, it seems to me, I sought after a miserable manner, which has made me sometimes since to question whether ever it issued in that which was saving, being ready to doubt whether such miserable seeking was ever succeeded. But yet I was brought to seek salvation in a manner that I never was before. I felt a spirit to part with all things in the world for an interest in Christ....

From about that time, I began to have a new kind of apprehensions and ideas of Christ, and the work of redemption, and the glorious way of salvation by him. I had an inward, sweet sense of these things that at times came into my heart, and my soul was led away in pleasant views and contemplations of them. And my mind was greatly engaged to spend my time in reading and meditating on Christ, and the beauty and excellency of his person, and the lovely way of salvation by free grace in him.

The Life and Character of Mr. Jonathan Edwards

C.S. Lewis
Enormous Bliss

As I stood beside a flowering currant bush on a summer day there suddenly arose in me without warning, and as if from a depth not of years but of centuries, the memory of that earlier morning at the Old House when my brother had brought his toy garden into the nursery. It is difficult to find words strong enough for the sensation which came over me; Milton's "enormous bliss" of Eden (giving the full, ancient meaning to "enormous") comes somewhere near it. It was a sensation, of course, of desire; but desire for what? Not, certainly, for a biscuit tin filled with moss, nor even (though that came into it) for my own past. ʼΙοῦ λίαν ποθῶ* and before I knew what I desired, the desire itself was gone, the whole glimpse withdrawn, the world turned commonplace again, or only stirred by a longing for the longing that had just ceased. It had taken only a moment of time; and in a certain sense everything else that had happened to me was insignificant in comparison.

The odd thing was that before God closed in on me, I was in fact offered what now appears a moment of wholly free choice. In a sense. I was going up Headington Hill on the top of a bus. Without words and (I think) almost without images, a fact about myself was somehow presented to me. I became aware that I was holding something at bay, or shutting something out. Or, if you like, that I was wearing some stiff clothing, like corsets, or even a suit of armor, as if I were a lobster. I felt myself being, there and then, given a free choice. I could open the door or keep it shut; I could unbuckle the armor or keep it on. Neither choice was presented as a duty; no threat or promise was attached to either, though I knew that to open the door or to take off the corslet meant the incalculable. The choice appeared to be momentous but it was also strangely unemotional. I was moved by no desires or fears. In a sense I was not moved by anything. I chose to open, to unbuckle, to loosen the rein. I say, "I chose," yet it did not really seem possible to do the opposite. On the other hand, I was aware of no motives. You could argue that I was not a free agent, but I am more inclined to think that this came nearer to being a perfectly free act than most that I have ever done. Necessity may not be the opposite of freedom, and perhaps a man is most free when, instead of producing motives, he could only say, "I am what I do." Then came the repercussion on the imaginative level. I felt as if I were a man of snow at long

---

*Oh, I desire too much.

last beginning to melt. The melting was starting in my back—drip-drip and presently trickle-trickle. I rather disliked the feeling.

Surprised by Joy

Father Reginald Garrigou-Lagrange, O.P., Dominican theologian
The Beginning of the Interior Life

The interior life, as we said, presupposes the state of grace, which is the seed of eternal life. Nevertheless the state of grace, which exists in every infant after Baptism and in every penitent after the absolution of his sins, does not suffice to constitute what is customarily called the interior life of a Christian. In addition, there are required a struggle against what would make us fall back into sin and a serious tendency of the soul toward God.

From this point of view, to give a clear idea of what the interior life should be, we shall do well to compare it with the intimate conversation that each of us has with himself. If one is faithful, this intimate conversation tends, under the influence of grace, to become elevated, to be transformed, and to become a conversation with God. This remark is elementary; but the most vital and profound truths are elementary truths about which we have thought for a long time, by which we have lived, and which finally become the object of almost continual contemplation....

As soon as a man ceases to be outwardly occupied, to talk with his fellow men, as soon as he is alone, even in the noisy streets of a great city, he begins to carry on a conversation with himself. If he is young, he often thinks of his future; if he is old, he thinks of the past, and his happy or unhappy experience of life makes him usually judge persons and events very differently.

If a man is fundamentally egotistical, his intimate conversation with himself is inspired by sensuality or pride. He converses with himself about the object of his cupidity, of his envy; finding therein sadness and death, he tries to flee from himself, to live outside of himself, to divert himself in order to forget the emptiness and the nothingness of his life. In this intimate conversation of the egoist with himself there is a certain very inferior self-knowledge and a no less inferior self-love.

He is acquainted especially with the sensitive part of his soul, that part which is common to man and to the animal. Thus he has sensible joys, sensible sorrows, according as the weather is pleasant or unpleasant, as he wins money or loses it. He has desires and aversions of the same sensible order, and when he is opposed, he has moments of impatience and anger prompted by inordinate self-love.

The Egoist. But the egoist knows little about the spiritual part of his soul, that which is common to the angel and to man. Even if he believes in the spirituality of the soul and of the higher faculties, intellect and will, he does not live in this spiritual order. He does not, so to speak, know experimentally this higher part of himself and he does not love it sufficiently. If he knew it, he would find in it the image of God and he would begin to love himself, not in an egotistical manner for himself, but for God. His thoughts almost always fall back on what is inferior in him, and though he often shows intelligence and cleverness which may even become craftiness and cunning, his intellect, instead of rising, always inclines toward what is inferior to it. It is made to contemplate God, the supreme truth, and it often dallies in error, sometimes obstinately defending the error by every means. It has been said that if life is not on a level with thought, thought ends by descending to the level of life. All declines, and one's highest convictions gradually grow weaker.

The intimate conversation of the egoist with himself proceeds thus to death and is therefore not an interior life. His self-love leads him to wish to make himself the center of everything, to draw everything to himself, both persons and things. Since this is impossible, he frequently ends in disillusionment and disgust; he becomes unbearable to himself and to others, and ends by hating himself because he wished to love himself excessively. At times he ends by hating life because he desired too greatly what is inferior in it.

If a man who is not in the state of grace begins to seek goodness, his intimate conversation with himself is already quite different. He converses with himself, for example, about what is necessary to live becomingly and to support his family. This at times preoccupies him greatly; he feels his weakness and the need of placing his confidence no longer in himself alone, but in God.

The Beginning of the Spiritual Life. While still in the state of mortal sin, this man may have Christian faith and hope, which subsist in us even after the loss of charity as long as we have not sinned mortally by incredulity, despair, or presumption. When this is so, this man's intimate conversation with himself is occasionally illumined by the supernatural light of faith; now and then he thinks of eternal life and desires it, although this desire remains weak. He is sometimes led by a special inspiration to enter a church to pray.

Finally, if this man has at least attrition for his sins and receives absolution for them, he recovers the state of grace and charity, the love of God and neighbor. Thenceforth when he is alone, his intimate conversation with himself changes. He begins to love himself in a holy manner, not for himself but for God, and to love his own for God; he begins to understand that he must pardon his enemies and love them, and to wish eternal life for them as he does for himself. Often, however, the intimate conversation of a man in the state of grace continues to be tainted with egoism, self-love, sensuality, and pride. These sins are no longer mortal in him, they are venial; but if they are repeated, they incline him to fall into a serious sin, that is, to fall back into spiritual death. Should this happen, this man tends again to flee from himself because what he finds in himself is no longer life but death. Instead of making a salutary reflection on this subject, he may hurl himself back farther into death by casting himself into pleasure, into the satisfactions of sensuality or of pride.

In a man's hours of solitude, this intimate conversation begins again in spite of everything, as if to prove to him that it cannot stop. He would like to interrupt it, yet he cannot do so. The center of the soul has an irrestrainable need which demands satisfaction. In reality, God alone can answer this need, and the only solution is straightway to take the road leading to Him. The soul must converse with someone other than itself. Why? Because it is not its own last end; because its end is the living God, and it cannot rest entirely except in Him. As St. Augustine puts it: "Our heart is restless, until it repose in Thee."

The interior life is precisely an elevation and a transformation of the intimate conversation that everyone has with himself as soon as it tends to become a conversation with God.

St. Paul says: "For what man knoweth the things of a man but the spirit of a man that is in him? So the things also that are of God no man knoweth, but the Spirit of God" (see 1 Cor. 2:11).

The Spirit of God progressively manifests to souls of good will what God desires of them and what He wishes to give them. May we receive with docility all that God wishes to give us! Our Lord says to those who seek Him: "Thou wouldst not seek Me if thou hadst not already found Me."

This progressive manifestation of God to the soul that seeks Him is not unaccompanied by a struggle; the soul must free itself from the bonds which are the results of sin, and gradually there disappears what St. Paul calls "the old man" and there takes shape "the new man."

He writes to the Romans: "I find then a law, that when I have a will to do good, evil is present with me. For I am delighted with the law of God, according to the inward man; but I see another law in my members, fighting against the law of my mind" (Rom. 7:21-23).

What St. Paul calls "the inward man" is what is primary and most elevated in us: reason illumined by faith and the will, which should dominate the sensibility, common to man and animals.

St. Paul also says: "For which cause we faint not; but though our outward man is corrupted, yet the inward man is renewed day by day" (see 2 Cor. 4:16). His spiritual youth is continually renewed, like that of the eagle, by the graces which he receives daily. This is so true that the priest who ascends the altar can always say, though he be ninety years old: "I will go in to the altar of God: to God who giveth joy to my youth" (Ps. 42:4).

St. Paul insists on this thought in his epistle to the Colossians: "Lie not one to another: stripping yourselves of the old man with his deeds, and putting on the new, him who is renewed unto knowledge, according to the image of Him that created him, where there is neither Gentile nor Jew ... nor barbarian nor Scythian, bond nor free. But Christ is all and in all" (Col. 3:9-11). The inward man is renewed unceasingly in the image of God, who does not grow old. The life of God is above the past, the present, and the future; it is measured by the single instant of immobile eternity. Likewise the risen Christ dies no more and possesses eternal youth. Now He vivifies us by ever new graces that He may render us like Himself. St. Paul wrote in a similar strain to the Ephesians: "For this cause I bow my knees to the Father of our Lord Jesus Christ ... that He would grant you, according to the riches of His glory, to be strengthened by His Spirit with might unto the inward man, that Christ may dwell by faith in your hearts; that, being rooted and founded in charity, you may be able to comprehend with all the saints, what is the breadth and length and height and depth; to know also the charity of Christ, which surpasseth all knowledge, that you may be filled unto all the fullness of God" (Eph. 3:14-19).

St. Paul clearly depicts in these lines the interior life in its depth, that life which tends constantly toward the contemplation of the mystery of God and lives by it in an increasingly closer union with Him. He wrote this letter not for some privileged souls alone, but to all the Christians of Ephesus as well as those of Corinth.

Furthermore, St. Paul adds: "Be renewed in the spirit of your mind: and put on the new man, who according to God is created in justice and holiness of truth.... And walk in love, as Christ also hath loved us, and hath delivered Himself for us, an oblation and a sacrifice to God for an odor of sweetness" (Eph. 4:23; 5:2).

In the light of these inspired words, which recall all that Jesus promised us in the beatitudes and all that He gave us in dying for us, we can define the interior life as follows: It is a supernatural life which, by a true spirit of abnegation and prayer, makes us tend to union with God and leads us to it.

It implies one phase in which purification dominates, another of progressive illumination in view of union with God, as all tradition teaches, thus making a distinction between the purgative way of beginners, the illuminative way of proficients, and the unitive way of the perfect.

The Three Ages of the Interior Life

Dag Hammarskjöld, Swedish statesman and
former secretary general of the United Nations
The Light of Love
We can reach the point where it becomes possible for us to recognize and understand Original Sin, that dark counter-center of evil in our nature—that is to say, though it *is* not our nature, it is *of* it—that something within us which rejoices when disaster befalls the very cause we are trying to serve, or misfortune overtakes even those whom we love.

Life in God is not an escape from this, but the way to gain full insight concerning it. It is not our depravity which forces a fictitious religious explanation upon us, but the experience of religious reality which forces the "Night Side" out into the light.

It is when we stand in the righteous all-seeing light of love that we can dare to look at, admit, and *consciously* suffer under this something in us which wills disaster, misfortune, defeat to everything outside the sphere of our narrowest self-interest. So a living relation to God is the necessary precondition for the self-knowledge which enables us to follow a straight path, and so be victorious over ourselves, forgiven by ourselves.

Markings

Mother Teresa of Calcutta
On Conversion

Conversion is love in action between God and the soul. The principal obstacle to conversion is sin. That is why the tenderness of God's love is so great that he gave us Jesus to wash away all our sins. He does this in confession through the merits of his Precious Blood. For that reason we go to confession and we become sinners without sin. This is true conversion: the love of God in the vivifying action of tender and merciful love. The pure of heart can see God in every person. Then naturally such a person will want to share the joy of love with one's own family and neighbors, especially those who have done us harm or those whom we have harmed. This is truly the fruit of authentic conversion, because where there is love, there is God.

Letter to the Eucharistic Congress at Seoul, South Korea, October 1989

TWO

Purification

Seek first his kingdom and his righteousness, and all these things shall be yours as well (Mt. 6:33).

Almost every well-articulated religious tradition leads its followers to a period of moral conversion or purification at the beginning of the spiritual journey. This purification is often symbolized in ritual and liturgical rites by cleansing ceremonies, for example, washings and even baptisms. It is the inner struggle for virtue and the rejection of sinful ways that is the real purification. Often in societies corrupted by wealth and indulgence, like ancient Rome, or in our own consumerist culture, people attempt a religious experience without practicing virtue. They focus narrowly on a few good qualities and leave out a total moral conversion. These good qualities, like selective concern for social justice or this or that good cause, are often displayed with a certain self-righteousness. Meanwhile, the whole range of virtues, natural and supernatural, is ignored. This is gnosticism at its worst. The following selections are aimed at the mists of New Age gnostic attitudes, which separate virtue from religious experience. They are also aimed at the silly vices of a silly time.

No religious faith is more deeply opposed to spirituality without morality than the Gospel of Jesus Christ. "If you love me, you will keep my commandments" (Jn. 14:15) is a very helpful challenge for the disciples of Christ to keep in mind in these days of worldly religiosity. This sobering truth is brought out in the following selections: There is no possibility of any genuine growth in the life given by the Holy Spirit without a long, painful struggle against one's own self-indulgence and self-seeking. Purification and repentance may seem to be rather grim ideas unless one approaches them with the spirit of Psalm 51:11-12: "Cast me not away from thy presence, and take not thy holy Spirit from me. Restore to me the joy of thy salvation, and uphold me with a willing spirit."

Gerald Heard, English spiritual writer
The First Step

We must start without delay on the painful, steep, humiliating path of undoing our busy, deliberately deluded selves. So only will the Kingdom come, where it must come fully and where we alone can decide whether it shall come—in ourselves. "The Kingdom of God is within you," yes, but only if we are prepared to let that powerful germ of eternal life grow, until it splits away and consumes this husk, our ego. Unless we, this person with his tightly bound triple self-love—love of his physical appetites and comforts, of his possessions, of his place, rank, and recognition—unless that hard and hardening nut is buried and rots and is eaten away by the new life's germ, there is no hope. Indeed we may say that the whole secret of the spiritual life is just this painful struggle to come awake, to become really conscious. And, conversely, the whole process and technique of evil is to do just the reverse to us: to lull us to sleep, to distract us from what is creeping up within us; to tell us that we are busy workers for the Kingdom when we are absent-mindedly (while we daydream of our importance) spreading death, not life....

That, then, is the first step, known by the grim technical term, purgation. I must start with myself, and stay with myself until some intention appears in my actions, some consistency between what I say and do. I must not escape into denunciation, coercion, or even superior concern for anyone else. I shall do so if I can; that is the invariable trick of the ego, trying to escape and save itself from its necessary death.... Then, after that complete abandonment of serving two masters—my view of myself as a master-builder gaining recognition by my active goodness, and of God—then comes the next step, illumination. I am still far below being capable of a creative act. That is God's prerogative, and He gives it only to those who have given themselves away that He may occupy the space they once filled. But I am permitted at last to see things as they are. Fear and hurry and anxiety leave me. Why? Because, though still extremely ignorant, I know one thing at last. I know that God exists. There is utter Reality, complete creative power holding the entire creation in its grasp. The whole of time and space is no more than an incident, a minute episode in the immeasurable order, power, and glory of complete Being. Once I have seen, really seen, that, once I am illuminated, then I have fully attained one step in approaching God's Kingdom and in letting it approach; I no longer am standing in the way. I cease to be a reason for people not believing in God.

The Creed of Christ

Father Rudolph S. Schnackenburg,
distinguished German Catholic Scripture scholar
Christ's Call to Conversion
We must let the words of Jesus stand in all their severity and ruggedness. Any mitigation, however well intended, is an attack on his moral mission. But how Jesus judges those who fall short of his demands is quite another matter. His behavior towards his disciples gives us an object lesson on this point. He took back even Simon Peter, who denied him three times and yet was the leader in the circle of the twelve, after Peter had bitterly repented his action, and He confirmed him in his position as chief of the disciples and shepherd of his sheep (cf. Luke 22:32; John 21:15-17). Admonition and mercy are found together. It is the mercy of God which always comes first. It comes definitively into history with the person and works of Jesus. But Jesus also longs to awaken the ultimate powers for good in those laid hold of by the love of God and saved from eternal ruin. They should now thankfully do the holy will of God in its totality, unalloyed. If in spite of everything they again succumb to human weakness and wretchedness, God's mercy will not fail if they turn back in penitence. To be sure, that is not stated explicitly in Jesus' sayings (He calls men to a first repentance and warns them against backsliding), but it is in line with his teaching as a whole (cf. the plenary power to forgive sins, John 20:23). The man who has a genuinely penitent outlook will not misunderstand the two facets of Jesus' mission—the proclamation of salvation to sinners and the call to complete submission to God. He will neither abuse the mercy of God and despise the commandments of Jesus, nor collapse under

the severity of his demands and despair of the grace of God. With the idea of the following of Christ, there is an even closer coincidence of God's guidance and his demands. "The living Christ is there to show the way to all who are ready to follow him. What is more, the strength to follow him is also there. The living Christ has two hands, one to point out the way, and the other to stretch out to help us onward" (T. W. Manson, *Ethics*, p.68).

The Moral Theology of the New Testament

Cardinal John Henry Newman
Original Sin—The Obvious Fact

If I looked into a mirror, and did not see my face, I should have the sort of feeling which actually comes upon me, when I look into this living busy world, and see no reflection of its Creator.... Were it not for this voice, speaking so clearly in my conscience and my heart, I should be an atheist, or a pantheist, or a polytheist when I looked into the world.... The sight of the world is nothing else than the prophet's scroll, full of "lamentations, and mourning, and woe."

To consider the world in its length and breadth, its various history, the many races of man, their starts, their fortunes, their mutual alienation, their conflicts; and then their ways, habits, governments, forms of worship; their enterprises, their aimless courses, their random achievements and acquirements, the impotent conclusion of long-standing facts, the tokens so faint and broken of a super-intending design, the blind evolution of what turn out to be great powers or truths, the progress of things, as if from unreasoning elements, not towards final causes, the greatness and littleness of man, his far-reaching aims, his short duration, the curtain hung over his futurity, the disappointments of life, the defeat of good, the success of evil, physical pain, mental anguish, the prevalence and intensity of sin, the pervading idolatries, the corruptions, the dreary hopeless irreligion, that condition of the whole race, so fearfully yet exactly described in the Apostle's words, "having no hope and without God in the world"....

What shall be said to this heart-piercing, reason-bewildering fact? I can only answer that either there is no Creator or this living society of men is in a true sense discarded from His presence.... *If* there be a God, *since* there is a God, the human race is implicated in some terrible aboriginal calamity. It is out of joint with the purposes of its Creator. This is a fact, a fact as true as the fact of its existence; and thus the doctrine of what is theologically called original sin becomes to me almost as certain as that the world exists, and as the existence of God.

Apologia pro Vita Sua

Father Cajetan of Bergamo, O.F.M. Cap.
The Beginning of Sin

If we examine all our falls into sin, whether venial or grave, the cause will always be found in some hidden pride; and true indeed are the words of the Holy Ghost: "For pride is the beginning of all sin" (Sirach 10:13). Of this truth our Lord Jesus Christ Himself has warned us in His Gospel where He says: "And whosoever shall exalt himself shall be humbled" (Matt. 23:12). God can give no greater humiliation to a soul than to allow it to fall into sin, because sin is the lowest depth of all that is base, vile and ignominious.

Therefore each time that we are humbled by falling into sin, it is certain that we must previously have exalted ourselves by some act of pride; because only the proud are threatened with the punishment of this humiliation: "And he humbled himself afterwards, because his heart had been lifted up" (2 Chron. 32:26). For thus it is written of King Hezekiah in holy Scripture, and the inspired writer has also said: "Before destruction the heart of man is exalted" (Prov. 18:12).

Humility of Heart

Growing in Virtue

In every world religion that teaches a spiritual path, the great step after initial conversion is purgation—the purifying of the heart and life of the individual from serious moral faults, sins, self-centered attitudes and, as far as possible, the voluntary indulgence of sinful inclinations. Christ summed up this requirement very succinctly and with Jewish directness, saying, "If you love me, you will keep my commandments" (Jn. 14:15). This process can and should be seen in a positive way as growth in the life of moral virtues or moral inclinations. Virtues are good traits consistently observable in a person's behavior. There are always some who enjoy an awareness of the divine or the transcendent, almost in a recreational way, but who never get their act together. They are religious, but they are never spiritual—a bad state of affairs.

The natural virtues—the consistent qualities of a good person—were outlined by the Greek philosophers among others, long before the Gospel. These natural virtues are generally grouped under four headings: prudence, justice, temperance, and fortitude or courage. One or several of these may be observed in the lives of those who are far from faith or any real religious commitment. There are prudent embezzlers and courageous crooks. A devout natural man without grace will struggle to have a coherent set of values, although as Garrigou-Lagrange points out, this effort will leave him deeply unsatisfied. His goal—a decent, peaceful life in the shadows of this world—must leave his heart restless. The so-called happy life is intrinsically unhappy because of its very passing nature. In a person of faith seeking to love and serve God, these same qualities, or virtues, will be raised to the level of supernatural qualities by the Holy Spirit. The goal will no longer be the happy life but eternal life in union with God. Then these same good qualities will be properly called supernatural Christian virtues.

Although they have the same names, and often the same results, the natural and supernatural virtues may clash dramatically. In the powerful play *A Man for All Seasons*, the king of England, Henry VIII, insists that his subjects sign an oath affirming that the king is the head of the Church in England. That decent chap the Earl of Essex tries to convince Thomas More that it is prudent to sign the oath because the king is dangerous and on the road to self-destruction. Thomas, while content that it does not bother the Earl of Essex to sign the oath, finds it is against his own faith and values to do so. He reminds Essex that if he—More—signs, he will go to hell, because he knows it is wrong. The faith and courage of Thomas in this world and his reward in the next are excellent illustrations of the difference between natural and supernatural virtues. As a person is more and more open to the Holy Spirit, the power of His action will be seen increasingly in the person's behavior. The following selections are entirely focused on the supernatural moral virtues, that is, on the qualities of behavior in Christians open to the operations of the Spirit. These few selections are chosen from an immense library of writings on the moral integrity of a true Christian life. We need to consider whether we are consistently following the Sermon on the Mount and the Gospel parables, which represent the purest teaching on the manner of life to which Christ has called us.

Often our actions are a mixture of natural and supernatural virtues. We have a foot in both camps. The Holy Spirit infuses our actions so that they may become more purely motivated and thereby are part of our spiritual journey. To act because of supernatural Christian virtue is to let that life be in us which was in Christ Jesus. These are important questions, essential for spiritual growth: How truly Christian is my life? How often do I act with a pure heart, with meekness, with poverty of spirit? If I fail to do so, do I complain that I am not blessed?

St. Francis de Sales, 17th-century bishop of Geneva
Every Virtuous Life Leads to God

When God the Creator made all things, he commanded the plants to bring forth fruit each according to its own kind; he has likewise commanded Christians, who are the living plants of his Church, to bring forth the fruits of devotion, each one in accord with his character, his station, and his calling.

I say that devotion must be practiced in different ways by the nobleman and by the working man, by the servant and by the prince, by the widow, by the unmarried girl, and by the married woman. But even this distinction is not sufficient; for the practice of devotion must be adapted to the strength, to the occupation, and to the duties of each one in particular.

Tell me, please, my Philothea, whether it is proper for a bishop to want to lead a solitary life like a Carthusian; or for married people to be no more concerned than a Capuchin about increasing their income; or for a working man to spend his whole day in church like a religious; or on the other hand for a religious to be constantly exposed like a bishop to all the events and circumstances that bear on the needs of our neighbor. Is not this sort of devotion ridiculous, unorganized and intolerable? Yet this absurd error occurs very frequently, but in no way does true devotion, my Philothea, destroy anything at all. On the contrary, it perfects and fulfills all things. In fact, if it ever works against, or is inimical to, anyone's legitimate station and calling, then it is very definitely false devotion.

The bee collects honey from flowers in such a way as to do the least damage or destruction to them, and he leaves them whole, undamaged and fresh, just as he found them. True devotion does still better. Not only does it not injure any sort of calling or occupation, it even embellishes and enhances it.

Moreover, just as every sort of gem, cast in honey, becomes brighter and more sparkling, each according to its color, so each person becomes more acceptable and fitting in his own vocation when he sets his vocation in the context of devotion. Through devotion your family cares become more peaceful, mutual love between husband and wife becomes more sincere, the service we owe to the prince becomes more faithful, and our work, no matter what it is, becomes more pleasant and agreeable.

It is therefore an error and even a heresy to wish to exclude the exercise of devotion from military divisions, from the artisans' shops, from the courts of princes, from family households. I acknowledge, my dear Philothea, that the type of devotion which is purely contemplative, monastic and religious can certainly not be exercised in these sorts of stations and occupations, but besides this threefold type of devotion, there are many others fit for perfecting those who live in a secular state.

Therefore, in whatever situations we happen to be, we can and we must aspire to the life of perfection.

The Introduction to the Devout Life

Father Gabriel of St. Mary Magdalen
True Prudence

True supernatural prudence consists in setting the highest value on each fleeting moment in view of our eternal goal. Human prudence values time as a means to accumulate earthly goods; supernatural prudence values it as a means to accumulate eternal goods. "Lay not up for yourself treasures on earth ... but lay up for yourselves treasures in heaven, where neither the rust nor moth consumes.... Seek ye therefore first the kingdom of God, and his justice, and all these things shall be added unto you" (Mt. 6:19,20,33). These are the chief rules of prudence, dictated by Jesus Himself.

St. Thérèse said to a religious who told her that she disliked doing a certain act of charity which required a great spirit of sacrifice, "I would have been glad to do it, since we are on earth to suffer. The more we suffer, the happier we are. How little you know about regulating your affairs!" Supernatural prudence teaches us how to regulate our affairs, not in view of earthly happiness, but of eternal beatitude; not in view of our own selfish interests, but in view of our progress in the way of perfection; and above all in view of the glory of God and the good of souls.

Supernatural prudence does not judge things according to the pleasure or displeasure they give us, but it evaluates them in the light of faith, in the light of eternity. "What is this worth in the light of eternity?" Whatsoever is not God, is nothing (St. Bernard).

Divine Intimacy

Monsignor Romano Guardini
Justice and the Judgment of God

A person is worthy of his humanity insofar as be strives to bring about justice in the place where he is; but as a whole, as that which it should be, as a condition of existence and an attitude of mankind, justice can never be attained. And here the idea of "progress" which has at present become a dogma, and the notion of the evolution of man beyond himself to ever greater heights must not confuse us. Personal experience as well as history tells another story. There is a basic disorder working in man which makes itself felt anew in every one who is born.

Only by God will true and complete justice be established, and only through His judgment. We should try to let the revelation that this judgment will be passed upon all mankind affect us deeply. The first thing that everyone who thinks of the judgment should say to himself is, "Judgment will be passed upon me!" But there will also be a judgment upon all the human institutions and powers about which we are so likely to feel that they are sovereign and subject to no examination: the state, civilization, history.

The judgment must be taken into account in all being and action. It is God's verdict upon every finite reality. Without it everything is half balanced in space. Only God determines it. He it is who sees through all, fearing nothing, bound by nothing, just in eternal truth. If a man does not believe in Him, his hunger and thirst shall never be satisfied.

The Virtues

William Law, English spiritual writer
Temperance and the Values of This World
Hence also appears the necessity of renouncing all those foolish and unreasonable expenses which the pride and folly of mankind have made so common and fashionable in the world. For if it is necessary to do good works as far as you are able, it must be as necessary to renounce those needless ways of spending money which render you unable to do works of charity.

You must therefore no more conform to these ways of the world than you must conform to the vices of the world; you must no more spend with those that idly waste their money as their own humor leads them than you must drink with the drunken, or indulge yourself with the epicure, because a course of such expenses is no more consistent with a life of charity than excess in drinking is consistent with a life of sobriety. When therefore anyone tells you of the lawfulness of expensive apparel, or the innocency of pleasing yourself with costly satisfactions, only imagine that the same person was to tell you that you need not do works of charity, that Christ does not require you to do good unto your poor brethren as unto Him, and then you will see the wickedness of such advice; for to tell you that you may live in such expenses as make it impossible for you to live in the exercise of good works is the same thing as telling you that you need not have any care about such good works themselves.

A Serious Call to a Devout and Holy Life

St. Dorotheos of Gaza, 6th-century Desert Father
Why Do We Fritter Away Our Lives?
Let us attend to ourselves, brothers, let us learn self-control while we have time. Why do we neglect ourselves? Let us be doing something good all the time so that we may find help in the time of trial. Why do we fritter away our lives? We are always hearing a great deal about the spiritual life and we don't care about it; we even despise it. We see our brothers snatched away from our midst and we don't abstain [from passion and excess] even when we know that in a little while we too shall be near death. Look! Since the time we sat down at this conference, we have used up two or three hours of our time and got that much nearer to death. Yet we take care to exclude time from our thoughts and we have no fear. Why do we not remember that saying of the

Senior that, "If a man lose gold and silver, he can always find more to replace it. Time once lost cannot be found again by living in idleness and negligence. No matter how hard we try to regain one hour of this time, we shall never find it." How many desire to hear the word of God and find no one to expound it, while we hear and despise it and are not stirred up by it. God knows, I am frightened by our imperviousness. We who can be saved, and do not even desire it. For we can cut off our unruly desires when they are newly born and we don't think about it; we allow them to grow up and harden against us, so that we make the last evil greater than the first. For, as I often tell you, it is one thing to uproot a blade of grass and another to uproot a great tree.

One of the great old men was at recreation with his disciples in a place where there were cypresses of different shapes and sizes, some large, some small. And he said to one of his disciples, "Pull up that cypress over there." It was a very small one and immediately the disciple pulled it up with one hand. Then the old man showed him another one, larger than the first, and he said, "Pull up that one." Working it backwards and forwards with both hands, he pulled it up. The old man showed him yet a larger one, and with much more trouble he pulled that up too. Then he showed him an even larger one and with much more labor, straining backwards and forwards and sweating profusely, he finally lifted that one too. Then the old man showed him a still larger one, but for all his energy and sweating he could not pull it up. And when the old man saw that he could not pull it up, he turned to another brother [and told him] to get up and help him, but even the two of them together could not pull it up. Then the old man said to all the brothers, "So it is with our evil desires: insofar as they are small to start with, we can, if we want to, cut them off with ease. If we neglect them as mere trifles they harden, and the more they harden, the more labor is needed to get rid of them. But if they grow to any degree of maturity inside us, we shall no longer be able to remove them from ourselves no matter how we labor unless we have the help of the saints interceding for us with God."

Discourses and Sayings

Monsignor Romano Guardini
Following the Courage of Christ

Have we ever thought about the truly divine courage of Christ? Have we understood the bravery that fired the heart of Jesus, when He, who came from the presence—St. John says "from the bosom"—of the Father, stepped into this earthly world? Into all the falsehood, the murderous cruelty, the pitiful narrowness of our existence? And He did this, not protected by the pride of the philosopher or secured by the tactics of the politician, not willing to repay guile with guile and blow with blow, but in the vulnerability of perfect purity.

Let us consider how we act amid the dangers of this world, how energetically we protect ourselves by all manner of means. Jesus never protected himself, but He accepted everything that the violence and unscrupulousness of men inflicted upon Him. We do not take the world as it is, but choose from it what pleases us. He accepted what the course of events brought upon Him, for this was the will of the Father. We know how to conform, to evade, and to seek advantages. His nature was such, and He spoke and acted in such a manner that what was most evil in men was challenged; that, as we read in Luke's Gospel, "the thoughts," the hidden disposition, "in the hearts of many were revealed" (Luke 2:35). He truly lived in the conditions of the world and endured them. The hour of Gethsemane lets us surmise what that meant. If we try to fathom all this, we may well shudder before what we can call the courage of God in Christ.

And He dared to live this life not in order to accomplish something of earthly grandeur, glorious heroism, or a noble work of art, but as a "redemption" for our sake. He lived so that we might gain the courage to be "Christians" in the world in which He was "Christ."

The Virtues

Mother Teresa of Calcutta
The Courage of Real Charity

To reach her Sisters in Beirut, long a cauldron of violence, [Mother Teresa] took a plane from Rome to Athens and then another plane to Cyprus. From Cyprus, the only means of reaching Beirut was a seventeen-hour boat trip. She found the six Sisters safe in Mar Takla, in East Beirut....

John de Salis, head of the Red Cross delegation in Lebanon, told Mother Teresa of the plight of mentally ill children in an asylum of the upper floor of Dar al-Ajaza Islamia, a home for the aged. The home, located near a camp of Palestinian refugees, had been damaged by bombs. The needs of the children for food, water, and adequate shelter were tragically acute. Mother Teresa decided that all the children could be housed with her Sisters who had already opened a refuge for the homeless and destitute. The problem was that Dar al-Ajaza was situated across the Green Line, the no-man's land separating that predominantly Muslim sector from East Beirut, home of the Christian Lebanese....

Mother Teresa insisted on crossing the line to evacuate the children. Against the advice even of church leaders, Mother Teresa traveled with four Red Cross vehicles into war-ravaged West Beirut to rescue the children. They found thirty-seven children, from seven to twenty-one, the most helpless examples of humanity. Among them were the deformed, the paralyzed, the severely mentally retarded, youngsters unaware of what was happening around them, but able to suffer hunger, thirst, and fear....

Mother Teresa went among them, embracing them and giving a handshake to the older children. Among the Muslim children were some Palestinians. One by one, Mother Teresa, the International Red Cross, and hospital workers picked up the children and carried or led them to the vehicles. The convoy crossed the Green Line at an Israeli-controlled checkpoint and rushed the children to the Mar Takla convent. Two days later, Mother Teresa crossed the Green Line again to evacuate another twenty-seven children.

One of the Red Cross officials commented: "What stunned everyone was her energy. She saw the problem, fell to her knees, and prayed for a few seconds, and then she was rattling off a list of supplies she needed.... We didn't expect a saint to be so efficient."

Eileen Egan,
Such a Vision of the Street:
Mother Teresa—The Spirit and the Work

Father Cajetan of Bergamo, O.F.M. Cap.
The Humility of Christ

Jesus Christ calls us all into His school to learn, not to work miracles nor to astonish the world by marvelous enterprises, but to be humble of heart. "Learn of Me, because I am meek and humble of heart" (Matt. 11:29). He has not called everyone to be doctors, preachers or priests, nor has He bestowed on all the gift of restoring sight to the blind, healing the sick, raising the dead or casting out devils, but to all He has said: Learn of Me to be humble of heart, and to all He has given the power to learn humility of Him. Innumerable things are worthy of imitation in the Incarnate Son of God, but He only asks us to imitate his humility....

Humility is in reality a confession of the greatness of God, who after His voluntary self-annihilation was exalted and glorified; wherefore Holy Writ says: "For great is the power of God alone, and He is honored by the humble" (Sirach 3:20)....

Humility is a virtue that belongs essentially to Christ, not only as man, but more especially as God, because with God to be good, holy and merciful is not virtue but nature, and humility is only a virtue. God cannot exalt Himself above what He is, in His most high Being, nor can He increase His vast and infinite greatness; but He can humiliate Himself as in fact He did humiliate and lower Himself. "He humbled Himself, He emptied Himself" (Phil. 2:7,8), revealing Himself to us through His humility as the Lord of all virtues, the conqueror of the world, of death, hell and sin.

No greater example of humility can be given than that of the only Son of God when the Word was made Flesh.

Humility of Heart

St. Augustine
The Challenge of Chastity

But now the voice of temptation was growing weaker. I had turned my face from it and, trembling, I could see the pure dignity of chastity serene and modestly joyful, summoning me in an honorable way so that I might come to her and not hesitate. She reached out to me with modest gestures so that I might join her and not run away. She beckoned to me, seeking to embrace me with pure hands, hands filled with so many examples of a virtuous life.

With her stood a crowd of young men and women and people of every age, mature widows and chaste single women, and in all of these there was a continence that was not barren but rather the mother of many children and these were the joyous satisfactions which had been given to her by you, O Lord, who are her spouse. She smiled at me, as if to say "Can't you do what all these others are doing? Remember, they can only do it with the help of the Lord their God. He, the Lord their God, gave them to me. Why do you rely on yourself and not stand at all? Cast yourself into His arms and don't be afraid. He will not drop you. Throw yourself trustingly into His arms, and He will embrace and heal you."

Confessions, Book 8

C.S. Lewis
Christian Chastity

Chastity is the most unpopular of the Christian virtues. There is no getting away from it: the Christian rule is, "Either marriage, with complete faithfulness to your partner, or else total abstinence." Now this is so difficult and so contrary to our instincts that obviously either Christianity is wrong or our sexual instinct, as it is now, has gone wrong. One or the other. Of course, being a Christian, I think it is the instinct which has gone wrong.

Monsignor Romano Guardini
Truth Belongs to God

This is a valid conclusion: He who holds to the truth holds to God. He who lies rebels against God and betrays the rational basis of existence.

In this world, the truth is weak. A trifle suffices to hide it. The most stupid persons can attack it. But some day the time will come when things will change. God will bring it about that truth will be as powerful as it is true; and this will be the judgment.

"Judgment" means that the possibility of lying ceases because omnipotent truth penetrates every mind, illumines every word and rules in every place. Then falsehood will be revealed as what it is. However expedient, clever, or elegant it may have been, it will be exposed as an illusion, as a nonentity.

We should let these thoughts occupy our minds, our understanding, and our hearts. Then we shall perhaps sense what truth is, its steadfastness, its calm radiance, its nobility. Then we will enter into union with it, through all that is most intimate and loyal within us. We will accept responsibility for the truth and expend our efforts in its behalf.

All this will suffer opposition and trials, because we are human. But our lives must testify to the fact that truth is the basis of everything—of the relation of man to man, of man to himself, of the individual to the community—and, above all, of man to God—no, of God to us.

The Virtues

Archbishop Fulton J. Sheen
Serenity

Spiritual joy is a serenity of temper in the midst of the changes of life, such as a mountain has when a storm breaks over it. To a man who has never rooted the soul in the Divine, every trouble exaggerates itself. He cannot put his full powers to any one thing, because he is troubled about many things.

Way to Happiness

THREE

Mature Faith

The apostles said to the Lord, "Increase our faith!" And the Lord said, "If you had faith as a grain of mustard seed, you could say to this sycamine tree, 'Be rooted up, and be planted in the sea,' and it would obey you" (Lk. 17:5-6).

Our Savior praises the faith of a little child because it is unquestioning. A child's faith must be complete because its world is filled with mysteries: "Why is the sky blue? Why did my grandmother have to die?" The child accepts the answer of trusted adults because of their authority. The faith of an adolescent often questions, and it must. Persons moving from childhood to maturity question what they have been told or the explanations they have received or at least how new knowledge fits in with what they already know to be true. To grow, adolescents must always be questioning and reorganizing their ideas because they are continually acquiring new information—some true, some half true, some mistaken or even deceptive. When it comes to religious belief, many people never get beyond this adolescent state of questioning. Consequently, they remain fixated in their efforts to understand all that they believe. Others are more fortunate. They achieve a level of maturity by surrendering to the mystery of God. Newman points out that this is an essential step if we are to continue making progress on the interior journey. A sense of mystery, or the psychological experience of awe at and acceptance of what goes beyond the mind of man in this world and the next, requires a certain humility and prayerfulness. When scholarly examination of theologically related matters ranging from Scripture to Church history is carried out without a sense of mystery, the individual gets stuck in a sterile mind game that may grasp details but never arrives at the whole Christian experience of the hidden God and the mystery of Christ. History indicates that this problem of intellectuals is to be expected in affluent societies like our own. In fact, this unhappy adolescent fixation can be seen in many talented religious people of our time. Perhaps this is why scholars often look so sad.

Mature faith, which requires only the intellectual application a person is capable of, moves far beyond the dust of the desks. It is alive, vital, always searching for new manifestations of the mystery of God, always ready to bow the stiff neck of pride before the Unknowable One. This is childlike faith. The truths of faith, based on divine revelation, are the rock on which the mature believer strives to evaluate all the opinions, discoveries, silly ideas, fads, hurdles, and distortions of the intellectual world. The believer can be in the world but never of it, in the sense that he stands on something altogether different—the rock of mature and unquestioning acceptance of the mystery of God. He may question how other things in experience relate to this mystery, but he does not question the mystery, as Newman points out. A God understood is an idol, a projection of the human mind, even if that idol is surrounded by the trappings of Christianity.

It is an observable phenomenon that maturity of faith is not simply the by-product of intelligence or hard-won scholarship. Maturity of faith comes through prayer and our willingness to accept the mysteriousness of God and the truths revealed by God. We must be willing to affirm these truths by faith and reason, and to allow faith alone to lift us beyond the final barriers to a place where intelligence cannot go. We are lifted up by the eagle wings of the Holy Spirit, and the mind, though limited, can repeatedly attempt to seek fresh analogies of divine things. The mind prayerfully looks through a glass darkly in a cautious and humble way. Otherwise theology becomes nothing more than an attempt to appease our doubts, or, worse, it is grandstanding with popular ideas that are grounded only in political correctness. This is a particularly embarrassing vice of our superficial times.

The just person, St. Paul tells us, lives guided by faith. When we face loss or rejection or even death because of our faith, then the depth of the maturity of our belief is revealed. The moving letter of Count von Moltke illustrates this strength in the face of death, which leads beyond faith to the beautiful, mysterious vision described by St. Ephrem of Syria.

Cardinal John Henry Newman
Preparing for Faith

Is not this the error, the common and fatal error, of the world, to think itself a judge of Religious Truth without preparation of heart? "I am the good Shepherd, and know My sheep, and am known of Mine." "He goeth before them, and the sheep follow Him, for they know His voice." "The pure in heart shall see God"; "to the meek mysteries are revealed"; "he that is spiritual judgeth all things." "The darkness comprehendeth it not." Gross eyes see not; heavy ears hear not. But in the schools of the world the ways towards Truth are considered high roads open to all men, however disposed, at all times. Truth is to be approached without homage. Everyone is considered on a level with his neighbor; or rather the powers of the intellect, acuteness, sagacity, subtleness, and depth, are thought the guides into Truth. Men consider that they have as full a right to discuss religious subjects as if they were themselves religious. They will enter upon the most sacred points of Faith at the moment, at their pleasure—if it so happen, in a careless frame of mind, in their hours of recreation, over the wine cup. Is it wonderful that they so frequently end in becoming indifferentists and conclude that Religious Truth is but a name, that all men are right and all wrong, from witnessing externally the multitude of sects and parties, and from the clear consciousness they possess within, that their own inquiries end in darkness?

Oxford University Sermons

I come then to this conclusion: If I must submit my reason to mysteries, it is not much matter whether it is a mystery more or a mystery less, when faith anyhow is the very essence of all religion, when the main difficulty to an inquirer is firmly to hold that there is a Living God, in spite of the darkness which surrounds Him, the Creator, Witness, and Judge of men. When once the mind is broken in, as it must be, to the belief of a Power above it, when once it understands that it is not itself the measure of all things in heaven and earth, it will have little difficulty in going forward. I do not say it will, or can, go on to other truths, without conviction; I do not say it ought to believe the Catholic faith without grounds and motives; but I say that when once it believes in God, the great obstacle to faith has been taken away—a proud, self-sufficient spirit. When once a man really, with the eyes of his soul and by the power of Divine grace, recognizes his Creator, he has passed a line; that has happened to him which cannot happen twice; he has bent his stiff neck and triumphed over himself. If he believes that God has no beginning, why not believe that He is Three yet One? if he owns that God created space, why not own also that He can cause a body to subsist without dependence on place? if he is obliged to grant that God created all things out of nothing, why doubt His power to change the substance of bread into the Body of His Son? It is as strange that, after an eternal rest, He should begin to create, as that, when He had once created, He should take on Himself a created nature; it is as strange that man should be allowed to fall so low, as we see before our eyes in so many dreadful instances, as that Angels and Saints should be exalted even to religious honors.

Discourses to Mixed Congregations

Matthias Joseph Scheeben, 19th-century German theologian
The Mystery of Christ

Christianity entered the world as a religion replete with mysteries. It was proclaimed as the mystery of Christ (Rom. 16:25-27; Col. 1:25-27), as the "mystery of the kingdom of God" (Mark 4:11; Luke 8:10). Its ideas and doctrines were unknown, unprecedented, and they were to remain inscrutable and unfathomable....

Even friends and zealous defenders of Christianity could not always suppress a certain dread when they stood in the obscurity of its mysteries. To buttress belief in Christian truth and to defend it, they desired to resolve it into a rational science, to demonstrate articles of faith by arguments drawn from reason, and so to reshape them that nothing would remain of the obscure, the incomprehensible, the impenetrable. They did not realize that by such a procedure they were betraying Christianity into the hands of her enemies and wresting the fairest jewel from her crown.

The greater, the more sublime, and the more divine Christianity is, the more inexhaustible, inscrutable, unfathomable, and mysterious its subject matter must be. If its teaching is worthy of the only-begotten Son of God, if the Son of God had to descend from the bosom of His Father to initiate us into this teaching, could we expect anything else than the revelation of the deepest mysteries locked up in God's heart? Could we expect anything else than disclosures concerning a higher, invisible world, about divine and heavenly things, which "eye hath not seen, nor ear heard," and which could not enter into the heart of any man (1 Cor. 2:9)? And if God has sent us His own Spirit to teach us all truth, the Spirit of His truth, who dwells in God and there searches the deep things of God (cf. John 16:13; 1 Cor. 2:10f), should this Spirit reveal nothing new, great, and wondrous, should He teach us no sublime secrets?

Far from repudiating Christianity or regarding it with suspicious eyes because of its mysteries, we ought to recognize its divine grandeur in these very mysteries. So essential to Christianity are its mysteries that in its character of truth revealed by the Son of God and the Holy Spirit it would stand convicted of intrinsic contradiction if it brought forward no mysteries. Its Author would carry with Him a poor recommendation for His divinity if He taught us only such truths as in the last analysis we could have learned from a mere man, or could have perceived and adequately grasped by our own unaided powers.

I would go even further: the truths of Christianity would not stir us as they do, nor would they draw us or hearten us, and they would not be embraced by us with such love and joy, if they contained no mysteries. What makes many a man recoil from the Christian mysteries as from sinister specters is neither the voice of nature nor the inner impulse of the heart nor the yearning for light and truth, but the arrogance of a wanton and overweening pride. When the heart thirsts after truth, when the knowledge of the truth is its purest delight and highest joy, the sublime, the exalted, the extraordinary, the incomprehensible all exercise an especial attraction. A truth that is easily discovered and quickly grasped can neither enchant nor hold. To enchant and hold us, it must surprise us by its novelty, it must overpower us with its magnificence; its wealth and profundity must exhibit ever new splendors, ever deeper abysses to the exploring eye. We find but slight stimulation and pleasure in studies whose subject matter is soon exhausted and so leaves nothing further for our wonderment. But how powerfully sciences enthrall us when every glance into them suggests new marvels to divine, and every facet of the object imprisons new and greater splendors! The greatest charm in knowledge is astonishment, surprise, wonderment.

The Mysteries of Christianity

Father Walter J. Ciszek, S.J., American missionary in Soviet Russia
Learning to Believe
There are moments of crisis in every life, moments of anxiety and fear, moments of frustration and opposition, moments sometimes even of terror. The kingdom of Christ—that kingdom of justice and peace, of love and of truth—has not yet been achieved here on earth; it has begun, but much remains to be done before it can reach its fullness and all creation will have again been made new according to the mind of the Father. Evil still exists alongside justice like the cockle among the wheat, hatred alongside love, the good with the bad, the sinner along with the saint. None of us, then, can escape the tensions of this imperfect world—neither sinner nor saint, good or bad, the weak or the strong, the healthy or the sick, the learned or the simple, the dedicated or the indifferent. Only by a lively faith can a man learn to live in peace among the tensions of this world, secure in his ability (with God's help) to weather the crises of life, whenever they come and whatever they may be, for he knows that God is with him. In the midst of suffering or failure or even sin, when he feels lost or overwhelmed by danger or temptation, his faith still reminds him of God. By faith he has learned to lift himself above the circumstances of this life and to keep his eyes fixed upon God, from whom he expects the grace and the help he needs, no matter how unworthy he may feel.

Faith, then, is the fulcrum of our moral and spiritual balance. The problems of evil or of sin, of injustice, of sufferings, even of death, cannot upset the man of faith or shake his trust and confidence in God. His powerlessness to solve such problems will not be a cause of despair or despondency for him, no matter how strong his concern and anxiety may be for himself and for those around him. At the core of his being there exists an unshakable confidence that God will provide, in the mysterious ways of his own divine providence.

He Leadeth Me

Cardinal John Henry Newman
Faith—Always a Gift

Faith is the gift of God, and not a mere act of our own, which we are free to exert when we will. It is quite distinct from an exercise of reason, though it follows upon it. I may feel the force of the argument for the divine origin of the Church; I may see that I ought to believe; and yet I may be unable to believe. This is no imaginary case; there is many a man who has ground enough to believe, who wishes to believe, but who cannot believe. It is always indeed his own fault, for God gives grace to all who ask for it, and use it, but still such is the fact, that conviction is not faith. Take the parallel case of obedience: many a man knows he ought to obey God, and does not and cannot,—through his own fault, indeed,—but still he cannot; for through grace alone can he obey. Now, faith is not a mere conviction in reason, it is a firm assent, it is a clear certainty greater than any other certainty and this is wrought in the mind by the grace of God, and by it alone.

Discourses to Mixed Congregations

Helmuth James, Count von Moltke,
German Lutheran statesman executed for opposition to Hitler
Faith—Our Victory Over the World
Tegel, January 10, 1945

Dear Heart: First I must tell you that quite evidently the last twenty-four hours of one's life are no different from any others. I had always imagined that it would come as a shock to say to oneself: "Now the sun is setting for the last time for you, now the hour hand will make only two more revolutions before twelve, now you are going to bed for the last time." Nothing of the sort. Perhaps I am a little cracked. For I cannot deny that I am in really high spirits. I only pray to God in heaven to sustain me in this mood, for surely it is easier for the flesh to die in this state. How merciful the Lord has been to me! Even at the risk of sounding hysterical—I am so full of thanks that there is actually no room for anything else. He has guided me so firmly and clearly during these two days. The whole courtroom might have roared, like Herr Freisler [president of the People's Court] himself, and all the walls might have rocked—it would have made no difference to me. It was just as is written in Isaiah 43:2: "When thou passest through the waters, I will be with thee; and through the rivers, they shall not overflow thee: when thou walkest through the fire, thou shalt not be burned; neither shall the flame kindle upon thee." That is to say: upon your soul. When I was called up for my last words, I was in such a frame of mind that I nearly said, "I have only one thing to add to my defense. Take my goods, my honor, my child and wife; the body they may kill; God's truth abideth still, his kingdom is for ever." But that would only have made it harder for the others; therefore I said only, "I do not intend to say anything, Herr President."

Therefore I can say only one thing, dear heart. May God be as merciful to you as to me.... I should be saying farewell to you—I can't do it. I should be mourning and regretting the drabness of your everyday life—I can't do it. I should indeed be thinking of the burdens that will now fall upon you—I can't do it. I can say only one thing to you: if you attain to a feeling of supreme security—if the Lord gives you that which, had it not been for this period in our lives and its conclusion, you would never have had, then I am leaving you a treasure that cannot be confiscated, a treasure compared to which even my life is of small account.

The decisive pronouncement in my trial was: "Count Moltke, Christianity and we National Socialists have one thing in common, and one thing only: we claim the whole man." Did he realize what he was saying?...

[God] ... permitted me to experience, to an unheard-of depth, the anguish of parting and the fear of death and the terror of hell—so that this too is over and done with. Then he endowed me with faith, hope, and love, all this in a plenitude truly lavish.... And then your husband was selected to be attacked and condemned, as a Protestant, above all because of his friendship with Catholics. And thus he stood before Freisler not as a Protestant, not as a landed proprietor, not as a nobleman, not as a Prussian, not as a German—all that was explicitly eliminated in the main hearing ... but as a Christian and as nothing else.

Letter written to his wife shortly before his execution by the Nazis

St. Ephrem of Syria, 4th-century Church Father and poet
Beyond Faith
As for that part of the Garden, my beloved,
which is situated so gloriously
at the summit of that height
where dwells the Glory,
not even its symbol
can be depicted in man's thought;
for what mind
has the sensitivity
to gaze upon it,
or the faculties to explore it,
or the capacity to attain to that Garden
whose riches are beyond comprehension.

Hymns on Paradise

Christoph Blumhardt, German pastor and theologian
In Times of Silence
And he said to me, "You are my servant, Israel, in whom I will be glorified." But I said, "I have labored to no purpose. I have spent my strength in vain and for nothing; yet surely my cause is with the Lord, and my reward is in God's hands."

Isaiah 49:3-4

Lord our God, we thank you for the help you have given us over and over again so that we can stand before you, rejoicing in the certainty of faith. We thank you for guiding and leading our lives and for letting us see a goal ahead, a goal to be revealed to all men. Be with us in times of silence when we seem to be alone. Keep us strong and steadfast through temptation and through all the turmoil of life. Help us to remain unshaken, for you walk with us holding us by the hand, and you can lift us above all that does not endure. Amen.

Lift Thine Eyes

FOUR

Hope and Trust in Darkness

Trust in him at all times, O people; pour out your heart
before him; God is a refuge for us (Ps. 62:8).

Faith in God's goodness and providence must precede hope; otherwise
hope is only a natural kind of optimism related to courage. Even the
strange adventure of chance that drives people to gamble may be mistaken
for hope. Hope begins with faith and leads to the next logical stage, that
is, trust in God for the things necessary for our own salvation or that of
those we care about. Hope and trust grow and increase only by trial, suffering, danger, sorrow, and, even if it comes, horror. For this reason, darkness is an essential part of the spiritual journey—darkness of many kinds.

For the believing Christian, trials must be evaluated in one of several
believing ways. Trials may be direct gifts of God, like the nights of the soul
spoken of by St. John of the Cross, or they may arise from the ordinary
happenings of life: sickness, failure, disappointment, or natural calamities
ranging from storms and fire to sickness and the effects of age. Or the worst
of disasters may result from the negligence, selfishness, or wickedness of
man. How many saints have come out of wars and persecutions! For the
Christian, all adversities accepted with faith and love are called collectively
the Cross. We choose to see them and realistically deal with them as part
of imitating the Divine Master, who challenges us to take up the cross and
follow Him (see Mk. 8:34). Christians of all persuasions have developed
key phrases for this faithful and trusting endurance of evil: "No cross, no

crown," or "God knows best," or simply "God's will be done." Perhaps the most impressive of these statements comes from the hymn to the Cross, written by the poet priest Venantius Fortunatus at the beginning of the Dark Ages: "*O Crux, ave, spes unica*—Hail, O Cross, our only hope."

Trials occur in every life, and the Cross comes to all. Beginners in the spiritual life usually spend much time and energy trying to pray the Cross away. And often enough God in His mercy lifts the Cross of suffering, as we see our Savior doing in the Gospel. But trusting that God will lift the Cross is only the beginning. The selections in this section are meant to show that the Christian making progress learns that in suffering and adversity there is much to be gained. Our Lord accepted His Cross when His hour came, and that Cross literally became the instrument of our salvation. Most people reading this anthology will still be wrestling with this great step of the spiritual life and will have yet to fully realize that in the Cross is life, hope, and the entrance into the way of light.

No section of the library of spirituality is more developed than the discussion of hope and trust. The call to trust God is the most frequent challenge given to the disciples by Christ, who accused them of little faith when they were timid or fearful. For this reason our selection of quotations on trust is longer and more varied than with other topics. For most readers this is an ongoing spiritual battle; this is the cutting edge. If you don't see this, then you are not there yet. If you trust easily in God, then you have made significant progress. But all need to remember that when darkness comes, the step of blind trust must be taken over and over again. "Thy will be done" expresses the single great practical step of the spiritual life. Some have called this trust the greatest act of worship we can perform, because it unites us in a most realistic way with the mystery of Christ.

Julian of Norwich, 14th-century English mystic and anchorite
Resting in Hope

Though we are in such pain, trouble and distress, that it seems to us that we are unable to think of anything except how we are and what we feel, yet as soon as we may, we are to pass lightly over it, and count it as nothing. And why? Because God wills that we should understand that if we know him and love him and reverently fear him, we shall have rest and be at peace. And we shall rejoice in all that He does.

I understood truly that our soul may never find rest in things below, but when it looks through all created things to find its Self, it must never remain gazing on its self, but feast on the sight of God its maker who lives within.

He did not say, "You shall not be tempest-tossed, you shall not be work-weary, you shall not be discomforted." But he said, "You shall not be overcome." God wants us to heed these words so that we shall always be strong in trust, both in sorrow and in joy.

In times of pain and grief He shows us the joy with which He embraced his own Cross and Passion, at the same time helping us to bear our troubles by his blessed strength. And in times of sin his compassion and pity are there to cheer us, powerfully protecting and defending us against all our enemies. These two are the everyday comforts He shows us in this life.

Sometimes a third comfort is mingled with the other two, his blissful joy which is a glimpse of heaven. By the touch of his grace enlightening our hearts and minds, we contemplate God in true faith, hope and love, with contrition and devotion, and He himself fills us with all manner of consolation and strength.

The more clearly the soul sees the blessed face by the grace of loving, the more it longs to see it fully.

Revelations of Divine Love

Dietrich von Hildebrand
The Perfection of Hope

We have seen ... that confidence in God constitutes man's adequate response to the omnipotence, the omniscience, and the charity of God, as well as to the merciful word which God has addressed to every one of us. It constitutes our central response to the God of Revelation: the response we *owe* to Him, together with that of love and adoration. Further, it represents an indispensable condition of our transformation in Christ.

Without confidence in God, neither our readiness to change nor our critical self-knowledge are of any avail; without confidence in God, neither true contrition nor humility are possible.

Without that basic surrender to God which implies a cheerful reliance on

Him, we could never advance along the path that leads to those goals. How could we risk that leap in the dark, the act of dying unto ourselves; how should we be ready to *lose our souls,* unless we knew that we were not to fall into the void but to be received by the mercy of God? How might we even dare to think of putting away the old man and becoming a new man, unless we relied on the message: "This is the will of God, your sanctification" (1 Thess. 4:3)? How could we bear the sight of our wretchedness and weakness, and in spite of our ever-recurrent relapses keep out discouragement, unless we were certain that God's mercy is infinite?—so that we may say with Thomas of Celano (in the *Dies Irae*): "Thou who hast absolved Mary and granted the thief's prayer, hast given hope also to me."

Not only is confidence in God a necessary condition of our transformation in Christ, in its perfection it is itself an integrating part thereof; an essential trait of holiness. Complete, unreserved, victorious confidence in God is a *fruit* of Faith, Hope and Charity. It is a manifest sign of our being "dead unto ourselves" and living "in and from God"; a mark of him that has "put on the new man, who according to God is created in justice and holiness of truth" (Eph. 4:24). And from confidence in God, again, issue the triumphant freedom of the saint, and the peace of Christ, which the world cannot give us.

Transformation in Christ

C.S. Lewis
Trials Are Reminders

My own experience is something like this. I am progressing along the path of life in my ordinary, contentedly fallen, and godless condition, absorbed in a merry meeting with my friends for the morrow or a bit of work that tickles my vanity today, a holiday or a new book, when suddenly a stab of abdominal pain that threatens serious disease, or a headline in the newspapers that threatens us all with destruction, sends this whole pack of cards tumbling down. At first I am overwhelmed, and all my little happinesses look like broken toys. Then, slowly and reluctantly, bit by bit, I try to bring myself into the frame of mind that I should be in at all times. I remind myself that all these toys were never intended to possess my heart, that my true good is in another world and my only real treasure is Christ. And perhaps, by God's grace, I succeed, and for a day or two become a creature consciously dependent on God and drawing its strength from the right sources. But the moment the threat is withdrawn, my whole nature leaps back to the toys: I am even anxious, God forgive me, to banish from my mind the only thing that supported me under the threat because it is now associated with the misery of those few days. Thus the terrible necessity of tribulation is only too clear. God has had me for but forty-eight hours and then only by dint of taking everything else away from me. Let Him but sheathe that sword for a moment and I behave like a puppy when the hated bath is over—I shake myself as dry as I can and race off to reacquire my comfortable dirtiness, if not in the nearest manure heap, at least in the nearest flower bed. And that is why tribulations cannot cease until God either sees us remade or sees that our remaking is now hopeless.

The Problem of Pain

Archbishop Fulton J. Sheen
The Meaning of the Cross

On the cross Our Lord shows that love can take no other form, when it is brought into contact with evil, than the form of pain. To overcome evil with good, one must suffer unjustly. The lesson of the Crucifix, then, is that pain is never to be isolated or separated from love. The Crucifix does not mean pain; it means sacrifice. In other words, it tells us, first, pain is sacrifice without love; and secondly, that sacrifice is pain with love.

First, pain is sacrifice without love. The Crucifixion is not a glorification of pain as pain. The Christian attitude of mortification has sometimes been misrepresented as idealizing pain, as if God were more pleased with us when we suffered than when we rejoiced. *No!* Pain in itself has no sanctifying influence! The natural effect of pain is to individualize us, center our thoughts on ourselves, and make our infirmity the excuse for every comfort and attention. All the afflictions of the body, such as penance, mortification, have no tendency in themselves to make men better. They often make a man worse. When pain is divorced from love, it leads a man to wish others were as he is; it makes him cruel, hateful, bitter. When pain is unsanctified by affection, it scars, burns up all our finer sensibilities of the soul, and leaves the soul fierce and brutal. Pain as pain, then, is not an ideal:

it is a curse, when separated from love, for rather than making one's soul better, it makes it worse by scorching it.

Now let us turn to the other side of the picture. Pain is not to be denied; it is not to be escaped. It is to be met with love and made a sacrifice. Analyze your own experience, and do not your heart and mind say that love is capable of overruling, in some way, your natural feelings about pain; that some things which otherwise might be painful are a joy to you when you find they benefit others. Love, in other words, can transmute pain and make it sacrifice, which is always a joy. If you lose a sum of money, is not your loss softened by the discovery that it was found by some very poor person whom you loved? If your head is racked with pain, your body wasted and worn from long vigils by the bedside of your child, is not the pain softened by the thought that through your love and devotion, the child was nursed back again to health? You could never have felt the joy, nor had the faintest idea of what your love was, if that sacrifice had been denied you. But if your love were absent, then the sacrifice would have been a pain, vexation, and annoyance.

The truth gradually emerges that our highest happiness consists in the feeling that another's good is purchased by our sacrifice; that the reason why pain is bitter is because we have no one to love and for whom we might suffer. Love is the only force in the world which can make pain bearable, and it makes it more than bearable by transforming it into the joy of sacrifice.

Now, if the dross of pain can be transmuted into the gold of sacrifice by the alchemy of love, then it follows the deeper our love, the less the sense of pain, and the keener our joy of sacrifice. But there is no love greater than the love of Him Who laid down His life for His friends. Hence, the more intensely we love His holy purposes, the more zealous we are for His kingdom, the more devoted we are to the greater glory of Our Lord and Savior, the more we will rejoice in any sacrifice that will bring even a single soul to His Sacred Heart. Such is the explanation of a Paul who gloried in his infirmities and of the Apostles who rejoiced that they could suffer for Jesus Whom they loved. That, too, is why the only recorded time in the life of Our Lord that He ever sang was the night He went out to His death for the love and redemption of men.

The Eternal Galilean

Venantius Fortunatus, 6th-century priest and poet
The Regal Dark Mysterious Cross
The regal dark mysterious cross
In song is lifted high,
The wood on which our God was raised
As Man against the sky.

Upon this wood his body bore
The nails, the taunts, the spear,
Till water flowed with blood to wash
The whole world free of fear.

At last the song that David sang
Is heard and understood:
"Before the nations God as king
Reigns from his throne of wood."

This wood now spread with purple wears
The pageantry of kings;
Of chosen stock it dares to hold
On high his tortured limbs.

O blessed Tree, upon whose arms
The world's own ransom hung;
His body pays our debt and life
From Satan's grasp is wrung.

O sacred Cross, our steadfast hope
In this our Passiontide,
Through you the Son obtained for all
Forgiveness as he died.

May every living creature praise
Our God both one and three,
Who rules in everlasting peace
All whom his cross makes free.

St. Dorotheos of Gaza
The Wisdom of a Monk of Old

God does not allow us to be burdened with anything beyond our power of endurance, and therefore, when difficulties come upon us, we do not sin unless we are unwilling to endure a little tribulation or to suffer anything unforeseen. As the Apostle says, "God is faithful and will not allow us to be tempted beyond what we are able [to endure]." But we are men who have no patience and no desire for a little labor and [no desire] to brace ourselves to accept anything with humility. Therefore we are crushed [by our difficulties]. The more we run away from temptations, the more they weigh us down and the less are we able to drive them away. Suppose a man for some reason dives into the sea: if he knows the art of swimming, what does he do when a great wave comes along? He ducks under until it goes past and then he goes on swimming unharmed. But if he is determined to set himself against it, it pushes him away and hurls him back a great distance, and when again he begins to swim forward, another wave comes upon him, and if again he tries to swim against it, again it forces him back, and he only tires himself out and makes no headway. But if he ducks his head and lowers himself under the wave, as I said, no harm comes to him and he continues to swim as long as he likes. Those who go on doing their work this way when they are in trouble, putting up with their temptations with patience and humility, come through unharmed. But if they get distressed and downcast, seeking the reasons for everything, tormenting themselves and being annoyed with themselves instead of helping themselves, they do themselves harm.

If painful experiences crowd in upon us, we ought not to be disturbed; allowing ourselves to be disturbed by these experiences is sheer ignorance and pride because we are not recognizing our own condition and, as the Fathers tell us, we are running away from labor. We make no progress because we have not squarely taken our own measure, we do not persevere in the work we begin, and want to acquire virtue without effort. Why should an emotional man find it strange to be disturbed by his emotions? Why should he be overwhelmed if he sometimes gives way to them? If you have them inside yourself, why are you disturbed when they break out? You have their seeds in you and yet you ask, why do they spring up and trouble me? Better to have patience and go on struggling with them and beg for God's help.

Discourses and Sayings

Archbishop François Fénelon, 17th-century French spiritual writer
On the Right Use of Trials

People find it very hard to believe that God heaps crosses on those He loves out of loving-kindness. "Why should He take pleasure in causing us to suffer?" they ask. "Could He not make us good without making us so miserable?" Yes, doubtless God could do so, for to Him all things are possible. His all-powerful hands hold the hearts of men and turn them as He pleases, as he who commands the source of a reservoir turns the stream whither he will. But though God could save us without crosses, He has not willed to do so, just as He has willed that men should grow up through the weakness and troubles of childhood, instead of being born fully developed men. He is the Master; we can only be silent and adore His infinite wisdom without understanding it. The one thing we do see plainly is that we cannot become really good save insofar as we become humble, unselfish, in all things turning from self to God.

Such a life of faith is necessary, not only to mold the good, by causing us to sacrifice our own reason amid a world of darkness, but also to blind those whose presumption misleads them. Such men behold God's works without comprehending them, and take them to be simply natural. They are without true understanding, since that is only given to those who mistrust their own judgment and the proud wisdom of man.

So it is to insure that the operation of grace may remain a mystery of faith that God permits it to be slow and painful. He makes use of the inconstancy, the ingratitude of men, the disappointments, the failures which attend human prosperity, to detach us from the creature and its good things. He opens our eyes by letting us realize our own weakness and evil in countless falls. It all seems to go on in the natural course of events, and this series of apparently natural causes consumes us like a slow fire. We would much rather be consumed at once by the flames of pure love, but so speedy a process would cost us nothing. It is utter selfishness that we desire to attain perfection so cheaply and so fast.

The Royal Way of the Cross

Father Jean-Pierre de Caussade, S.J., 18th-century French spiritual writer
Surrender and Trust

If we wish to enjoy an abundance of blessings, we have only one thing to do: purify our hearts by emptying them of all desire for created things and surrender ourselves wholly to God. By doing this we shall get all we want. Let others, Lord, ask you for all sorts of gifts. Let them increase their prayers and entreaties. But I, my Lord, ask for one thing only and have only a single prayer—give me a pure heart! How happy we are if our hearts are pure! Through the ardor of our faith we see God as He is. We see Him in everything and at every moment working within and around us. And in all things we are both his subject and his instrument. He guides us everywhere and leads us to everything. Very often we do not think about it, but He thinks for us. It is enough that we have desired what is happening to us and must happen to us by his will. He understands our readiness. We are bewildered and seek to find this desire within ourselves, but we cannot. He, though, sees it very clearly. How silly we are! Surely we know what a well-disposed heart is: one where God is found. He sees all the good intentions there and consequently knows that this heart will always be submissive to his will. He is also aware that we do not know what is useful for us, so He makes it his business to give it to us. He cares nothing about thwarting us. If we are going eastward, He makes us turn to the west. If we are about to run onto the rocks, He takes the helm and brings us into port. We have neither map nor compass, know nothing of winds or tides, yet we always make a prosperous voyage. If pirates try to board us, an unexpected gust of wind sweeps us beyond their reach.

Good will and a pure heart! Jesus well knew what He was doing when He set you among the Beatitudes. Can there be a greater happiness than to possess God if He also possesses us? It is a state of charmed delight in which the soul sleeps peacefully in the bosom of providence, plays innocently with the divine wisdom (Prov. 8:30), and feels no anxiety about the voyage which continues on its even, happy way in spite of rocks and pirates and continual storms.

A pure heart and good will! The one foundation of every spiritual state!
Abandonment to Divine Providence

St. Thomas More,

16th-century English statesman, spiritual writer, and martyr

A Prayer Facing Death: From the Tower of London

Give me thy grace, good Lord,

To set the world at nought,

To set my mind fast upon thee,

And not to hang upon the blast of men's mouths.

To be content to be solitary.

Not to long for worldly company.

Little and little utterly to cast off the world,

And rid my mind of all the business thereof.

Not to long to hear of any worldly things,

But that the hearing of worldly phantasies may be to me displeasant.

Gladly to be thinking of God,

Piteously to call for his help,

To lean unto the comfort of God.

Busily to labour to love him.

To know mine own vility and wretchedness,

To humble and meeken myself under the mighty hand of God,

To bewail my sins passed,

For the purging of them, patiently to suffer adversity.

Gladly to bear my purgatory here,

To be joyful of tribulations,

To walk the narrow way that leadeth to life.

To bear the cross with Christ,

To have the last thing in remembrance,

To have ever afore mine eye my death that is ever at hand,

To make death no stranger to me

To foresee and consider the everlasting fire of hell,

To pray for pardon before the judge come.

To have continually in mind the passion that Christ suffered for me,

For his benefits uncessantly to give him thanks.

To buy the time again that I before have lost.

To abstain from vain confabulations,

To eschew light foolish mirth and gladness,

Recreations not necessary to cut off.

Of worldly substance, friends, liberty, life and all, to set the loss at right nought, for the winning of Christ.

To think my most enemies my best friends.

For the brethren of Joseph could never have done him so much good with their love and favour as they did him with their malice and hatred.

These minds are more to be desired of every man than all the treasure of all the princes and kings, Christian and heathen, were it gathered and laid together all upon one heap.

Father Walter J. Ciszek, S.J.,
Hope in a Slave Labor Camp

The desire for survival was uppermost in the minds of everyone in the slave camps of Siberia. To live through it all and see freedom in the end was the secret hope everyone cherished. The instinct to live, to survive, especially for those who had a family or loved ones to return to, was the strongest motivation of every hour of every day. How conscious these men were of every day they lived. They counted it both as one day less in their sentence and yet one day less in their lives. No one wished, even for his bitterest enemy, the misfortune of dying in these camps away from everything a man held dear. And yet each day, they knew, was a step in the long slow march toward death.

It was to such men as these that I had been chosen, and was privileged, to bring the bread of life. "Unless you eat my flesh and drink my blood," Christ said to his disciples, "you shall not have life in you. He who eats my flesh and drinks my blood shall have life and have it more abundantly." These men, with simple and direct faith, grasped this truth and they believed in it. They could not explain it as a theologian might, but they accepted it and lived by it and were willing to make voluntary sacrifices even in a life of almost total deprivation, in order to receive this bread of life. Mass and the Blessed Sacrament were a source of great consolation to me; they were the source of my strength and joy and spiritual sustenance. But it was when I realized what the Holy Eucharist meant to these men, what sacrifices they were willing to make for it, that I felt animated, privileged, driven to make it possible for them to receive this bread of life as often as they wished. No danger, no risk, no retaliation could prevent my saying Mass each day for them. "As often as you do this, do it in memory of me." Life in the labor camps was Calvary for these men in many ways every day; there was nothing I would not do to offer the sacrifice of Calvary again for them each day in the Mass.

He Leadeth Me

St. John of the Cross
All Are Mine—Even in the Darkness
Mine are the heavens
And mine is the earth
The angels are mine
And the Mother of God;
And God himself is mine and for me,
Because Christ is mine
And all for me.

Yours is all of this,
My soul.
Go forth and exult
In your glory!
Hide yourself in it and rejoice!

St. Teresa's Bookmark
Let nothing disturb you,
Let nothing frighten you,
Though all things pass
God does not change.
Patience wins all things.
But he lacks nothing
Who possesses God;
For God alone suffices.

Father Eugene Hamilton,
a young seminarian ordained in the hour of death
The Cross, Our Only Hope

I guess you could say those are the days where all you can really do is cling to that which is in front of you and yet also it disappears from your sight. And what you're clinging to is that Cross of Christ. When I say it disappears, the various events and the pain and the diagnostic reports or the bad test results that might come in seem to make that vision of the Cross more difficult to see. And yet in your heart of hearts, in your very soul, you somehow know it's there and you somehow instinctively reach out to it and try to hold on to it at the same time, in an effort because you hope and pray that stretching out on the other side is that hand of Jesus and hopefully He is willing to take you into his hand.

A Priest Forever

Hope and Humility

Hope is a theological virtue by which we believe that God will give the means of salvation to ourselves and to all whom we love and care about, even to great multitudes whom we don't know. But such an act of faith is obviously a gift of God because our own daily experience will point in the opposite direction. If we are honest with ourselves, experience may lead us to despair. Like faith, hope is a pure gift. But as we have seen, hope requires trust—and adversity recruits hope, as Kierkegaard points out so powerfully.

Unfortunately, the opportunity to trust is often missed because of our lack of true humility. We tell ourselves we don't deserve what is happening to us, and that may be true enough. The life of Christ and of most of His great disciples is filled with injustice. We can easily spend our time railing against the injustice done to us rather than using our energy to grow by humbly accepting the Cross. This does not mean that we should not protest injustice, but it tells us a great deal about how we should do this. A painful question presents itself here. Christ was quite capable of protesting injustice and even confronting evil head-on. But when His hour came, He accepted His Passion and death with incredible meekness, humility, and forgiveness. For this reason He is mystically portrayed in St. John's Gospel and in the New Testament book of Revelation as both the Lamb slain and sacrificed and the Lamb upon God's throne. May I suggest that if you think for a moment you have this mystery all figured out, you're wrong! Based on Revelation, I suspect we will spend our eternity plumbing the depths of the humility of God and of the Lamb. St. Augustine does not hesitate to claim in a letter to Egyptian monks that only by contemplating the humility of God on the Cross are we able to come to any real knowledge of the Holy Trinity.

For most of us, life has many humiliations, and for a thoughtful person the greatest of these are totally interior, since they concern what we really think of ourselves. "My sin is always before me" can be an expression of true humility; often, however, it is a sad counterfeit, merely self-hate, that sweet poison of the neurotic mind. Once when I had failed to get something done, Mother Teresa asked me how I felt about the whole thing. I told her I was humiliated but unfortunately not humbled. I added the observation that it was my lot in life often to be humiliated but rarely humbled. With a twinkle in her eye she said, "Well, cheer up! Humiliation can be a road to humility." The following sections may be very helpful if read with this in mind.

Dietrich von Hildebrand
Humility: The Liberation From Self

We have two great enemies to combat within us: pride and concupiscence. The two are mostly intertwined in some definite manner. Men tainted by pride alone are seldom to be met with. It is these two enemies that render us blind to value. But they are not of equal importance: it is not concupiscence but pride that constitutes the primal evil in our souls. Satan's original gesture is the act of absolute pride that rebels against God, the embodiment of all values, in an impotent attempt to appropriate His power and dominion. True, in the sinfulness of many men (indeed, of most men) concupiscence plays a more conspicuous part; but, nevertheless, it falls short of being the primal evil. That is why in the Gospels even the sin of impurity, however grave, is less severely judged than that of pride. Christ denounced pride and obduracy in far more incisive terms than the sins of the flesh. Thus, pride is the deepest root of the malignancy within ourselves, which is entirely consonant with the fact that Adam's sin, too, consisted in an act of disobedience inspired not by concupiscence, which was only to be a consequence of the Fall, but by pride.

The fact alone that pride is the primal source of all moral evil clearly demonstrates the paramount importance of humility. What is most essential in the process of dying to ourselves is the conquest of pride and that liberation from one's self, whose name is *humility*. On the degree of our humility depends the measure in which we shall achieve freedom to participate in God's life and make it possible for the supernatural life received in holy Baptism to unfold in our souls.

Transformation in Christ

Father Cajetan of Bergamo, O.F.M. Cap.
Gaining Humility

It is possible that a tormenting doubt might arise in the mind of someone who might say: "If I must judge myself to be wanting in humility, I must conclude that I am lost, and such a judgment would lead me to despair." But do you not perceive the error? To speak wisely you ought to say: "I know I am wanting in humility; therefore I must try and obtain it; for without humility I am a reprobate, and it is necessary to be humble in order to be among the elect."

There would indeed be cause for despair if on the one hand humility were necessary for salvation and on the other it were unattainable. But nothing is more natural to us than humility, because we are drawn towards it by our own misery; and nothing is easier, since it is enough for us to open our eyes and to know ourselves; this is not a virtue we need go far to seek, as we can always find it within ourselves, and we have an infinity of good reasons in ourselves for doing so. Nevertheless, we must labor as long as life lasts to acquire humility, nor must we ever imagine that we have acquired it; and even should we have obtained it in some degree, we must still continue to strive after it as though we did not possess it, in order that we may be able to keep it. Let us have a true desire to be humble; let us not cease to implore God that He may give us the grace to be humble; and let us often study the motives that may help to make us humble of heart;

and let us not doubt the divine Goodness, but conform to the advice given us in Holy Writ: "Think of the Lord in goodness" (Wisdom 1:1).

Humility of Heart

St. Isaac of Syria
The Source of Humility

Now humility of heart comes about in a person for two causes: either from precise knowledge of his sins, or from recollection of the greatness of God.

I mean, how exceedingly the greatness of the Lord of all lowered itself, so that in such ways as these he might converse with and admonish men.

He humbled himself so far as to assume a human body; he endured men and associated with them, and showed himself so despised in the world, he who possesses ineffable glory above with God the Father, and at whose sight the angels are struck with awe, and the glory of whose countenance shines throughout their orders.

The Heart of Compassion: Daily Readings With St. Isaac of Syria

Monsignor Romano Guardini
The Humility of Jesus

The apostle said of you, O Lord, that from all eternity you were "in the rank of Godhead," the Son of the Father, the image of his holiness and partaker of his glory. But you did not regard this "God-likeness" as a theft that a robber anxiously clings to, but generously you "dispossessed yourself. You took the nature of a slave, fashioned in the likeness of man and presenting yourself to us in human form. You lowered your own dignity, accepted an obedience which brought you to death, death on a cross."

You followed man in his remoteness from God. Your humility descended into the lost depths and brought us back. Therefore God has "raised you to such a height, has given you that name which is greater than any other name; so that everything in heaven and on earth must bend the knee before the name of Jesus, and every tongue must confess Jesus Christ as the Lord."

And therefore I, too, bend my knee in your name, O Lord, and confess:

you are the Lord, the redeemer and bringer of salvation.

Sin is blindness: and so I beseech you, my redeemer, rid me of the error of arrogance. Teach me to see who I am and who you are. Move my heart that it may feel what you have done.

In the hour when you changed our fate, O Lord, you were quite alone. No one was with you; there was no comprehension and no love. Alone you carried our guilt before God's justice. But now you have taken us up in your redemption, and I beseech you to grant that I know of you and be with you with my love.

Amen.

Prayers From Theology

St. Augustine
Humility and the Knowledge of the Trinity
There is the Invisible Creator, origin and cause of all we see, from whom all being comes; He is supreme, eternal, unchanging and comprehended only by Himself. There is One by whom this supreme Ruler reveals Himself—The Word equal to Him by whom He is begotten and made known. There is One who is Holiness itself, who makes holy all that is sanctified. He is the inseparable and undivided communion between the unchanging Word and that First Cause and Creator who proclaims Himself by this Word. And they are all equal to each other.

Who can contemplate with calm and pure mind this whole being and, blessed by this contemplation, press on to the sight of that which is beyond all known by our perception—to be clothed with everlasting life and obtain eternal salvation? Who can do this but someone who has admitted his sins, leveled his pride to the dust, and knelt in meekness to receive God as his teacher?

This can only happen by getting rid of pride by humility of spirit so that we can be lifted up. Such a humility was provided for us in a way that was filled with glory but most gentle, converting our haughty hearts by persuasion rather than by force. This was done by the Word by whom God the Father reveals Himself to angels, His Son who is his Power and Wisdom, hidden from human hearts blinded by worldly desires, humbling Himself to come in human form. This humble example of God makes us more afraid of being proud than of being humiliated like Him.

Therefore, the Christ who is preached throughout the world is not wearing an earthly crown, nor a rich Christ, but Christ crucified. At first this Christ was ridiculed by many, and the ridicule goes on. A few believed at first but now whole nations. Because when Christ, despite the ridicule of men, was first preached, the lame walked, the dumb spoke, the deaf heard, and even the dead came back to life. This finally convinced some of the proud that even among the visible forces of the physical world there is nothing more powerful than the Humility of God. All this took place that we might struggle to be humble, shielded from the contemptible assaults of human pride by the example of a humble God.

Letter 232

Fyodor Dostoyevsky,
19th-century Russian novelist
Humility and Love
The words of Father Zossima

At some thoughts one stands perplexed, especially at the sight of men's sin, and wonders whether one should use force or humble love. Always decide to use humble love. If you resolve on that once for all, you may subdue the whole world. Loving humility is marvelously strong, the strongest of all things and there is nothing else like it.

Every day and every hour, every minute, walk round yourself and watch yourself, and see that your image is a seemly one. You pass by a little child, you pass by, spiteful, with ugly words, with wrathful heart; you may not have noticed the child, but he has seen you, and your image, unseemly and ignoble, may remain in his defenseless heart. You don't know it, but you may have sown an evil seed in him and it may grow, and all because you were not careful before the child, because you did not foster in yourself a careful, actively benevolent love. Brothers, love is a teacher; but one must know how to acquire it, for it is hard to acquire, it is dearly bought, it is won slowly by long labor. For we must love not only occasionally, for a moment, but for ever. Every one can love occasionally, even the wicked can.

The Brothers Karamazov

FIVE

The Illuminative Way, Part 1: The Love of Neighbor

In thy light we shall see light (Ps. 36:9, *Douay-Rheims Version*).

We ought to pay close attention to the second way, or phase, of the interior journey because although it is an intermediate step, it is as far as most of us are going to get. The illuminative way, so called because the mind and heart of the individual are opening to the light of the divine presence, in some ways is the most beautiful part of the spiritual journey. Dawn and sunrise, corresponding to the illuminative way, are often the most beautiful parts of the day. Obviously, the unitive way that follows represents the highest human perfection, because it is the most complete surrender to the sanctifying or hallowing grace of Christ. But that way has not only its high mountains but its terrifying valleys, incredible darknesses as well as transforming light. The illuminative way also has its trials, demands, and struggles, but nothing like the ultimate death of self described by the saints as they reach the higher levels in the journey to the summit of the mountain of God.

An illustration drawn from St. John of the Cross may help. The soul immersed in a life of sin is like a window covered with mud and grime. Although the sun is shining on the window, no light gets through because it is caked with mud. The incredible brightness of the sun lighting up the whole earth and solar system is blocked out by a film of slop, just as the human soul is kept from the light of God by sin and sinful attachments. But then, by the grace of God, and only by grace, and the individual's coopera-tion with it (a grace in itself), the window becomes partially clean. The light, dimly at first, begins to shine through. The hard work and struggle of the purgative way have cleaned some of the window of the soul. When a muddy window is being cleaned or when doors are opened a crack, and sunlight penetrates a darkened room, the initial rays of light seem extremely beauti-ful and bright. They are like the first rays of the sun after a storm. This is the beginning of the illuminative way.

It may easily happen that an individual so blessed will overestimate the degree of his spiritual progress. Many mistake this experience for the begin-ning of the unitive way, because souls at this level are easily deceived by rem-nants of self-love and misled by the persistent residue of pride. This mistake can also be made by others who are unfamiliar with real sanctity. They may observe changes in terms of greater generosity and more prayerfulness, but these do not indicate that a person is already in the unitive way. Because a person in the illuminative way is more active and generous, he or she is more likely to be thought saintly than someone who has entered into the silent union with God in the unitive way.

Because of the similarity in behavior of a person motivated by Christian kindness and compassion, which are supernatural Christian moral virtues, and the theological virtue of charity, it is often all but impossible to distin-guish them. There is, however, one acid test: the theological virtue of char-ity makes it possible for us to love our enemies and to do good to those who hate us and to pray for those who persecute and calumniate us. This is the law of charity given by our Savior in the Sermon on the Mount (see Matthew 5).

A spontaneous and free-flowing love of neighbor, followed by a greater love of God, are the two most important characteristics in the illuminative way. These two emphases, one following on the other, are significant enough that we may identify these as two distinct phases of the illuminative way. The theological virtue of charity, which is totally a gift of God, operates as the dominant virtue in this way of the spiritual life. Charity is quite dif-ferent from the natural virtues of kindness and religion with which it is often confused, even when these virtues are infused by the Holy Spirit. As super-natural Christian virtues, kindness and compassion may fall short of charity. We practice these virtues, along with charity, but real charity is revealed now in its entire divine splendor.

Generosity, zeal, ease at prayer, and recollection are all signs of a person growing in this way. The pull of the all-encompassing love of God is ever more strongly felt. God is experienced as a consuming fire. Others who would do better to remain silent will counsel the person in the illuminative way to observe moderation, common sense, balance. In a word, they will try to impose the mediocrity that they themselves have become comfortable with. The lives of the saints such as St. Teresa of Avila suggest that they suffer much at the hands of advisers who are themselves stuck somewhere in the purgative way, usually struggling with an incomplete and timid attempt to trust God and to accept His will.

The illuminated soul is much more free than it had been. Human relations and understanding the needs of others are bathed in the divine light. Prayer and contemplative meditation become easier. Parenthetically, it should be mentioned that the illuminated soul becomes something of an environmentalist, but not a naturalist. As Chesterton observes of St. Francis, souls in the illuminative way are supernaturalists, that is, they see God's presence in the natural world. St. Bonaventure speaks of their seeing the footprints of God in creation. For them, not only do the heavens proclaim God's glory, but so does the smallest flower. Not only does the beautiful speak of God, but the broken, the suffering, the hurt, and even the ugly shout out the presence of the Creator. Cardinal Terence Cooke, a former Archbishop of New York and now a candidate for beatification, expressed this attitude in a letter shortly before his death: "Life is no less beautiful when it is accompanied by illness or weakness, hunger or poverty, physical or mental diseases, loneliness or old age." This observation, which we will return to later, is all the more meaningful when we know that he had terminal cancer for the last nine years of his life.

With all this, the person in the illuminative way is only halfway along the journey. Although sin is deeply rejected, it remains a possibility both by reason of weakness and unperceived egocentric desires. But despite it all, the soul perceives ever brighter light as the window is cleansed and the eyes of the heart become clearer. Christ becomes a constant companion. He is experienced everywhere. All things speak of Him. The following poem, written by the devout Irish patriot Joseph Mary Plunkett, expresses very well that Christ-centered vision of the person who has come to experience the meaning of the words "I am the light of the world; he who follows me will not walk in darkness."

I see His blood upon the rose
And in the stars the glory of His eyes,
His body gleams amid eternal snows,
His tears fall from the skies.
I see His face in every flower;
The thunder and the singing of the birds
Are but His voice—and carven by His power
Rocks are His written words.

All pathways by His feet are worn,
His strong heart stirs the ever-beating sea,
His crown of thorns is twined with every thorn,
His cross is every tree.

Love of Neighbor, First Focus of the Illuminative Way
True Generosity

I assume that no one reading this anthology needs to be convinced of the necessity of love of neighbor. This is surely an aspect of the Gospel that is most universally recognized. But at the beginning of the illuminative way, love of neighbor moves from being simply an aspect of Christianity to being its strongest focus, and for a very good reason. The person who has come to deep trust in God is only then free enough from fear and insecurity to be able to give an unequivocal love to neighbor and even to the stranger.

Love of neighbor must be practiced from the moment of conversion. But despite all efforts, that love will remain qualified and limited by the needs and expectations of the individual believer. When we meet one of those whom God has chosen as an apostle of charity—a Mother Teresa or Father Solanus Casey—we realize that their charity is all-encompassing. They do not *practice* charity; they have *become* a being of generosity and giving. In a revealing remark to a friend, Father Solanus once said that all that he wanted to do was give and give, because God had given him so much. Not all are called to be apostles of charity, but all are called to give more and more generously of themselves, because God is love. The very life of the three Persons of the Trinity is an eternal and mutual giving, each to the others. The first epistle of St. John puts it succinctly: "God is love, and he who abides in love abides in God, and God abides in him" (1 Jn. 4: 16).

The reader may never doubt that true generosity, which is not based on likes and dislikes, on convenience or simple duty, is a sign of genuine growth toward or in the illuminative way. This can be a very humbling and disconcerting truth. Léon Bloy, the early twentieth-century French writer and prophetic figure, put it very well when he said that we know how much we love God by how we treat ungrateful beggars. The following passages should contribute to our own realization that we must give more and more. As St. Paul says so beautifully, "Love bears all things, believes all things, hopes all things, endures all things. Love never ends" (1 Cor. 13:7-8).

St. Augustine
The Bond of Charity

Do not think of the poor as only those with no money. Look at each person's needs. Perhaps you are well off in something when someone else is in need of just that. Perhaps you give someone a helping hand—and this is far more important than money. You may give advice without toil or loss, but you have given an alms.

Friends, since we are teaching, it is as if you, the congregation, are the poor, because God has given us what we can bestow on you. But we all receive everything from Him who alone is rich. This is how the Church, the Body of Christ, maintains itself. We the members are held together and are made one in charity and in the bond of peace when each one gives what he has to the one who lacks it. It is what you have that makes you rich: it is what you lack that makes you poor. In this way we can all be truly affectionate to one another and to all around us who are in need.

Sermon on Psalm 125

John Wesley
Charity Unfeigned

Charity cannot be practiced right unless, first, we exercise it the moment God gives the occasion; and, secondly, retire the instant after to offer it to God by humble thanksgiving. And this for three reasons: first, to render him what we have received from him. The second, to avoid the dangerous temptation which springs from the very goodness of these works. And the third, to unite ourselves to God, in whom the soul expands itself in prayer, with all the graces we have received, and the good works we have done, to draw from him new strength against the bad effects which these very works may produce in us, if we do not make use of the antidotes which God has ordained against these poisons. The true means to be filled anew with the riches of grace is thus to strip ourselves of it; and without this it is extremely difficult not to grow faint in the practice of good works.

Works, Volume 11

St. John Vianney, the Curé of Ars
Complete Charity

All our religion is but a false religion, and all our virtues are mere illusions and we ourselves are only hypocrites in the sight of God, if we have not that universal charity for everyone—for the good and for the bad, for the poor and for the rich, and for all those who do us harm as much as for those who do us good.

Quoted in *Voice of the Saints*

Cardinal John Henry Newman
Love Depends on Practice

It is obviously impossible to love all men in any strict and true sense. What is meant by loving all men, is to feel well-disposed to all men, to be ready to assist them, and to act towards those who come in our way as if we loved them. We cannot love those about whom we know nothing; except indeed we view them in Christ, as the objects of His Atonement, that is, rather in faith than in love. And love, besides, is a habit and cannot be obtained without actual *practice*, which on so large a scale is impossible. We see then how absurd it is when writers (as is the manner of some who slight the Gospel) talk magnificently about loving the whole human race with a comprehensive affection, of being the friends of all mankind, and the like. Such vaunting professions, what do they come to? that such men have certain benevolent *feelings* towards the world—feelings and nothing more—nothing more than unstable feelings, the mere offspring of an indulged imagination, which exist only when their minds are wrought upon, and are sure to fail them in the hour of need. This is not to love men, it is but to talk about love. The real love of man *must* depend on practice and, therefore, must begin by exercising itself on our friends around us; otherwise it will have no existence. By trying to love our relations and friends, by submitting to their wishes, though contrary to our own, by bearing with their infirmities, by overcoming their occasional waywardness by kindness, by dwelling on their excellences, and trying to copy them, thus it is that we form in our hearts that root of charity, which, though small at first, may, like the mustard seed, at last even overshadow the earth.

Parochial and Plain Sermons

Søren Kierkegaard,
19th-century Danish philosopher and theologian
Loving Others As Yourself
Christ commands you to "love your neighbor as yourself." But this "as yourself"? Certainly no wrestler can get so tight a grasp upon his opponent as that which this commandment gets on our selfish hearts. The commandment is so easy to understand, and yet we must be broken in spirit to follow it. As Jacob limped after be has wrestled with God, so shall our selfishness be broken when it has wrestled with this commandment. Yet this commandment does not teach that a man should not love himself. Rather, it teaches him the proper kind of self-love. Christianity presupposes that a man loves himself, and adds that in loving himself he should also love his neighbor.

The Duty of Love
Only when love is a duty is it eternally secure. The sense of duty drives out all doubt and anxiety, because it excludes all possibility of change; whereas love based on emotion and feeling can change, and so is not secure.

Emotional love may for a period be so intense that the heart burns with passion, but in that passion there is always anxiety that eventually the fire will burn itself out. This anxiety leads us constantly to test the other's love, to reassure oneself that all is well. But this testing is a sign of lack of confidence. Yet if love is a duty, a binding commitment before God, then there is no need to test. Emotions and feelings may come and go; but dutiful love lasts forever.

Quoted in *Daily Readings with Søren Kierkegaard*

Forgiveness

Every person who ever meditated on the Lord's Prayer knows that forgiveness is a very special Christian obligation. And so we struggle to forgive, but often reach only the desire to forgive, without real forgiveness. This desire and the attempts that forgiveness inspires are good acts in themselves, but they are not the fullness of charity. This remarkable quality is reserved for the person in the illuminative way who now realizes that there is nothing to lose and everything to gain by forgiving and wishing the best even for his worst enemies. Hostility is an immediate response to the fear of being hurt, but the person illuminated by the irresistible and unquestioned presence of God knows in fact that he has nothing to lose. Then forgiveness flows along with mercy, understanding, and magnanimity, or boundless generosity. Not only can the person say, "It is no longer I who live, but Christ who lives in me" (Gal. 2:20); he can also say, "It is no longer I who forgive, but Christ who forgives in me."

The writers in this section were chosen to illustrate the fact that the ability to forgive is a grace that must be personally accepted by all who struggle to forgive. The quotation of St. Thomas More recorded by eyewitnesses following his condemnation for treason is a remarkable act of forgiveness in every way. It is worthwhile noting that most contemporary psychological theorists are completely in the dark when it comes to real forgiveness. They may wisely counsel walking away from those who have hurt us or simply letting things go, or, to use the popular expression, "getting the monkey off your back." This is wise, but it is not the virtue of charity. Christ speaks of the virtue when He tells you to love your enemies, do good to those who hate you, and pray for those who persecute and calumniate you. To the secular psychologist this may sound like self-hate or passive aggression. With faith in the love of Christ for all, and His universal will to forgive and embrace a sinful world, forgiveness is the closest possible imitation of Christ, who spoke of forgiveness of sins at the Last Supper, on the Cross, and in His first words to His disciples when He rose from the dead.

St. Pius X
Forgiveness and the Interior Life
Without an interior life, we will never have strength to persevere in sustaining all the difficulties inseparable from any apostolate, the coldness and lack of cooperation even on the part of virtuous men, the calumnies of our adversaries, and at times even the jealousy of friends and comrades in arms.... Only a patient virtue, unshakably based upon the good, and at the same time smooth and tactful, is able to move these difficulties to one side and diminish their power.

Encyclical *Manete in Me* (*Remain in Me*), 1905

Anonymous
A Meditation on Forgiveness
The task for me is to bring what I find in myself and in my relationships to the eternal Thou, where I can experience forgiving. To say, "I forgive you," has in it always the danger of inflation. I am not the forgiver. I must try to participate in that which is making forgiveness possible.

I need to have an "altar," someplace where I can feel the Presence, and to that "altar," whether in a church, in my house, or in a personal symbol, I can bring whatever I have done to another, or what another has done to me, and there I can feel accepted, forgiven or forgiving, despite what I have done or what has been done to me. What has been done, by me or by another, must be faced; not that the results will be eradicated, but that they may be altered and energy pent up in them released. All of it must be accepted, worked with lovingly, and thus eventually transformed. And it can be transformed if it is brought to an "altar"—wherever that may be for me.

Catherine de Hueck Doherty
A Prayer of Forgiveness

Beloved, my heart is torn by sorrow. I love You. I want to serve You. But human beings tear my heart to pieces. Give me strength, humility, understanding. Above all, give me forgiveness—never to hold a grudge against anyone, to love all alike. O Jesus, please! I do want to serve You in humility. Give me love of Yourself, humility, purity of intention, the gift of prayer. O Beloved, I will besiege You for these gifts for they will bring me nearer to You.

Diary

Fyodor Dostoyevsky
Judge Not

The words of Father Zossima

Remember particularly that you cannot be a judge of any one. For no one can judge a criminal, until he recognizes that he is just such a criminal as the man standing before him, and that he perhaps is more than all men to blame for that crime. When he understands that, he will be able to be a judge. Though that sounds absurd, it is true. If I had been righteous myself, perhaps there would have been no criminal standing before me. If you can take upon yourself the crime of the criminal your heart is judging, take it at once, suffer for him yourself, and let him go without reproach. And even if the law itself makes you his judge, act in the same spirit so far as possible, for he will go away and condemn himself more bitterly than you have done. If, after your kiss, he goes away untouched, mocking at you, do not let that be a stumbling-block to you. It shows his time has not yet come, but it will come in due course. And if it come not, no matter; if not he, then another in his place will understand and suffer, and judge and condemn himself, and the truth will be fulfilled. Believe that, believe it without doubt; for in that lies all the hope and faith of the saints.

The Brothers Karamazov

St. Thomas More

A Great Act of Forgiveness

The dreaded words having been uttered, More was given one final opportunity to speak—a chance to plead for mercy customarily given to convicts after sentencing. But More did not ask for mercy; instead he offered forgiveness:

More have I not to say, my lords, but that like as the blessed Apostle St. Paul, as we read in the Acts of the Apostles, was present, and consented to the death of St. Stephen, and kept their clothes that stoned him to death, and yet be they now both twain holy Saints in heaven, and shall continue there friends forever, so I verily trust, and shall therefore right heartily pray, that though your lordships have now here in earth been judges to my condemnation, we may yet hereafter in heaven merrily all meet together, to our everlasting salvation.

Quoted in *The King's Good Servant But God's First*

Zeal

The love of neighbor in the illuminative way brings with it a practical urgency, an impulse to help others which is steady, unwavering, and generally fitted to the needs of those whom we meet. In this respect zeal goes far beyond the enthusiasm that one may encounter in those on the purgative way. That first enthusiasm is legitimate and necessary but in reality expresses mostly the subconscious needs of the person who experiences it. For this reason zealous beginners often are unsteady, unreliable, and prone to give to others what their own internal needs suggest. The zealous apologist may only be shoring up his own faith while trying to convince others of his point of view, which just happens to agree with the Gospel. In fact, it is not difficult to find such enthusiasts in other religions and even in political and social causes. If the beginner's own needs and perceptions change, this zeal may evaporate or go elsewhere. Almost all Christian churches have had zealous apostles who turned into enemies of the Gospel. Their zeal may have been a natural quality, but it did not reach the level of true charity. Natural zeal, which is related to enthusiasm and the natural virtue of courage, can easily become bitter zeal—the zeal of the silly or of the absurd television evangelist or, worse, the zeal of an inquisitor.

The zealous charity of the illuminative way is gentle, kind, understanding, and most of all attentive to God's grace. It is a universally held although often underappreciated belief of Christians that grace, and especially the grace of faith, is a pure gift of God. No one can give someone else faith. We are called to be witnesses of faith. You may be able to convince people of the superiority of Communism or the need for vitamins or of some nonrevealed religion, but you cannot convince them of the Christian faith unless they receive the call of God's grace. On the basis of our arguments, some people may form a positive opinion of Christianity, but that does not mean that they have automatically received the gift of faith. Zealous, mature Christians are willing to give all their energy and time to works of hope and charity and to being witnesses to the Gospel. However, their experience of mature faith does not permit them to preach their own importance. The mature Christian knows what it means "to spend oneself and to be spent for the Gospel."

Cardinal Terence Cooke
This Grace-Filled Moment

It is at times when life is threatened—such as times of serious illness—that the Lord gives us a special grace to appreciate "the gift of life" more deeply as an irreplaceable blessing which only God can give and which God must guide at every step. From the beginning of human life, from conception until death and at every moment between, it is the Lord Our God who gives us life, and we, who are His creatures, should cry out with joy and thanksgiving for this precious gift....

The gift of life, God's special gift, is no less beautiful when it is accompanied by illness or weakness, hunger or poverty, mental or physical handicaps, loneliness or old age. Indeed, at these times human life gains extra splendor as it requires our special care, concern, and reverence. It is in and through the weakest of human vessels that the Lord continues to reveal the power of His love....

I call on you to rededicate your efforts for the sanctity of all human life and to work to counteract the contemporary threats to life. I urge you to increase and to strengthen the programs in our parishes and communities for the poor, the elderly, the handicapped, the rejected, the homeless, the suffering, the unwanted, the unborn.

At this grace-filled time of my life, as I experience suffering in union with Jesus, Our Lord and Redeemer, I offer gratitude to Almighty God for giving me the opportunity to continue my apostolate on behalf of life. I thank each one of you, my sisters and brothers in the Archdiocese of New York and throughout our nation, for what you have done and will do on behalf of human life. May we never yield to indifference or claim helplessness when innocent human life is threatened or when human rights are denied.

Pastoral Letter, October 1983

Christoph Blumhardt
Christ Is Risen

When we hear about the resurrection of Jesus Christ, it should shake us to the bones. "What? Somebody has risen from the dead? Who is it? That can't be! The whole world has to change if this is true!" Anyone who is not struck in this way has no idea what it means to be crucified and then to rise again. This must sink so deeply into our hearts that we gain a new attitude to life. It must strike us so powerfully that we make this risen one our Lord and accept Him as the Lord of the world. We must acknowledge that all things belong to Jesus. Why? Because He has risen from the dead. Therefore all knees must bend before Him and all tongues must confess that Jesus Christ is the Lord. There cannot be any creature either in heaven or under the earth which is anything beside Him. For this we live and strive.

The only real Christians are those who under the impression of the resurrection of Jesus Christ lay claim to the whole world in the name of the risen one. For they alone know that it will be only a short time before Jesus Christ becomes the ruler. He who merely assumes that Christ died and rose again is no Christian. He is simply a man with certain opinions.

A Christian, then, a warrior and fighter, is one who concludes from the resurrection of Jesus Christ that the world will now come under the rulership of God. He knows that as a Christian he must help toward this goal. We, as the living church of Christ, must live in constant struggle towards the great rulership of the King, Jesus Christ. This makes us Christians.

Christoph Blumhardt and His Message

Dom Jean-Baptiste Chautard, a Trappist abbot
Zeal for God and Souls

The saints have often been extremely outspoken against error, the contagion of loose living, and hypocrisy. Take St. Bernard, for example. This oracle of his own time was one of those saints who showed most firmness in his zeal for God. But the attentive reader of his life will be able to see to what an extent the interior life had made this man of God selfless. He only fell back on strong measures when he had clear evidence that all other means were useless. Often, too, he varied between gentleness and strength. After having shown his great love for souls by avenging some principle with holy indignation and stern demands for remedies, reparation, guarantees, and promises, he would at once display the tenderness of a mother in the conversion of those whom his conscience had forced him to fight. Pitiless towards the errors of Abelard, he speedily became the friend of the one whom his victory had reduced to silence.

When it was a matter of choosing means, if he saw that no principle was necessarily involved, he always stood before the hierarchy of the Church as a champion of nonviolent procedure. Learning that there was a movement on foot to ruin and massacre the Jews of Germany, he left his cloister without a moment's delay and hurried to their rescue, preaching a crusade of peace. Fr. Ratisbonne quotes a document of great significance in his *Life of St. Bernard*. It is a statement of the most exalted Rabbi of that land, expressing his admiration for the monk of Clairvaux, "without whom," he says, "there would not be one of us left alive in Germany." And he urges future generations of Jews never to forget the debt of gratitude they owe to the holy abbot. On this occasion St. Bernard uttered the following words: "We are the soldiers of peace, we are the army of the peacemakers, fighting for God and peace: *Deo et paci militantibus.* Persuasion, good example, loyalty to God are the only arms worthy of the children of the Gospel."

There is no substitute for the interior life as a means of obtaining this spirit of selflessness which characterizes the zeal of every saint.

The Soul of the Apostolate

St. Francis de Sales
Love and Sacrifice

Our Divine Master gave us His life not only to heal the sick, to work miracles, and to teach us what we ought to do to be saved or to be pleasing to Him. He also spent His entire life even shaping His cross, suffering a thousand thousand persecutions from the very ones to whom He was doing so much good and for whom He laid down His life. We must do the same, says the holy Apostle, that is, we too should shape our cross in suffering for one another as the Savior taught us; in giving our life for those very ones who would take it from us, as He so lovingly did; in spending ourselves for our neighbor, not only in agreeable things, but also in those which are painful and disagreeable such as bearing lovingly these persecutions which might in some fashion cool our heart towards our brothers.

There are some who say: "I greatly love my neighbor and would wish, indeed, to render him some service." That is very good, says St. Bernard, but it is not enough; we must go further. "Oh! I love him so much! I love him so much that I would gladly sacrifice all my possessions for him." That is going further and is certainly better, but still it is not enough. "I love him, I assure you, so greatly that I would willingly expend myself for him in whatever he wanted from me." This is certainly a very good sign of your love, but you must go still further; for there is a still higher degree in this love, as St. Paul teaches us, when he wrote: "Be imitators of me as I imitate Christ" (1 Cor. 11:1). And in one of his epistles he wrote thus to his most dear children: "I am ready to give my life for you, and give of myself so completely that I make no reservation in proving to you how dearly and tenderly I love you. Yes, I am even ready to agree to all that anyone would want of me in your behalf" (2 Cor. 12:14-15, 19). In this he teaches us that to spend ourselves even so far as to give our life for the neighbor is not as much as to allow ourselves to be spent at the will of others, either by them or for them.

This is what he had learned from our dear Savior, who spent Himself for our salvation and our redemption (Phil. 2:8), and afterwards allowed Himself to be spent so as to perfect this Redemption and to win eternal life for us, even permitting Himself to be fastened to the Cross by the very persons for whom He died. He spent Himself during His whole life, but in His death He allowed Himself to be spent, permitting not His friends, but His enemies, to do with Him all that they wished. They put Him to death with a fury insupportably wicked. Nevertheless, He did not resist at all but allowed Himself to be pulled and turned in every direction as prompted by the cruelty of these malicious executioners (Isa. 50:5). For He beheld in all this the will of His heavenly Father, which was that He should die for humankind, and to which He submitted with an incomparable love, one more worthy of being adored than imagined or understood.

Sermon for the Third Sunday of Lent

St. Maximilian Kolbe
Trust and Zeal—A Martyr's Encouragements from Prison

All brothers must pray very much and well. Work with fervor and don't worry too much about us, because nothing can happen to us without the permission of God and the Immaculata.

From postcard of March 13, 1941, after his arrest

Let us promise to let ourselves be led more and more completely how and where the Mother of God wishes, so that, fulfilling our duty to the utmost, we may through love save all souls.

From postcard of May 12, 1941
His last communication before being transferred to Auschwitz

Love for the Poor

Christ emphatically identifies love and care of the poor with love for Himself—both His humanity and His divinity. The mystics of the Church, all of them people of profound contemplative spirit, are characteristically identified with the oppressed, the disadvantaged, the poorest of the poor. This identification with the poor is often their most attractive feature to others.

Because the materially and socially poor are often noisy and distracting, even demanding, the care of the poor is frequently distasteful to those struggling along the way. They do not realize that it is this very disturbing aspect of caring for the poor that contributes to the transcendence of self and the death of narcissism. St. Francis of Assisi's experience with the leper brings out beautifully this aspect of caring for the poor. Every reader who has come this far needs to ask, Am I letting Jesus pass me by when I do not recognize Him in the poor, the needy, the disadvantaged, and the oppressed?

Catherine de Hueck Doherty
True Charity

"If you love me, keep my commandments" (John 14:15).

Beloved, I try so hard, but somehow I never seem to succeed. I work so hard at Your works of mercy, but I seem to have no charity. Efficiency, kindness, goodness of heart—yes. But I have nothing like real charity—that elusive tenderness and sensitivity to the feelings of others that mark true charity.

O Beloved, when I read about how gentle and kind You were, I see myself as I am. How far I am from that understanding, that profound insight into others that would give me gentleness of touch in healing spiritual wounds.

For the sake of Your poor and unfortunate children, give it to me, Beloved. Light my soul with the gift of prayer. Give me an understanding and practice of humility. Have mercy on me, Master!

Diary

Fyodor Dostoyevsky
Universal Charity
The words of Father Zossima

Brothers, have no fear of men's sin. Love a man even in his sin, for that is the semblance of Divine love and is the highest love on earth. Love all God's creation, the whole world and every grain of sand in it. Love every leaf, every ray of God's light. Love the animals, love the plants, love everything. If you love everything you will perceive the divine mystery in things. Once you perceive it, you will begin to comprehend it better every day. And you will come at last to love the whole world with an all-embracing love. Love the animals: God has given them the rudiments of thought and joy untroubled. Do not trouble it, don't harass them, don't deprive them of their happiness, don't work against God's intent. Man, do not pride yourself on superiority to the animals; they are without sin, and you, with your greatness, defile the earth by your appearance on it and leave traces of your foulness after you—alas, it is true of almost every one of us! Love children especially, for they too are sinless like the angels; they live to soften and purify our hearts and, as it were, to guide us. Woe to him who offends a child! Father Anfim taught me to love children. The kind, silent man used often on our wanderings to spend the farthings given us on sweets and cakes for the children. He could not pass by a child without emotion, that's the nature of the man.

The Brothers Karamazov

Mother Teresa of Calcutta
Christ Among the Poor

The poor have no need of our pity. The poor need our help and assistance. What they give us is more than we give them. Christ said: "I was hungry, and you gave me to eat." He hungered not only for bread but for love that makes one understand that one is loved, is known, is somebody for someone. He was naked not only in reference to clothing but also in reference to human dignity, because of the injustice that is done to the poor, who are disdained simply because they are poor. Christ knew the abandonment of those in prison, those who are rejected, those who are not wanted, those who walk through this world devoid of all help.

Quoted in *Teresa of Calcutta: A Pencil in God's Hand*

Dom Helder Camara,
20th-century Archbishop of Recife, Brazil
United With All

Do you know what I thank the Creator and Father for most of all? I thank Him for uniting me, in Christ, with all human beings of every race, every color and creed....

Christ teaches us more and more that all of us, absolutely all of us, without exception, have the same father; and that, consequently, we are all brothers! And further, we human beings sense that our fraternity extends to include all creatures, animated or inert, great or small. All of us emerged from the hands of the Creator!

Lending our voices joyfully to the stones and the seas, to the winds and the stars, to the trees and the animals, we are aware that above all we are brothers to our fellowmen, sharing adventures and dangers, misery and glory....

It is a pity, O Century, our friend, that as we begin to reach out towards the stars, we leave behind us on earth an absurdity, a folly, an aberration: more than two-thirds of humanity living in subhuman conditions, suffering from poverty and starvation....

But what a joy it is, O Century, to see that God really isn't selfish. How the Creator and Father rejoices to make man His co-creator, how the Son of God, the Redeemer of man and the universe, rejoices to make us His co-liberators!

Christ, the Son of God made man, who made Himself our brother, urges us today more than ever to liberate ourselves and liberate our brothers and sisters from sin and the consequences of sin, from selfishness and the consequences of selfishness.

It is a pity, O Century, that, as we continue to extend the limits of our intelligence and creativity, we continue to be so limited, so grossly selfish, and so incapable of imagining a world without empires to control and subjugate it. Incapable of imagining a world without oppressors and oppressed....

Nevertheless, O Century, in every country, and every race, and every religion, in every human group, the Spirit of God continues to inspire minorities who are resolved to make any sacrifice in order to create a world that is better to live in, more just and more humane: in order to liberate the world from the increasingly heavy and stifling structures that oppress practically all men....

Among the oppressed you will find a profusion of divisions, splits, distrust and conflict.... Oppressors are skillful at sowing discord among the oppressed. It was no coincidence that at the supreme moment of His life Christ asked His Father for unity among His people.

Suggest, teach, persuade: the day will come when all the world's minorities will unite to construct a world that is more just and more humane, the day when we shall finally discover the nuclear force of Love!

The Conversions of a Bishop

St. Francis of Assisi
Friend of the Poor

In all the poor this model of Christian poverty beheld the image of Christ, and so when he had received as an alms things necessary for the body, he not only liberally bestowed them upon any poor man whom he met on the way, but accounted that he was thus restoring to him what was rightfully his own. It happened once that he met a poor man, as he was returning from Siena wearing, by reason of sickness, a cloak over his habit. Beholding with a pitiful eye the misery of this poor man, "It is fitting," said he to his companion, "that we should restore this cloak to this poor man, for it is his, and I accepted it only until I should find someone poorer than myself." But his companion, considering the necessity of the compassionate Father, pertinaciously objected to his relieving others and neglecting himself. But he answered: "I should be accounted a thief by the great Almsgiver were I to withhold that which I wear from him who has greater need of it than I." Therefore, he was accustomed to ask permission of those who relieved his corporal necessities, to give away that which he received from them to any he should meet with in any greater need than himself. He spared nothing, neither cloak, nor tunic, nor books, nor even the ornaments of the altar, but would give all these things to the poor to fulfill the office of mercy. Oftentimes when he met a poor man on the way, laden with a heavy burden, he would take it on his own weak shoulders and carry it for him.

The consideration of the common origin of all creatures filled him with overflowing tenderness for all; and he called them all his brothers and sisters, because they had all one origin with himself. But he bore the sweetest and strongest affection to those whose natural qualities set forth the sweet meekness of Christ, and by which He is therefore signified in Holy Scripture. He would frequently redeem lambs which were being led to the slaughter, in memory of that most meek Lamb Who, to redeem sinners vouchsafed to be led forth to die.

St. Bonaventure, The Life of St. Francis of Assisi

Cardinal John Henry Newman
Prayer for Love of Neighbor

Dear Jesus, help me to spread your fragrance everywhere I go. Flood my soul with your spirit and life. Penetrate and possess my whole being so utterly that my life may be only a radiance of yours.

Shine through me and be so in me that every soul I come in contact with may feel your presence in my soul. Let them look up, and see no longer me, but only Jesus!

Stay with me and then I shall begin to shine as you shine, so to shine as to be a light to others. The light, O Jesus, will be all from you, shining on others through me. Let me thus praise you in the way which you love best, by shining on those around me.

Let me preach you without preaching, not by my words, but by my example, by the catching force, the sympathetic influence of what I do, the evident fullness of the love my heart bears to you. Amen.

Meditations on Christian Doctrine

SIX

The Illuminative Way: Part II
The Love of God

I have come as light into the world, that whoever believes
in me may not remain in darkness (John 12:46).

L ove for God is the ultimate and supreme experience of the human
being, and yet its very meaning is difficult to comprehend. Do we simply love the works of God, or the cause of God, or those who represent
God's goodness to us? To do God's will and to accept the decrees of His
providence is certainly a kind of love for God. But beyond this, there is an
experience of loving God which draws us out of ourselves and fills us with
the delight of love.

The following selections, carefully chosen from a great array of Christian
writings of all three major traditions, suggest that the experience of divine
love does not differ much from one to another. There is a surprising similarity in the descriptions, suggesting that the love of God that characterizes
the illuminative way is more dependent on divine grace than it is on any
characteristics of an individual.

As you read, you may find that some of the descriptions will resonate with
you. This recognition does not mean that you are a mystic, but simply that
you are being drawn on by the promise that Christ gives to hearts open to
Him, namely, that He and the Father will come and take up their dwelling
and remain in you (see John 14:23).

St. Jane Frances de Chantal
A Plan for Holiness

My very dear Lord,

Since God, in His eternal goodness, has moved you to consecrate all your love, your actions, your works, and your whole self to Him utterly without any self-interest but only for His greater glory and His satisfaction, remain firm in this resolve. With the confidence of a son, rest in the care and love which divine Providence has for you in all your needs. Look upon Providence as a child does its mother who loves him tenderly. You can be sure that God loves you incomparably more. We can't imagine how great is the love which God, in His goodness, has for souls who thus abandon themselves to His mercy and who have no other wish than to do what they think pleases Him, leaving everything that concerns them to His care in time and in eternity.

After this, every day in your morning exercise, or at the end of it, confirm your resolutions and unite your will with God's in all that you will do that day and in whatever He sends you. Use words like these: "O most holy Will of God, I give You infinite thanks for the mercy with which You have surrounded me; with all my strength and love I adore You from the depths of my soul and unite my will to Yours now and forever, especially in all that I shall do and all that You will be pleased to send me this day, consecrating to Your glory my soul, my mind, my body, all my thoughts, words, and actions, and my whole being. I beg You, with all the humility of my heart, accomplish in me Your eternal designs and do not allow me to present any obstacle to this. Your eyes, which can see the most intimate recesses of my heart, know the intensity of my desire to live out Your holy will, but they can also see my weakness and limitations. That is why, prostrate before Your infinite mercy, I implore You, my Savior, through the gentleness and justice of this same will of Yours, to grant me the grace of accomplishing it perfectly, so that, consumed in the fire of Your love, I may be an acceptable holocaust which, with the glorious Virgin and all the saints, will praise and bless You forever. Amen."

During the activities of the day, spiritual as well as temporal, as often as you can, my dear lord, unite your will to God's by confirming your morning resolution. Do this either by a simple, loving glance at God, or by a few words spoken quietly and cast into His heart, by assenting in words like:

"Yes, Lord, I want to do this action because You want it," or simply, "Yes, Father," or "O Holy Will, live and rule in me," or other words that the Holy Spirit will suggest to you. You may also make a simple sign of the cross over your heart, or kiss the cross you are wearing. All this will show that above everything you want to do the holy will of God and seek nothing but His glory in all that you do.

Letter to her brother, André Frémyot, Archbishop of Bourges

Evelyn Underhill
Recollection and Silence

The true asceticism is a gymnastic not of the body, but of the mind. It involves training in the art of recollection; the concentration of thought, will, and love upon the eternal realities which we commonly ignore. The embryo contemplative, if his spiritual vision is indeed to be enlarged, and his mind kindled, as Dionysius says, to "the burning of love," must acquire and keep a special state of inward poise, an attitude of attention, which is best described as "the state of prayer"; that same condition which George Fox called "keeping in the Universal Spirit." If we do not attend to reality, we are not likely to perceive it. The readjustments which shall make this attention natural and habitual are a phase in man's inward conflict for the redemption of consciousness from its lower and partial attachments. This conflict is no dream. It means hard work: mental and moral discipline of the sternest kind. The downward drag is incessant, and can be combated only by those who are clearly aware of it, and are willing to sacrifice lower interests and joys to the demands of the spiritual life. In this sense mortification is an integral part of the "purgative way." Unless the self's "inclination to true wisdom" is strong enough to inspire these costing and heroic efforts, its spiritual cravings do not deserve the name of mysticism.

The Essentials of Mysticism

Theophan the Recluse
Recollection and Love

I have often reminded you, my dear sister, about the remembrance of God, and now I tell you again: unless you work and sweat to impress on your heart and mind this awe-inspiring Name, you keep silence in vain, you sing in vain, you fast in vain, you watch in vain. In short, all a nun's work will be useless without this activity, without recollection of God. This is the beginning of silence for the Lord's sake, and it is also the end. This most desirable Name is the soul of stillness and silence. By calling it to mind we gain joy and gladness, forgiveness of sins, and a wealth of virtues. Few have been able to find this most glorious Name, save only in stillness and silence. Man can attain it in no other way, even with great effort. Therefore, knowing the power of this advice, I entreat you for the love of Christ always to be still and silent, since these virtues enrich remembrance of God within us.

Quoted in *The Art of Prayer*

St. Isaac of Syria
Love Silence

Love silence above everything else, for it brings you near to fruit which the tongue is too feeble to expound.

First of all we force ourselves to be silent, but then from out of our silence something else is born that draws us into silence itself.

May God grant you to perceive that which is born of silence! If you begin in this discipline I do not doubt how much light will dawn in you from it.

After a time a certain delight is born in the heart as a result of the practice of this labor, and it forcibly draws the body on to persevere in stillness.

A multitude of tears is born in us by this discipline, at the wondrous vision of certain things which the heart perceives distinctly, sometimes with pain, and sometimes with wonder.

For the heart becomes small and becomes like a tiny babe: as soon as it clings to prayer, tears burst forth.

The Heart of Compassion: Daily Readings with St. Isaac of Syria

St. Thomas Aquinas
The Silence of a Great Mind

The last word of St. Thomas is not communication but silence. And it is not death which takes the pen out of his hand. His tongue is stilled by the superabundance of life in the mystery of God. He is silent, not because he has nothing further to say; he is silent because be has been allowed a glimpse into the inexpressible depths of that mystery which is not reached by any human thought or speech.

The acts of the canonization process record: On the feast of St. Nicholas, in the year 1273, as Thomas turned back to his work after Holy Mass, he was strangely altered. He remained steadily silent; he did not write; he dictated nothing. He laid aside the *Summa Theologica* on which he had been working. Abruptly, in the middle of the treatise on the Sacrament of Penance, he stopped writing. Reginald, his friend, asks him, troubled: "Father, how can you want to stop such a great work?" Thomas answers only, "I can write no more.... All that I have hitherto written seems to me nothing but straw ... compared to what I have seen and what has been revealed to me."

This silence lasted throughout a whole winter. The great teacher of the West had become dumb. Whatever may have imbued him with a deep happiness, with an inkling of the beginning of eternal life, must have aroused in the men in his company the disturbing feeling caused by the uncanny.

At the end of this time, spent completely in his own depths, Thomas began the journey to the General Council at Lyons. His attention continued to be directed inward....

The prayer of St. Thomas that his life should not outlast his teaching career was answered. On the way to Lyons he met his end.

The mind of the dying man found its voice once more, in an explanation of the Canticle of Canticles for the monks of Fossanova. The last teaching of St. Thomas concerns, therefore, that mystical book of nuptial love for God, of which the Fathers of the Church say: the meaning of its figurative speech is that God exceeds all our capabilities of possessing Him, that all our knowledge can only be the cause of new questions, and every finding only the start of a new search.

Joseph Pieper, *The Silence of St. Thomas*

Jonathan Edwards
An Appearance of Divine Glory

After this my sense of divine things gradually increased and became more and more lively and had more of that inward sweetness. The appearance of everything was altered; there seemed to be, as it were, a calm, sweet cast, or appearance of divine glory, in almost everything. God's excellency, his wisdom, his purity and love, seemed to appear in everything: in the sun, moon, and stars, in the clouds, and blue sky, in the grass, flowers, trees, in the water and all nature, which used greatly to fix my mind. I often used to sit and view the moon for a long time; and so in the daytime, spent much time in viewing the clouds and sky, to behold the sweet glory of God in these things; in the meantime singing forth with a low voice, my contemplations of the Creator and Redeemer. And scarce anything among all the works of nature was so sweet to me as thunder and lightning: formerly, nothing had been so terrible to me. I used to be a person uncommonly terrified with thunder, and it used to strike me with terror when I saw a thunderstorm rising. But now, on the contrary, it rejoiced me. I felt God at the first appearance of a thunderstorm, and used to take the opportunity at such times to fix myself to view the clouds, and see the lightnings play, and hear the majestic and awful voice of God's thunder, which oftentimes was exceeding entertaining, leading me to sweet contemplations of my great and glorious God; and while I viewed, used to spend my time, as it always seemed natural to me, to sing or chant forth my meditations, to speak my thoughts in soliloquies, and speak with a singing voice.

I felt then a great satisfaction as to my good estate, but that did not content me. I had vehement longings of soul after God and Christ, and after more holiness, wherewith my heart seemed to be full, and ready to break; which often brought to my mind the words of the Psalmist, "My soul breaketh for the longing it hath" (Ps. 119:28). I often felt a mourning and lamenting in my heart that I had not turned to God sooner, that I might have had more time to grow in grace. My mind was greatly fixed on divine things; I was almost perpetually in the contemplation of them. Spent most of my time in thinking of divine things, year after year, and used to spend abundance of my time in walking alone in the woods and solitary places for meditation, soliloquy, and prayer, and converse with God: and it was always my manner at such times to sing forth my contemplations; and was almost constantly in ejaculatory prayer wherever I was. Prayer seemed to be natural to me, as the breath by which the inward burnings of my heart had vent.

The delights which I now felt in things of religion were of an exceeding different kind from those forementioned, that I had when I was a boy. They were totally of another kind; and what I then had no more notion or idea of, than one born blind has of pleasant and beautiful colours. They were of a more inward, pure, soul-animating, and refreshing nature. Those former delights never reached the heart, and did not arise from any sight of the divine excellency of the things of God, or any taste of the soul-satisfying and life-giving good there is in them....

I had great longings for the advancement of Christ's kingdom in the world. My sacred prayer used to be in great part taken up in praying for it. If I heard the least hint of anything that happened in any part of the world that appeared to me, in some respect or other, to have a favorable aspect on the interest of Christ's kingdom, my soul eagerly catched at it; and it would much animate and refresh me. I used to be earnest to read public newsletters mainly for that end, to see if I could not find some news favorable to the interest of religion in the world....

I had then, and at other times, the greatest delight in the holy scriptures, of any book whatsoever. Oftentimes in reading it, every word seemed to touch my heart. I felt a harmony between something in my heart and those sweet and powerful words. I seemed often to see so much light exhibited by every sentence, and such a refreshing ravishing food communicated, that I could not get along in reading. Used oftentimes to dwell long on one sentence, to see the wonders contained in it, and yet almost every sentence seemed to be full of wonders.

The Life and Character of Mr. Jonathan Edwards

Watchman Nee
Restore to Me the Joy of Salvation
Of all the parables in the Gospels, that of the prodigal son affords, I think, the supreme illustration of the way to please God. The father says:

"It was meet to make merry and be glad" (Luke 15:32), and in these words Jesus reveals what it is that, in the sphere of redemption, supremely rejoices his Father's heart. It is not an elder brother who toils incessantly for the father, but a younger brother who lets the father do everything for him. It is not an elder brother who always wants to be the giver, but a younger brother who is always willing to be the receiver. When the prodigal returned home, having wasted his substance in riotous living, the father had not a word of rebuke for the waste nor a word of inquiry regarding the substance. He did not sorrow over all that was spent; he only rejoiced over the opportunity the son's return afforded him for spending more.

God is so wealthy that his chief delight is to give. His treasure-stores are so full that it is pain to Him when we refuse Him an opportunity of lavishing those treasures upon us. It was the father's joy that he could find in the prodigal an applicant for the robe, the ring, the shoes, and the feast; it was his sorrow that in the elder son he found no such applicant. It is a grief to the heart of God when we try to provide things for Him. He is so very, very rich. It gives Him true joy when we just let Him give and give and give again to us. It is a grief to Him, too, when we try to do things for Him, for He is so very, very able. He longs that we will just let Him do and do and do. He wants to be the Giver eternally, and He wants to be the Doer eternally. If only we saw how rich and how great He is, we would leave all the giving and all the doing to Him.

Sit, Walk, Stand

Dag Hammarskjöld
Echoing Silence
Echoing silence
Darkness lit up by beams
Light
Seeking its counterpart
In melody
Stillness
Striving for liberation
In a word
Life
In dust
In shadow
How seldom growth and blossom
How seldom fruit

God does not die on the day when we cease to believe in a personal deity, but we die on the day when our lives cease to be illumined by the steady radiance, renewed daily, of a wonder, the source of which is beyond all reason.

Markings

St. Augustine
If All Things Grew Silent

If to any man the tumult of the flesh grew silent, silent the images of earth and sea and air: and if the heavens grew silent, and the very soul grew silent to herself and by not thinking of self mounted beyond self: if all dreams and imagined visions grew silent, and every tongue and every sign and whatsoever is transient—for indeed if any man could hear them, he should hear them saying with one voice: We did not make ourselves, but He made us who abides forever: but if, having uttered this and so set us to listening to Him who made them, they all grew silent, and in their silence He alone spoke to us, not by them but by Himself: so that we should hear His word, not by any tongue of flesh nor the voice of an angel nor the sound of thunder nor in the darkness of a parable, but that we should hear Himself whom in all these things we love, should hear Himself and not them: just as we two had but now reached forth and in a flash of the mind attained to touch the eternal Wisdom which abides over all: and if this could continue, and all other visions so different be quite taken away, and this one should so ravish and absorb and wrap the beholder in inward joys that his life should eternally be such as that one moment of understanding for which we had been sighing—would not this be: *Enter Thou into the joy of Thy Lord?* But when shall it be? Shall it be when *we shall all rise again* and *shall not all be changed?*

Confessions, Book 9

St. Augustine
What Do I Love When I Love God?

Without doubts and with certainty do I love you, Lord. You have pierced my heart with your words, and I have loved you.... But what do I love, when I love you? Not the beauty of bodies, not the fair harmony of time nor the brightness of the light, so gladsome to our eyes, not the sweet melodies of different songs, nor the fragrant smell of flowers and ointments and spices, not manna and honey, not limbs which can be caught in the embraces of the flesh. None of these do I love, when I love my God. And yet I do love a kind of light, and melody, and fragrance, and meat, and embrace, when I love my God, the light, melody, fragrance, meat, the embraces of my inner man, where a light shines in my soul that space cannot contain, where there sounds what time cannot steal away, where there is a fragrance that breathing cannot disperse, where there is a taste that eating cannot diminish, and there clings what no fullness of any kind can take from me. This is what I love when I love my God....

What, then, do I love, when I love my God? Who is he who stands above the head of my soul? By my very soul will I ascend to him. I will pass beyond that power which unites me to my body, and fill its whole frame with the force of life.... I will pass, then, over and beyond this power of my nature also, rising by degrees to him who made me.... These things I do within myself, in that vast court of my memory. For there are present within me the heavens, the earth, the sea, and everything I could think about them, except for what I have forgotten. There I meet myself and recall myself.

Confessions, Book 10

At last I love you alone, you alone do I follow, you alone do I seek. You alone am I ready to serve, for you alone, by right, are ruler. Under your rule do I wish to be. Command me, I pray you, and order what you will, but first heal and open my ears that I may hear your commands, heal and open my eyes that I may see your every movement. Remove all unsoundness from me so that I may recognize you. Tell me where to look so that I may look upon you, and I shall hope to do all the things you command!

Soliloquies

Too late have I loved you, O beauty so ancient and yet so new! Too late have I loved you. And behold, you were within me and I was away and I was away outside, and there I searched for you, deformed, plunging, absorbed in those beautiful things which you had made. You were with me, but I was not with you. Things held me far from you, things which would not have existed at all except for you. You called, you shouted, and burst in on my deafness. You shone and gleamed brightly at me and dispersed my blindness.

You breathed forth fragrances, and I drew in my breath, and still I pant for you. I tasted much, and I hunger and thirst for more. You touched me, and I burned for your peace.

Confessions, Book 10

St. Dmitri of Rostov
Great Love

No unity with God is possible except by an exceedingly great love. This we can see from the story of the woman in the Gospel, who was a sinner: God in His great mercy granted her the forgiveness of her sins and a firm union with Him, "for she loved much" (Luke 7:47). He loves those who love Him, He cleaves to those who cleave to Him, gives Himself to those who seek Him, and abundantly grants fullness of joy to those who desire to enjoy His love.

To kindle in his heart such a divine love, to unite with God in an inseparable union of love, it is necessary for a man to pray often, raising the mind to Him. For as a flame increases when it is constantly fed, so prayer, made often, with the mind dwelling ever more deeply in God, arouses divine love in the heart. And the heart, set on fire, will warm all the inner man, will enlighten and teach him, revealing to him all its unknown and hidden wisdom, and making him like a flaming seraph, always standing before God within his spirit, always looking at Him within his mind, and drawing from this vision the sweetness of spiritual joy.

Quoted in *The Art of Prayer*

St. Bernard of Clairvaux
Growing in Love of God

If you look back on your own experience, is it not in that victory by which your faith overcomes the world, in your "exit from the horrible pit and out of the slough of the marsh" (Psalm 39:3) that you yourselves sing a new song to the Lord for all the marvels he has performed? Again, when he purposed to "settle your feet on a rock and to direct your steps" (Psalm 39:3-4), then too, I feel certain, a new song was sounding on your lips, a song to our God for his gracious renewal of your life. When you repented, he not only forgave your sins but even promised rewards, so that rejoicing in the hope of benefits to come, you sing of the Lord's ways: how great is the glory of the Lord! (Psalm 137:5). And when, as happens, texts of Scripture hitherto dark and impenetrable at last become bright with meaning for you, then, in gratitude for this nurturing bread of heaven, you must charm the ears of God with a voice of exultation and praise, a festal song. In the daily trials and combats arising from the flesh, the world, and the devil, that are never wanting to those who live devout lives in Christ, you learn by what you experience that man's life on earth is a ceaseless warfare, and are impelled to repeat your songs day after day for every victory won. As often as temptation is overcome, an immoral habit brought under control, an impending danger shunned, the trap of the seducer detected, when a passion long indulged is finally and perfectly allayed, or a virtue persistently desired and repeatedly sought is ultimately obtained by God's gift; so often, in the words of the prophet, let thanksgiving and joy resound (Isaiah 51:3). For every benefit conferred, God is to be praised in his gifts....

Again I think that your own experience reveals to you the meaning of those psalms, which are called not Songs of Songs but Songs of the Steps, in that each one, at whatever stage of growth he be, in accord with the upward movements of his heart may choose one of these songs to praise and give glory to him who empowers you to advance. I don't know how else these words could be true: "There are shouts of joy and victory in the tents of the just" (Psalm 117:15). And still more that beautiful and salutary exhortation of the Apostle: "With psalms and hymns and spiritual canticles, singing and chanting to the Lord in your hearts" (Ephesians 5:19).

But there is that other song which, by its unique dignity and sweetness, excels all those I have mentioned and any others there might be; hence by every right do I acclaim it as the Song of Songs. It stands at a point where all the others culminate. Only the touch of the Spirit can inspire a song like this, and only personal experience can unfold its meaning. Let those who are versed in the mystery revel in it; let all others burn with desire rather to attain to this experience than merely to learn about it. For it is not a melody that resounds abroad but the very music of the heart, not a trilling on the lips but an inward pulsing of delight, a harmony not of voices but of wills. It is a tune you will not hear in the streets; these notes do not sound where crowds assemble; only the singer hears it and the one to whom he sings—

the lover and the beloved. It is preeminently a marriage song telling of chaste souls in loving embrace, of their wills in sweet concord, of the mutual exchange of the heart's affections.

The novices, the immature, those but recently converted from a worldly life do not normally sing this song or hear it sung. Only the mind disciplined by persevering study, only the man whose efforts have borne fruit under God's inspiration, the man whose years, as it were, make him ripe for marriage—years measured out not in time but in merits—only he is truly prepared for nuptial union with the divine partner.

Sermon on the Song of Songs

SEVEN

The Dark Night

Remember Jesus Christ, risen from the dead, descended from David, as preached in my gospel, the gospel for which I am suffering and wearing fetters like a criminal. But the word of God is not fettered. Therefore I endure everything for the sake of the elect, that they also may obtain salvation in Christ Jesus with its eternal glory. The saying is sure: If we have died with him, we shall also live with him; if we endure, we shall also reign with him (2 Tm. 2:8-12).

The Night of the Senses

Much has been written about the place of suffering on the spiritual journey. We must carry the Cross, and we feel the weight of the Cross most of the time. However, beyond the expected trials of any life of virtue there are specific experiences of darkness and aridity that are integral parts of the spiritual journey. Their purpose is explicitly to draw us away from our own self-love and self-indulgence (called narcissism in psychology) and to help us become more pure in our love of God. Darkness teaches us to seek God for Himself alone and not for any personal enjoyment. It seems to me—and I cautiously depart from some traditional writers—that this spiritual darkness may be related to causes that are not exclusively supernatural. The effect of the body on the mind and the complexity of the mind itself have been better understood in recent decades. Often a true spiritual darkness is occasioned providentially by something that is apparently unrelated to the spiritual life, such as a dietary deficiency, loss of employment, rejection or the demise of a loved one, or physical illness. Certainly the great darkness of St. Thérèse was intimately connected with her terminal illness: profound depression usually accompanies the acute tubercular states. Wherever darkness comes from, it can be used to turn our hearts from self-indulgence and self-love to God. We should learn not to fear darkness nor to run away from it. Most people who have been on the spiritual journey for a while have learned that life's best blessings often come wrapped in dirty newspaper. Eugene Hamilton, a young seminarian, found a direct road to God through terminal cancer. Although only minimally familiar with St. John of the Cross and probably unaware of St. Theophan, he learned the theology of suffering explicitly from Pope John Paul's apostolic letter which teaches that suffering is an integral part of discipleship. Eugene's experience is especially enlightening to us because he is a child of our own times. Nevertheless, he found the same strength and help that St. Teresa found four hundred years before—the knowledge that Christ is there as a supporting friend whenever we are willing to let Him be.

St. John of the Cross
The Night of the Senses and the Night of the Spirit

Since the conduct of these beginners in the way of God is lowly and not too distant from love of pleasure and of self, as was explained, God desires to withdraw them from this base manner of loving and lead them on to a higher degree of divine love. And He desires to liberate them from the lowly exercise of the senses and of discursive meditation, by which they go in search of Him so inadequately and with so many difficulties, and lead them into the exercise of spirit, in which they become capable of a communion with God that is more abundant and freer of imperfections. God does this after beginners have exercised themselves for a time in the way of virtue and have persevered in meditation and prayer. For it is through the delight and satisfaction they experience in prayer that they have become detached from worldly things and have gained some spiritual strength in God. This strength has helped them somewhat to restrain their appetites for creatures, and through it they will be able to suffer a little oppression and dryness without turning back. Consequently, it is at the time they are going about their spiritual exercises with delight and satisfaction, when in their opinion the sun of divine favor is shining most brightly on them, that

God darkens all this light and closes the door and spring of the sweet spiritual water they were tasting as often and as long as they desired. For since they were weak and tender, no door was closed to them, as St. John says in the Apocalypse. [Rev. 3:8] God now leaves them in such darkness that they do not know which way to turn in their discursive imaginings; they cannot advance a step in meditation, as they used to, now that the interior sensory faculties are engulfed in this night. He leaves them in such dryness that they not only fail to receive satisfaction and pleasure from their spiritual exercises and works, as they formerly did, but also find these exercises distasteful and bitter. As I said, when God sees that they have grown a little, He weans them from the sweet breast so that they might be strengthened, lays aside their swaddling bands, and puts them down from His arms that they may grow accustomed to walking by themselves. This change is a surprise to them because everything seems to be functioning in reverse.

The Dark Night, Book 1, Chapter 8

St. Claude de la Colombière
Trust in the Darkness

The time of desolation and dryness is the best for gaining merit. A soul that seeks God easily bears this state and rises above all that passes before the imagination and in the inferior part of the soul where consolation is mostly to be found. It does not cease to love God, to humble itself, and to accept this state even forever. There is nothing so dangerous and so much to be suspected as sweetness. Sometimes we attach ourselves to it, and when it is passed we find we have less instead of more fervor in doing good. It is a real consolation for me to think that in the midst of aridity and temptation my heart is free and that it is only by my heart (that is, my will) that I can merit or demerit; that I neither please nor displease God by things which are beyond my control, such as sensible sweetness and importunate thoughts which come into my mind in spite of myself.

Therefore during this time of suffering and desolation I say to God: My Lord, let the world and even the devil take for themselves what I cannot prevent them having, but they shall never have anything to do with my heart, my will that thou hast left in my possession—this belongs to thee: take it, it is thine, and do what thou wilt with it. A man to whom God has given a real desire to please him need never trouble about anything. "Peace to men of good will" (Lk 2:14).

Retreat Notes, 1674

Theophan the Recluse
How to Behave in the Darkness

You undertake different tasks, so you tell me, "in most cases unwillingly and without any eagerness—I have to force myself." But this, after all, is a basic principle in the spiritual life—to set yourself in opposition to what is bad and to force yourself to do what is good. This is the meaning of the Lord's words, "The kingdom of heaven suffereth violence, and the violent take it by force" (Matt. 11:12). This is why following the Lord is a yoke. If all were done eagerly, where would be the yoke? Yet in the end it so comes about that everything is done easily and willingly.

You say, "A dull insensitivity holds me fast; I become like an automaton—without thoughts or feelings."

Such states come sometimes as a punishment because we have inclined in thought or feeling to something evil; and sometimes they come as an education—chiefly to teach us humility, to accustom us not to expect anything from our own powers, but to wait on God alone. A few such experiences undermine confidence in self; and so, when we are delivered from heaviness, we know where the help comes from, and we realize on whom to rely in everything. This is a depressing state, but it must be endured with the thought that we do not deserve anything better, that we have earned it. There are no remedies against it, and deliverance from it depends on God's will. All we can do is to cry to the Lord: Thy will be done! Have mercy! Help me! But on no account should we allow ourselves to grow slack, for this is harmful and destructive. The holy Fathers describe such states as cooling off or dryness; and they agree in regarding them as something inevitable for anyone trying to live according to God's will, for without them we quickly become presumptuous.

Quoted in *The Art of Prayer*

Pope John Paul II
Redemptive Suffering

The mystery of the Redemption of the world is in an amazing way rooted in suffering, and this suffering in turn finds in the mystery of the Redemption its supreme and surest point of reference....

And so there should come together in spirit beneath the Cross of Calvary all suffering people who believe in Christ, and particularly those who suffer because of their faith in Him who is the crucified and risen One, so that the offering of their sufferings may hasten the fulfillment of the prayer of the Savior Himself that all may be one. Let there also gather beneath the Cross all people of good will, for on this Cross is the "Redeemer of man," the Man of Sorrows, who has taken upon Himself the physical and moral sufferings of the people of all times, so that in love they may find the salvific meaning of their sorrow and valid answers to all of their questions.

On the Christian Meaning of Human Suffering

St. Thomas More
The Savior's Darkness in Gethsemane

For a huge mass of troubles took possession of the tender and gentle body of our most holy Savior. He knew that His ordeal was now imminent and just about to overtake Him: the treacherous betrayer, the bitter enemies, binding ropes, false accusations, slanders, blows, thorns, nails, the cross, and horrible tortures stretched out over many hours. Over and above these, He was tormented by the thought of His disciples' terror, the loss of the Jews, even the destruction of the very man who so disloyally betrayed Him, and finally the ineffable grief of His beloved mother. The gathered storm of all these evils rushed into His most gentle heart and flooded it like the ocean sweeping through broken dikes.

The Sadness of Christ

Father Eugene Hamilton
United with Christ in the Darkness

When I asked Gene about his concept of victim in our December 1996 interview, his answer was most illuminating:

"I guess it's an understanding, a realization that in the particular human condition that we're in, because of original sin, evil has entered the world. As a result of that we have human suffering, and yet at the same time we have hope because we've been redeemed by Jesus Christ. And He specifically chose the plan of God, that He would redeem the world through His suffering on the Cross and by dying and then rising to new life. And so it is through the passion, death, and resurrection that is re-presented in the Eucharistic sacrifice and that we proclaim in the Scriptures that we realize that it is in dying that we become born into eternal life. And so we've regained that life through the Cross of Christ through His resurrection. While we're on this pilgrimage here on earth, the Cross gives us a better understanding of the fact that this is not the end, but it is merely a part of that pilgrimage towards our ultimate goal and what the Lord wants for us—eternal life with Him forever. And so I believe that those who suffer in this life can be assured that Jesus is very, very close to them in their suffering. That Jesus will always hold out his hand to them in their suffering and that He will be with them in their suffering and that they can unite that suffering with His on the Cross. Therefore suffering takes on that salvific meaning for the salvation of others so that merit and grace can be given for others. It permits us basically to take a very active role in God's plan of redemption."

A Priest Forever

St. Teresa of Avila
Christ the Friend in the Darkness

Alone I was, without a single friend to give me a word of encouragement, I could neither pray nor read, but there I remained, for hours and hours together, uneasy in mind and afflicted in spirit on account of the weight of my trouble, and of the fear that perhaps after all I was being tricked by the devil, and wondering what in the world I could do for my relief. Not a gleam of hope seemed to shine upon me from either earth or heaven; except just this: that in the midst of all my fears and dangers I never forgot how Our Lord must be seeing the weight of all I endured.

O my Lord Jesus Christ! What a true friend You are, and how powerful! For when You wish to be with us, You can be, and You always do wish it, if only we will receive You. May everything created, O Lord of all the world, praise You and bless You! If only I could tramp the whole world over, proclaiming everywhere with all the strength that is in me what a faithful friend You are to those who will be friends with You! My dear Lord, all else fails and passes away. You, the Lord of them all, never fail, never pass away. What You allow those who love You to suffer is all too little. O my Lord, how kindly, how nobly, how tenderly, how sweetly You succeed in handling and making sure of Your own! Oh, if only one could secure that one would love nothing but just You alone! You seem, my dear Lord, to put to the trial with rods and agonies one who loves You, only that, just when You have brought her to the last extreme of endurance, she may understand all the more the boundless limits of Your love.

Autobiography, Chapter 25

St. John of the Cross
Trusting in God During Darkness

If there is no one to understand these persons, they either turn back and abandon the road or lose courage, or at least they hinder their own progress because of their excessive diligence in treading the path of discursive meditation. They fatigue and overwork themselves, thinking that they are failing because of their negligences or sins. Meditation is now useless for them, because God is conducting them along another road, which is contemplation and which is very different from the first. For the one road belongs to discursive meditation and the other is beyond the range of the imagination and discursive reflection.

Those who are in this situation should feel comforted; they ought to persevere patiently and not be afflicted. Let them trust in God Who does not fail those who seek Him with a simple and righteous heart; nor does He fail to impart what is needful for the way until getting them to the clear and pure light of love. God will give them this light by means of that other night, the night of spirit, if they merit that He place them in it.

The Dark Night, Book 1, Chapter 10

The Night of the Spirit

And when the sixth hour had come, there was darkness over the whole land until the ninth hour. And at the ninth hour Jesus cried with a loud voice, "Eloi, Eloi, lama sabachthani?" which means, "My God, my God, why hast thou forsaken me?" And some of the bystanders hearing it said, "Behold, he is calling Elijah." And one ran and, filling a sponge full of vinegar, put it on a reed and gave it to him to drink, saying, "Wait, let us see whether Elijah will come to take him down." And Jesus uttered a loud cry, and breathed his last. And the curtain of the temple was torn in two, from top to bottom. And when the centurion, who stood facing him, saw that he thus breathed his last, he said, "Truly this man was the Son of God!" (Mark 15:33-37).

Just as it is ultimately impossible to describe the experience of infused contemplation to someone who has never received the gift, it is equally impossible to describe the dark night of the spirit, which prepares for it. The objective description of St. John of the Cross surely has the ring of authority about it. There is no doubt that he is describing what he knows from experience. The description of St. Thérèse is direct and subjective, given to her prioress at the time, and might leave one hoping for physical martyrdom as an easier way out of this world. Is such purgation necessary for the human soul before it enters into the light of God? An interesting question, to which there is no certain answer.

Certainly there are great Christians who have gone through the doors of death without ever giving evidence of having experienced such profound darkness. But neither do they give evidence of the level of contemplative prayer that John and Thérèse attained. Perhaps not everyone is called to such a high degree of contemplation and, consequently, may not have to go through such things. On the other hand, it may be that the very strength of character and personality possessed by the great mystics requires a far deeper experience of the death of self, even if that self has been faithful to the service of God and continues in a generous discipleship.

Letters from St. Thérèse to a troubled seminarian were recently published which the saint wrote during the period of incredible darkness described in her autobiography. The letters, however, give no evidence of the relentless illness that was dragging her down and depriving her of every physical comfort, or of the spiritual darkness she endured for several months before her death.

It is perhaps not helpful for most of us to dwell on this stage of the spiritual life, because indeed we will not arrive at it. On the other hand, those who experience a long, painful illness in the process of dying may do well to keep in mind this experience of the dark night of the spirit. If the terminally ill approach their relentless physical deterioration with faith and trust, and rely as completely as possible on the Holy Spirit, they may, in fact, make great spiritual progress in a very short time. I am sure that I have seen this occur.

For the sake of clarity I have written of the night of the senses and the night of the spirit together. In fact, they occur separately, the second as part of the unitive way. While there is no agreement on when they occur, there is total agreement that their purpose is the final purification of the soul. The descriptions of the night of the spirit included here pertain to the unitive way. It is important to note that these periods of darkness may not even appear to the person undergoing them as a darkness to be endured, but rather as a sacrifice in union with Christ to be offered to the Father.

St. John of the Cross
God Leads the Soul

If God intends to lead the soul on, He does not put it in this dark night of spirit immediately after its going out from the aridities and trials of the first purgation and night of sense. Instead, after having emerged from the state of beginners, it usually spends many years exercising itself in the state of proficients. In this new state, as one liberated from a cramped prison cell, the soul goes about the things of God with much more freedom and satisfaction of spirit and with more abundant interior delight than it did in the beginning before entering the night of sense. Its imagination and faculties are no longer bound to discursive meditation and spiritual solicitude, as was their custom. The soul readily finds in its spirit, without the work of meditation, a very serene, loving contemplation and spiritual delight. Nonetheless, since the purgation of the soul is not complete (the purgation of the principal part, that of the spirit, is lacking, and without it the sensory purgation, however strong it may have been, is incomplete because of a communication existing between the two parts of the soul which form only one *suppositum*), certain needs, aridities, darknesses, and conflicts are felt. These are sometimes far more intense than those of the past and are like omens or messengers of the coming night of the spirit.

The Dark Night, Book 2, Chapter 1

St. John of the Cross
Death and Resurrection

The two extremes, divine and human, which are joined here, produce the third kind of pain and affliction the soul suffers here. The divine extreme is the purgative contemplation and the human extreme is the soul, the receiver of this contemplation. Since the divine extreme strikes in order to renew the soul and divinize it (by stripping it of the habitual affections and properties of the old man to which it is strongly united, attached, and conformed), it so disentangles and dissolves the spiritual substance—absorbing it in a profound darkness—that the soul at the sight of its miseries feels that it is melting away and being undone by a cruel spiritual death; it feels as if it were swallowed by a beast and being digested in the dark belly, and it suffers an anguish comparable to Jonas's when in the belly of the whale (Jonah 2:1-3). It is fitting that the soul be in this sepulcher of dark death in order that it attain the spiritual resurrection for which it hopes....

God does all this by means of dark contemplation. And the soul not only suffers the void and suspension of these natural supports and apprehensions, which is a terrible anguish (like hanging in midair, unable to breathe), but it is also purged by this contemplation. As fire consumes the tarnish and rust of metal, this contemplation annihilates, empties, and consumes all the affections and imperfect habits the soul contracted throughout its life. Since these imperfections are deeply rooted in the substance of the soul, it usually suffers besides this poverty and this natural and spiritual emptiness an oppressive undoing and an inner torment. Thus the passage of Ezechiel may be verified: "Heap together the bones, and I shall burn them in the fire, the flesh shall be consumed, and the whole composition burned, and the bones destroyed" (Ezek. 24:10). He refers here to the affliction suffered in the emptiness and poverty of both the sensory and the spiritual substance of the soul. And he then adds: "Place it also thus empty on the embers that its metal may become hot and melt and its uncleanness be taken away from it and its rust consumed" (Ezek. 24:11). This passage points out the heavy affliction the soul suffers from the purgation caused by the fire of this contemplation. For the prophet asserts that in order to burn away the rust of the affections the soul must, as it were, be annihilated and undone in the measure that these passions and imperfections are connatural to it.

Because the soul is purified in this forge like gold in the crucible, as the Wise Man says (Wis. 3:6), it feels terrible annihilation in its very substance and extreme poverty as though it were approaching its end. This experience is expressed in David's cry: "Save me, Lord, for the waters have come in even unto my soul; I am stuck in the mire of the deep, and there is nowhere to stand; I have come unto the depth of the sea, and the tempest has overwhelmed me. I have labored in crying out, my throat has become hoarse, my eyes have failed while I hope in my God" (Ps. 68:2-4).

The Dark Night, Book 2, Chapter 6

St. Thérèse of Lisieux
A Saint Approaches Death

When I want to rest my heart, wearied by the darkness which surrounds it, by the memory of the luminous country to which I aspire, my torment redoubles; it seems to me that the darkness, borrowing the voice of sinners, says mockingly to me, "You are dreaming about the light, about a country fragrant with the sweetest perfumes; you are dreaming about the *eternal* possession of the Creator of all these things; you believe that one day you will walk out of this fog which surrounds you! Dream on, dream on; rejoice in death which will give you not what you hope for, but even deeper night, the night of nothingness."

I may perhaps appear to you to be exaggerating my trial. In fact, if you go by the sentiments I express in my little poems composed this year, I must appear to you as a soul filled with consolations and one for whom the veil of faith is almost torn aside. It is no longer a veil for me, it is a wall which reaches right up to the heavens and hides the starry firmament. When I sing of the happiness of heaven, of the eternal possession of God,

I feel no joy in this, for I sing simply what *I want to believe.*

The Story of a Soul

St. Thérèse of Lisieux
Ready to Leave
St. Thérèse wrote this letter when she was in the darkest part of her journey to God.
August 10, 1897
Carmel of Lisieux
Jesus +
My dear little Brother,

I am now all ready to leave. I have my passport for Heaven, and it is my dear father who has obtained this grace for me. On the 29th he gave me the assurance that I would soon go to join him. The next day the doctor, astonished by the progress the sickness had made in two days, said to Mother that it was time to grant my wish to receive Extreme Unction. So I had this happiness on the 30th, and also that of seeing Jesus in the Blessed Sacrament leave the tabernacle to come to me, Whom I received as Viaticum for my long voyage! This Bread of Heaven has strengthened me. Just look, it seems as if my pilgrimage can't get to its destination. Far from complaining about this, I rejoice that God still lets me suffer for love of Him. Ah, how good it is to let yourself go in His arms, with neither fears nor desires.

I have to tell you, little brother, that we don't understand Heaven in the same way. You think that, once I share in the justice and holiness of God, I won't be able to excuse your faults as I did when I was on earth. Are you then forgetting that I shall also share in the infinite mercy of the Lord? I believe that the Blessed in Heaven have great compassion for our miseries. They remember that when they were weak and mortal like us, they committed the same faults themselves and went through the same struggles, and their fraternal tenderness becomes still greater than it ever was on earth. It's on account of this that they never stop watching over us and praying for us.

Now my dear little brother, I must tell you about the inheritance you will come into after my death. Here is the share which our Mother will give you: (1) the reliquary which I received on the day I took the habit and which has never left me since then; (2) a little crucifix which is incomparably more dear to me than the large one, for the one I have now is no longer the first one that I was given. In Carmel we sometimes exchange holy objects; it is a way of keeping us from getting attached to them. Let me come back to the little Crucifix. It is not beautiful; the face of Christ has disappeared. You won't be surprised at this when I tell you that since I was 13 years old this souvenir from one of my sisters has followed me everywhere. It was especially during my voyage in Italy that this Crucifix became dear to me. I touched it to all the famous relics I had the joy of venerating, which were more than I can count, and moreover it was blessed by the Holy Father. Ever since I've been sick, I hold our dear little Crucifix almost constantly in my hands, and as I look at it now, I think with joy that, after having received my kisses, it will go to claim those of my little brother. Look then what a heritage you will have! In addition, our Mother will give you the last picture that I painted.

Dear little brother, let me end where I should have begun, by thanking you for the great pleasure you gave me by sending me your photograph.

A Dieu, dear little brother, may God give us the grace to love Him and to save souls for Him. This is the wish of your unworthy little Sister Thérèse of the Child Jesus and of the Holy Face. r.c.i.

Letter to Maurice Bellière, seminarian for the diocese of Bayeux

EIGHT

The Unitive Way

If then you have been raised with Christ, seek the things
that are above, where Christ is, seated at the right hand of
God (Col. 3:1).

Our reasons for including the unitive, or highest, way of the spiritual
life are very different from the motive for including the other two
ways. No one who is truly in the unitive way needs to read about it; in fact,
they should not waste time with a book. They should be busy praying for
the rest of us. The very power of divine presence in the unitive way will be
all the direction the person ordinarily needs.

There are two reasons for including selections that illustrate the unitive
way. First, we need a sense of completion, an idea of where we are going,
even if we don't expect to get there. More important is the realization that
in any process of development, the final state exists in a tentative and
subtle way all through the process. Not only is the child the father of the
man, but all through development the final maturation is beginning to
emerge ever so subtly. Readers who are seriously interested in spiritual
development should be filled with a sense of attraction to the awesome
union with God. They should also be examining their own present performance to see if they are really seeking the treasure hidden in the field
and the pearl of great price.

A valuable result of having some familiarity with the writings of the great
mystics is that we may be able to recognize a truly advanced soul, one who
is really close to God. Cardinal Newman warns that we may have lived with

saints without recognizing their holiness. Since the vast majority of truly advanced souls are not mystical theologians like St. John of the Cross, or writers of profound psychospiritual autobiography like St. Teresa, or stigmatics like St. Francis, we tend to miss them. We have all known humble and silent souls who have surrendered themselves completely to God and, as a consequence, are in union with Him. They have begun the reality of eternal life epitomized by our Savior when He said, "that they may all be one; even as Thou, Father, art in me, and I in thee, that they also may be in us" (Jn. 17:21).

Many writers make a distinction between the two phases of the unitive way—simple union and transforming union. The first refers to a state that many describe as one in which the individual places no obstacles at all in the way of God's control and is unfailingly docile to His actions and inspiration. Life has become a simple response to God—even when there comes the final darkness at the end of all ego activity. The transforming union that follows leaves the soul "like a stone that has reached the center of the earth." The soul will have attained the highest degree of love. According to St. John of the Cross, the love of God will wound it in its inmost center; then the soul will be transformed and enlightened in the highest degree in its substance, functioning, and strength, until it becomes most like unto God.

The unitive way is one of dazzling light, in contrast to the terror of the dark night. Those appear to do best in it who trust in the Lord like St. Thérèse of Lisieux. They will to believe even when the experience of faith is lost in the darkness. It takes an incredible trust to live through the annihilation of the self-centered ego. This third way includes the darkness of Calvary and the white radiance of the Resurrection. Yet in it all, no one is expected to give up the works of virtue and charity of the previous ways. As these brief selections indicate, souls in the unitive way are much more active than we assume.

Many spiritual writers and directors have thought it wise not even to discuss this highest realm with those along the way because, as Archbishop Goodier observes, those along the way may dream that they are in this state when they are actually far off. At times most devout struggling souls feel that they are in a simple union with God. It may be the case, but it does not last, because they actually have not made that much progress. Few would even have a hint of what transforming union apparently means from those who have described it from their own experience.

It is best for the serious reader who has persevered with this book up to now to stand back and lovingly admire the great snow-covered peaks of the unitive way. Most of us are not even to the tree line of the second dark night. We are still on the lower slopes where the inviting clumps of mountain flowers bloom amid daunting rocks and deep ravines.

Let's be grateful to have come this far and keep before us the advice of St. Paul: Press on!

Gerald Heard, English spiritual writer
The Call of the Few

The Light shines through those who have so opened themselves, or rather let themselves be opened. Thank God we have all of us known one or two of them. And there may be more of them than we notice, for they are the reverse of showy. They may be very active, but when we think of them it is not of their activity, physical or mental, of which we think. It is of some still, firm quality, some essence deeper than deeds, that we see in them. They see Reality, are always looking at it, and, through that seeing, there is in them a quality of entire Being.

Is there anything beyond that stage? That is indeed much.... The first stage is that of servantship, when we learn not to disobey. The second stage is one of friendship, when we learn why we have had to obey, and to abstain from much that seemed harmless and even, in its way, right.... Then comes the third stage, that of creative action, the station and work of sons.... They are not merely privileged onlookers, they are co-workers. This is the well-known (but seldom climbed) ladder of the mystics.... If we think that goal anything less than the highest, that can be because we have never met any of that highest third rank—as well may be. They are themselves rare and, like all supreme masterpieces, those who would understand them must in themselves have already something of the nature they would appreciate. If we are quite blind, however intense the sun, we shall still see only darkness.... Theirs is of the essential nature of their Father, a quality, an intensity of Being, which is, unless they screen it from us, disquieting, uncanny. Real creativeness is far more terrible than what we call destruction.

Can we ourselves hope to climb this tremendous way to the Kingdom? Certainly: we are called, all of us, to do so. Certainly: there will be no Kingdom unless and until we do so climb to that station. For only those who have attained may safely be given the powers, the spiritual powers whereby, and only whereby, God's Kingdom may come on earth. How can we learn to climb to such immense heights? We have seen the first steps. The very first is to know that I as I am, am an obstacle to the Kingdom. I must start, before anything else, by clearing myself out of the way. I must learn, right down to my reflexes, to say and mean and know, "Let my name perish, so Thy Kingdom come."

The Creed of Christ

Archbishop Alban Goodier, S.J.
Signs of the Contemplative

When we come across souls who seem to possess Infused Contemplation in some form, we must needs be cautious, for the simple reason that there are few states more easy to counterfeit, or rather more open to delusion. The difficulty is increased for the director because, almost always, the self-deluded soul is not aware that delusion is possible. It takes itself seriously; it has learnt to look at itself from a peculiar angle, which it thinks supernatural; it may have had some emotional experience which, it is convinced, has come from God. For such a soul the angel of darkness easily transforms himself into an angel of light. So long as there is the slightest doubt, caution is always safer than encouragement; we may see how the earliest guides of St. Teresa treated her with this caution, even those who, like Fr. Balthasar Alvarez, believed in her from the first. Still it is not wise and, as St. John of the Cross very pointedly repeats, it can do much harm to check altogether such souls as are not clearly deluded. While we doubt, we must also hesitate and not condemn. For a real contemplative, perfect and genuine, is worth far more than any active worker; in the end his influence, however hidden, and even despised as not consonant with the times, will be far greater than that of one who has merely done much. *Porro unum est necessarium* ("One thing is needful"—Luke 10:42). Moreover, we may add that the contemplative has more to suffer, in soul and usually in body, than have the rest of us, however well they may conceal it; and to increase that suffering by any lack of sympathy or understanding on our part is worse than merely a misfortune.

Lastly, apart from those few to whom is given the full grace of Infused Contemplation, there are very many who may be said to have a contemplative bent or mentality; who see life as with the eyes of God, who find Him living in the world around them, whose way of prayer is not external, speaking as it were to another, but internal, to God whom they have found within them, occupying all they are. To withdraw such souls from what some might call their dreamland would be unfortunate, to put them on more 'practical' lines would be to load them with chains; the contemplative mind, internal realization, the life of union of being, is a seed ground of prayer which, when discovered, should never be contemned.

An Introduction to the Study of Ascetical and Mystical Theology

Theophan the Recluse
Everything in Its Own Time

The Lord, having entered into union with the spirit of man, does not immediately fill him completely or dwell in him wholly. This is not because of any reluctance on His part—for He is ready to fill everything—but because of us: it is because the passions are still mixed with the powers of our nature, not yet separated from them and not yet replaced by their opposite virtues.

While fighting the passions with all zeal, we must have the eyes of the mind turned towards God. This is the first principle to be maintained in building a way of life pleasing to God. By it we should test the straightness or crookedness of the rules and the ascetic feats which we may have in mind and undertake.

This necessity of being turned inwardly towards God must be fully recognized, because all the errors in the active life seem to come from ignorance of this principle. Not seeing its significance, some people stop short at the exterior stage of devout exercises and ascetic efforts; others stop short at the habitual practice of good deeds, without rising any higher. Others again attempt to pass directly to contemplation. All these things are required of us, but everything must be done in its own time. At the beginning there is only a seed, which afterwards develops—not exclusively, but in its general tendency—into one form of life or another. Gradualness is necessary—the orderly ascent from exterior to interior deeds, and then from both to contemplation. Such is always the sequence—never vice versa.

Quoted in *The Art of Prayer*

Jonathan Edwards
The Perfect Holiness of Heaven

The heaven I desired was a heaven of holiness; to be with God, and to spend my eternity in divine love, and holy communion with Christ. My mind was very much taken up with contemplations on heaven, and the enjoyments of those there, and living there in perfect holiness, humility, and love. And it used at that time to appear a great part of the happiness of heaven, that there the saints could express their love to Christ. It appeared to me a great clog and hindrance and burden to me, that what I felt within, I could not express to God, and give vent to as I desired. The inward ardor of my soul seemed to be hindered and pent up, and could not freely flame out as it would. I used often to think how in heaven this sweet principle should freely and fully vent and express itself. Heaven appeared to me exceeding delightful as a world of love. It appeared to me that all happiness consisted in living in pure, humble, heavenly, divine love.

I remember the thoughts I used then to have of holiness. I remember I then said sometimes to myself, I do certainly know that I love holiness, such as the Gospel prescribes. It appeared to me there was nothing in it but what was ravishingly lovely. It appeared to me to be the highest beauty and amiableness, above all other beauties, that it was a *divine* beauty, far purer than anything here upon earth, and that everything else was like mire, filth, and defilement in comparison of it.

Holiness, as I then wrote down some of my contemplations on it, appeared to me to be of a sweet, pleasant, charming, serene, calm nature. It seemed to me it brought an inexpressible purity, brightness, peacefulness, and ravishment to the soul; and that it made the soul like a field or garden of God with all manner of pleasant flowers; that is, all pleasant, delightful, and undisturbed, enjoying a sweet calm and the gently vivifying beams of the sun. The soul of a true Christian, as I then wrote my meditations, appeared like such a little white flower as we see in the spring of the year, low, and humble on the ground, opening its bosom to receive the pleasant beams of the sun's glory; rejoicing as it were in a calm rapture; diffusing around a sweet fragrancy; standing peacefully and lovingly, in the midst of other flowers round about; all in like manner opening their bosoms to drink in the light of the sun.

There was no part of creature-holiness that I then, and at other times, had so great a sense of the loveliness of, as humility, brokenness of heart, and poverty of spirit: and there was nothing that I had such a spirit to long for. My heart, as it were, panted after this, to lie low before God, and in the dust; that I might be nothing, and that God might be all; that I might become as a little child.

The Life and Character of Mr. Jonathan Edwards

Concepción Cabrera de Armida (Conchita)
A Soul Simply United with Christ

Conchita was being prepared for her special mission, a sacrificial priesthood for the salvation of souls. On June 21, 1906, Jesus says to her:

"You will be my altar and at the same time my victim. Offer yourself in union with me, offer me at each moment to the eternal Father, with the so exalted purpose of saving souls and of glorifying him. Forget everything, and above all, forget yourself. Let that be your constant occupation. You have received a sublime mission, the mission of a priest. Admire my bounty and show your gratitude. Without your knowing it, I have given you what you desired so much, and much, much more than that: the ability to be a priest, not that of holding me in your hands but in your heart, and the grace of never separating myself from you. Achieve the grandiose finality of this grace. As you see, it is not for you alone but universal, obliging you with all possible purity to be at one and the same time altar and victim, consumed in holocaust with the other Victim, the sole Host which may be agreeable to God and which may save the world."

Quoted in *Revelations of Women Mystics*

St. John of the Cross
Transforming Union

Fire or a stone tend by their natural force to the center of their sphere.... When a stone shall have reached the center of the earth, and is incapable of further motion of its own, we say of it that it is then in its inmost or deepest center.

The center of the soul is God. When the soul shall have reached Him, according to its essence, and according to the power of its operations, it will then have attained to its ultimate and deepest center in God. This will be when the soul shall love Him, comprehend Him, and enjoy Him with all its strength. When, however, the soul has not attained to this state ... it is not in the deepest center, because there is still room for it to advance.... But if the soul shall have attained to the highest degree of love, the love of God will then wound it in its inmost depth or center, and the soul will be transformed and enlightened in the highest degree in its substance, faculties, and strength, until it shall become most like unto God. The soul in this state may be compared to crystal, lucid and pure; the greater the light thrown upon it, the more luminous it becomes by the concentration thereof, until at last it seems to be all light and indistinguishable from it; it being then so illumined, and to the utmost extent, that it seems to be one with the light itself.

The Living Flame of Love, Stanza 1

St. Francis of Assisi
The Stigmata

By the seraphic ardor of his desires, he was being borne aloft into God; and by his sweet compassion he was being transformed into Him who chose to be crucified because of the excess of his love (Eph. 2:4). On a certain morning about the feast of the Exaltation of the Cross, while Francis was praying on the mountainside, he saw a Seraph with six fiery and shining wings descend from the height of heaven. And when in swift flight the Seraph had reached a spot in the air near the man of God, there appeared between the wings the figure of a man crucified, with his hands and feet extended in the form of a cross and fastened to a cross. Two of the wings were lifted above his head, two were extended for flight, and two covered his whole body. When Francis saw this, he was overwhelmed, and his heart was flooded with a mixture of joy and sorrow. He rejoiced because of the gracious way Christ looked upon him under the appearance of the Seraph, but the fact that he was fastened to a cross pierced his soul with a sword of compassionate sorrow (Luke 2:35).

He wondered exceedingly at the sight of so unfathomable a vision, realizing that the weakness of Christ's passion was in no way compatible with the immortality of the Seraph's spiritual nature. Eventually he understood by a revelation from the Lord that divine providence had shown him this vision so that, as Christ's lover, he might learn in advance that he was to be totally transformed into the likeness of Christ crucified, not by the martyrdom of his flesh, but by the fire of his love consuming his soul.

As the vision disappeared, it left in his heart a marvelous ardor and imprinted on his body markings that were no less marvelous. Immediately the marks of nails began to appear in his hands and feet just as he had seen a little before in the figure of the man crucified. His hands and feet seemed to be pierced through the center by nails, with the heads of the nails appearing on the inner side of the hands and the upper side of the feet and their points on the opposite sides. The heads of the nails in his hands and his feet were round and black; their points were oblong and bent as if driven back with a hammer, and they emerged from the flesh and stuck out beyond it. Also his right side, as if pierced with a lance, was marked with a red wound from which his sacred blood often flowed, moistening his tunic and underwear.

When Christ's servant realized that he could not conceal from his intimate companions the stigmata that had been so visibly imprinted on his flesh, he feared to make public the Lord's secret (Tob. 12:7) and was thrown into an agony of doubt whether to tell what he had seen or to be silent about it. He called some of the friars and, speaking in general terms, presented his doubt to them and sought their advice. One of the friars, who was named Illuminato and was illumined by grace, realized that Francis had had a miraculous vision because he seemed still completely dazed. He said to the holy man: "Brother, you should realize that at times divine secrets are revealed to you not for yourself alone but also for others. You have every reason to fear that if you hide what you have received for the profit of many, you will be blamed for burying that talent" (Matt. 25:25). Although the holy man used to say on other occasions: "My secret is for myself" (Isa. 24:16), he was moved by Illuminato's words and then with much fear recounted the vision in detail, adding that the one who had appeared to him had told him some things which he would never disclose to any man as long as he lived.

St. Bonaventure, *The Life of St. Francis of Assisi*

St. Thérèse of Lisieux
The Vision at the End

An account of St. Thérèse's death by Mother Agnes of Jesus

Her breathing suddenly became weaker and more labored. She fell back on the pillow, her head turned towards the right. The infirmary bell was rung and, to allow the nuns to assemble quickly, Mother Marie de Gonzague said in a loud voice: "Open all the doors." Hardly had the nuns knelt at her bedside when she pronounced very distinctly her final act of love: "Oh! I love him," she said, looking at her crucifix. Then a moment later: "My God, I love you!"

We thought that was the end, when suddenly she raised her eyes, eyes that were full of life and shining with an indescribable happiness 'surpassing all her hopes.' Sister Marie of the Eucharist approached with a candle to get a better look at that sublime gaze, which lasted for the space of a Credo. The light from the candle passed back and forth in front of her eyes did not cause any movement in her eyelids....

Then she closed her eyes, and the whiteness of her face, which had become more accentuated during the ecstasy, returned to normal. She appeared ravishingly beautiful and had a heavenly smile....

We did not have to close her eyes, for she had closed them herself after the vision. Mother Prioress then had the community retire, and Sister Aimée, Sister Marie of the Sacred Heart, and I prepared the Servant of God for burial. Her face had a childlike expression, and she didn't seem any more than twelve years old.

The Passion of Thérèse of Lisieux

St. John of the Cross
The Living Flame

"O living flame of love that tenderly wounds my soul." This is like saying: O enkindled love, with your loving movements you are pleasantly glorifying me according to the greater capacity and strength of my soul, bestowing divine knowledge according to all the ability and capacity of my intellect, and communicating love according to the greater power of my will, and rejoicing the substance of my soul with the torrent of your delight by your divine contact and substantial union, in harmony with the greater purity of my substance and the capacity and breadth of my memory!...

O flame of the Holy Spirit that so intimately and tenderly pierces the substance of my soul and cauterizes it with Your glorious ardor! Previously, my requests did not reach Your ears, when, in the anxieties and weariness of love in which my sense and my spirit suffered because of considerable weakness, impurity, and lack of strong love, I was praying that You loose me and bring me to Yourself, because my soul longed for You, and impatient love did not allow me to be so conformed to the conditions of this life in which you desired me still to live. The previous impulses of love were not enough, because they did not have sufficient quality for the attainment of my desire; now I am so fortified in love that not only do my sense and spirit no longer faint in You, but my heart and my flesh, reinforced in You, rejoice in the living God (Ps 83:3), with great conformity between the sensory and spiritual parts. What you desire me to ask for, I ask for; and what you do not desire, I do not desire, nor can I, nor does it even enter my mind to desire it. My petitions are now more valuable and estimable in Your sight, since they come from You, and You move me to make them, and I make them in the delight and joy of the Holy Spirit, my judgment now issuing from Your countenance (Ps 16:2), that is, when You esteem and hear my prayer. Tear, then, the thin veil of this life and do not let old age cut it naturally, that from now on I may love You with plenitude and fullness my soul desires forever and ever.

The Living Flame of Love, 1:17,36

St. Teresa of Avila
A Dialogue of Love

Now I see, my Bridegroom, that You are mine. I cannot deny it. You came into the world for me; for me You underwent severe trials; for me You suffered many lashes; for me You remain in the most Blessed Sacrament; and now you grant me so many wonderful favors. How can I be Yours, my God? What can one who has used so unskillfully the favors You have granted do for You? What can be expected of her services? Since with Your help she does something, consider what a poor worm will be able to do. Why does a Lord so powerful need her?

Oh, love! How I would want to say this word everywhere because love alone is that which can dare say with the bride, I am my Beloved's. He gives us permission to think that He, this true Lover, my Spouse and my Good, needs us. Since He gives us permission, let us repeat, daughters, my Beloved is mine and I am my Beloved's. You are mine, Lord? If You come to me, why do I doubt that I will able to serve You? From here on, Lord, I want to forget myself and look only at how I can serve You and have no other desire than to do Your will.

But my desire is not powerful, my God; You are the powerful One. What I can do is be determined; thus from this very moment I am determined to serve You through deeds.

Meditations on the Song of Songs, 4:10-12

St. Bonaventure
Not Light but Fire

In this passing over,
if it is to be perfect,
all intellectual activities must be left behind
and the height of our affection
must be totally transferred and transformed
into God.
This, however, is mystical and most secret,
which "no one knows
except him who receives it,"
no one receives
except him who desires it,
and no one desires except him
who is inflamed in his very marrow by the fire of the Holy Spirit
whom Christ sent into the world.
And therefore the Apostle says that
this mystical wisdom is revealed
by the Holy Spirit.

Since, therefore, in this regard
nature can do nothing
and effort can do but little,
little importance should be given to inquiry,
but much to unction;
little importance should be given to the tongue,
but much to inner joy;
little importance should be given to words and to writing,
but all to the gift of God,
that is, the Holy Spirit;
little or no importance should be given to creation,
but all to the creative essence,
the Father, Son and Holy Spirit,
saying with Dionysius
to God the Trinity:
"Trinity,
superessential, superdivine, and supereminent
overseer of the divine wisdom of Christians,
direct us into
the super-unknown, superluminous, and most sublime
summit
of mystical communication.
There
new, absolute, and unchangeable mysteries of theology
are hidden
in the superluminous darkness
of a silence
teaching secretly in the utmost obscurity
which is supermanifest—
a darkness which is super-resplendent
and in which everything shines forth
and which fills to overflowing
invisible intellects
with the splendors of invisible goods
that surpass all good."...

But if you wish to know how these things come about,
ask grace not instruction,
desire not understanding,
the groaning of prayer not diligent reading,
the Spouse not the teacher,
God not man,
darkness not clarity,
not light but the fire
that totally inflames and carries us into God
by ecstatic unctions and burning affections....

Whoever loves this death
can see God
because it is true beyond doubt that
"man will not see me and live."
Let us, then, die
and enter into the darkness;
let us impose silence
upon our cares, our desires, and our imaginings.
With Christ crucified
let us pass "out of this world to the Father"
so that when the Father is shown to us,
we may say with Philip:
"It is enough for us."
Let us hear with Paul:
"My grace is sufficient for you."

The Soul's Journey Into God

PART TWO

Provisions for the Journey

NINE

Grief and Contradiction

Simon Peter said to him, "Lord, where are you going?"
Jesus answered, "Where I am going you cannot follow me
now; but you shall follow afterward." Peter said to him,
"Lord, why cannot I follow you now? I will lay down my
life for you." Jesus answered, "Will you lay down your life
for me? Truly, truly, I say to you, the cock will not crow, till
you have denied me three times."

"Let not your hearts be troubled; believe in God, believe
also in me. In my Father's house are many rooms; if it were
not so, would I have told you that I go to prepare a place
for you? And when I go and prepare a place for you, I will
come again and will take you to myself, that where I am you
may be also" (Jn. 13:36-14:3).

The spiritual life can be described as a road, as we have done here. But
this analogy may give rise to some misleading conclusions, namely, that
whoever takes the road and follows all the maps, completes the stages, and
fills in all the blanks at the various passport offices along the way will have a
nice, safe, tranquil journey. Nothing could be further from the truth. Jacob
wrestled with the angel of the Lord and limped away wounded. Moses never
got across the Jordan. Peter betrayed Christ. Judas hanged himself. And
Paul cried out, "Who is weak, and I am not weak? Who is scandalized, and

I am not on fire?" (2 Cor. 11:29, *Douay-Rheims Version*). St. Francis near death prayed that he would not be lost, and St. Alphonsus Liguori wondered if the last visit to the chapel before his death would be the last time he was to be in Christ's presence. If you are quite sure of yourself and confident about how easy it all is, you have much to learn about the spiritual life.

The following selections come from a wide variety of people, including a condemned murderer, a reluctant atheist, a repentant sinner who recalls Christ moving away from him before his conversion, a mystical poet who was a drug addict, and another mystical poet who fought bleak depression all his life. And just for good measure, to make sure you get the point, we have included a painful act of contrition written by one of the greatest saints, and a poem written by a fool. So there! Watch out for complacency.

If you suspect you have become complacent, if you are sure of yourself as one of God's special people or think of yourself as spiritually and psychologically integrated, which is the Pharisaism of our time, if you have a tendency to be judgmental or self-righteous, I suggest the following cure. Open the Gospels to any page and read carefully for at least three minutes, and you will come across some words of Christ Himself that will demolish your self-reliance. He alone is our salvation and sanctification. Whenever we are tempted to think that we are doing any more than reluctantly letting His Holy Spirit operate in us, we are sadly mistaken. He will, providentially, out of His great mercy, allow us to fall and fail so that we may know that He alone is our light and our salvation. When we have learned a little, we will rejoice and be glad that He has let us fail, so that we may put all our trust in Him.

Jacques Fesch
The Murderer Meets His Savior

At la Santé, in the cell from which he would leave directly for the scaffold, Jacques was with his God. In these last moments he was living the agony of the Garden of Olives, and interiorly he shed drops of blood, for even with God close, death is always death.

But Christ was there. He was with Jacques to the end. For one last time, Jacques received from Him an extraordinary grace: the certain knowledge that he would go straight to heaven. He wrote:

"I am calmer than before, because Jesus has promised me that He will take me straight to heaven....

"My Lord and my God, I am going to see You face to face. Happy those whom God honors with martyrdom! If only I could give my life like the martyrs, who died rather than deny their faith! As for me, I am guilty.... May my blood, which will soon flow, be accepted by God as a holocaust. May each drop wipe out a mortal sin. Like Jesus, I implore heaven that no sin may be laid to anyone's charge because of me, but that every action, every thought, every word may serve to glorify my God. Jesus, I love you! ...

"Jesus is very near to me. He draws me closer and closer to Himself, and I can only adore Him silently, longing to die of love.

"I wish, like little St. Thérèse of the Child Jesus, to renew with each heartbeat this offering to become 'a victim of His merciful love, until that day when, the shadows having passed away, I may repeat my love to Him in an eternal encounter.'

"The execution will take place tomorrow, at around four in the morning. May God's will be done in all things. I am sure that in His goodness Jesus will give me a Christian death, so that I can bear witness to Him to the very end. I must glorify His Holy Name, and I know that I shall glorify it.... I must be steadfast, and so I think of the procession of all the beheaded who give luster to the Church. Shall I be weaker than they? God will preserve me from that!

"Suddenly the thought comes: no matter what I do, Paradise is not for me! Satan is behind this. He wants to discourage me. I throw myself at Mary's feet and it is better....

"Bitterness of all bitterness! I mustn't forget that whatever my feelings may be, I can always overcome them with my will. And then, God is faithful, I mustn't forget that....

"In five hours, I shall see Jesus! How good He is, our Lord! He doesn't even wait until eternity to reward His chosen ones. He draws me ever so gently to Himself, giving me a peace which is not of this world....

"Good Jesus, who suffered so much for me and who still carries all my sorrow! Happy the one who puts his trust in the Lord. He will never be disappointed. God is love!

"Peace has gone now. It has given place to anguish! It is horrible! My heart is pounding madly in my breast. Holy Virgin, have pity on me! Yet, with a little more effort I believe I shall succeed in overcoming this anguish. But I'm suffering all the same!

"I hear disturbing noises. God grant that I may sustain the blow. Holy Virgin, be with me! Farewell to all, and may the Lord bless you....

"I wait in the dark, and in peace. I await love!" ...

Jacques watched and prayed all night. He was standing when they entered his cell. He embraced his lawyer, but did not say a word. His face was drenched with suffering.

After having received final absolution from the prison chaplain, he received Communion, together with his lawyer.

At 5:30, Jacques' head fell.

This was the man men judged, condemned, and executed. This was the one whom the Lord, I have no doubt, called to "enter into life."

Light Over the Scaffold

Søren Kierkegaard
Lasting and Growing Repentance

It is told that there was once a man who through his misdeeds deserved the punishment which the law meted out to him. After he had suffered for his wrong acts, he went back into ordinary society, improved. Then he went to a strange land, where be was not known, and where he became known for his worthy conduct. All was forgotten. Then one day there appeared a fugitive that recognized the distinguished person as his equal back in those miserable days. This was a terrifying memory to meet. A deathlike fear shook him each time this man passed. Although silent, this memory shouted in a high voice until through the voice of this vile fugitive it took on words. Then suddenly despair seized this man, who seemed to have been saved. And it seized him just because repentance was forgotten, because the improvement toward society was not the resigning of himself to God, so that in the humility of repentance he might remember what he had been. For in the temporal and sensual and social sense, repentance is in fact something that comes and goes during the years. But in the eternal sense, it is a silent daily anxiety. It is eternally false, that guilt is changed by the passage of a century. To assert anything of this sort is to confuse the Eternal with what the Eternal is least like—with human forgetfulness....

It is not a gain that guilt should be wholly forgotten. On the contrary, it is loss and perdition. But it is a gain to win an inner intensity of heart through a deeper and deeper inner sorrowing over guilt. It is not a gain to notice, because of a man's forgetfulness, that he is growing older. But it is a gain to notice that a man has grown older by the deeper and deeper penetration into his heart of the transformation wrought by remorse. One should be able to tell the age of a tree from its bark; in truth one can also tell a man's age in the Good by the intensity of his repentance. There is a battle of despair that struggles—with the consequences. The enemy attacks constantly from behind, and yet the fighter shall continue to advance. When this is so, the repentance is still young and weak....

But when, in spite of this, more confident steps are made along the way, when punishment itself becomes a blessing, when consequences even become redemptive, when progress in the Good is apparent; then is there a milder but deep sorrow that remembers the guilt. It has wearied out and overcome what could deceive and confuse the sight. Therefore it does not see falsely, but sees only the one sorrowful thing. This is the older, the strong, and the powerful repentance....

And it must be said of repentance that, if it is forgotten, then its strength was only an immaturity; but the longer and the more deeply one treasures it, the better it becomes. For guilt looks most terrifying the nearer at hand one sees it. But repentance is most acceptable to God, the further away repentance views the guilt, along the way of the Good.

Purity of Heart Is to Will One Thing

Benjamin Tucker Tanner
Hidden Grief
Oh, the untold, secret grief,
That draws back from all relief,
Will not deign to have a cure—
Grieves and says: I must endure.

Ah, the tear—soon wiped away—
Wipes in haste with no delay

Lest some sympathizing eye
Might the weeping sad espy.

Ah, the heart's great heaving groan
Quickly silenced lest the moan
Might attack some friendly heart
And to save, at once to start.

God of mercy, known alone
To Thee is the saddening groan
To Thee is the falling tear,
God of mercy, hear, oh hear.

Conversations with God

Francis Thompson
Pursued by God

Now of that long pursuit
Comes on at hand the bruit;
That Voice is round me like a bursting sea:
'And is thy earth so marred,
Shattered in shard on shard?
Lo, all things fly thee, for thou fliest Me!
Strange, piteous, futile thing!
Wherefore should any set thee love apart?
Seeing none but I makes much of naught' (He said),
'And human love needs human meriting:
How hast thou merited—
Of all man's clotted clay the dingiest clot?
Alack, thou knowest not
How little worthy of any love thou art!
Whom wilt thou find to love ignoble thee,
Save Me, save only Me?
All which I took from thee I did but take,
Not for thy harms,
But just that thou might'st seek it in My arms.
All which thy child's mistake

Fancies as lost, I have stored for thee at home:
  Rise, clasp My hand, and come!'

  Halts by me that footfall:
  Is my gloom, after all,
Shade of His hand, outstretched caressingly?
  'Ah, fondest, blindest, weakest,
  I am He Whom thou seekest!
Thou dravest love from thee, who dravest Me.'

The Hound of Heaven

Anonymous
A Fool's Prayer
I had thought to do something good,
Noble, lasting, to make a contribution.
But I failed. Some did not see it that way,
But an outward show misled them.
Inside I knew: I took more than I gave.

I had tried to do something—something good.
They told me, "Be a good boy."
They tried themselves and did some good;
Others fooled themselves a bit.
Yes, some good things happened and remained,
But I could have ruined it all.

And now the road comes to an end,
And even the fool sees it right,
Sees himself a stray dog with matted hair,
Searching for scraps at the side of the road
All alone in the twilight rain.

And the fool is a fool no more.
We do not do good, but we can allow
Good to come through us.

I wait like a stray, with ears uplifted,
Believing Someone will call in a friendly way,
A pat on the head, a bowl of warm food,
And I will have found my home again.

The Farmer calls, His Son pats my wet head
And points to a bed by the fire.

And the stray is a stray no more. Amen.

Miguel de Unamuno
The Atheist's Prayer
Hear my petition you, God who do not exist
And into your nothingness gather these my griefs again
You who never abandoned unhappy men
Without the consolation of illusion. Do not resist

Our petition; may our longing by you be dressed.
When you remove yourself furthest from my sight,
The fairy-tales to sweeten my sad night
Told by my soul, I then remember best.

How great you are, my God! So great you are
That you are not, except as an idea.
How narrow the reality, though it expands so far

In order to include you. I suffer from your mere
Non-existence, God, since if it were that you
Were to exist, then I would really too.

St. Teresa of Avila
Prayer of Someone Fallen Into Sin

O my Jesus! What a sight it is when You through Your mercy return to offer Your hand and raise up a soul that has fallen in sin after having reached this stage! How such a soul knows the multitude of Your grandeurs and mercies and its own misery! In this state it is in truth consumed and knows Your splendors. Here it doesn't dare raise its eyes, and here it raises them up so as to know what it owes You. Here it becomes a devotee of the Queen of heaven so that she might appease You; here it invokes the help of the saints that fell after having been called by You. Here it seems that everything You give it is undeserved because it sees that it doesn't merit the ground on which it treads. Here, in approaching the sacraments, it has the living faith to see the power that God has placed in them; it praises You because You have left such a medicine and ointment for our wounds and because this medicine not only covers these wounds but also takes them away completely. It is amazed by all this. And who, Lord of my soul, wouldn't be amazed by so much mercy and a favor so large for a betrayal so ugly and abominable? I don't know why my heart doesn't break as I write this! For I am a wretched person!

Life, Chapter 19

TEN

Religious Experience

As a hart longs
    for flowing streams,
so longs my soul
    for thee, O God.
My soul thirsts for God,
    for the living God,
When shall I come and behold
    the face of God?
    (Ps. 42:1-2).

What can be known about God is plain to them, because
God has shown it to them. Ever since the creation of the
world his invisible nature, namely, his eternal power and
deity, has been clearly perceived in the things that have
been made (Rom. 1:19-20).

Religious experience is one of the most profound and influential
elements of human life, and one of the least studied. It built the pyra-
mids, and in our time it has vigorously survived the Nazi and Communist
attempts to destroy belief in God. Like all human things, religious experience can be creative or destructive, uplifting or damaging, sane or mad. On
the one hand, religious experience can be manipulated, fabricated out of
human need, and then denied. On the other hand, it leads many of those
who are moved by it to conclude, in the words of C.S. Lewis, that they
were "made for another world." The hatred and disdain for religion on the
part of some is often so uncharacteristic of the rest of their behavior that

one concludes that they must have had a history of negative religious experience. For example, Bertrand Russell, otherwise a supporter of liberal and enlightened values, thought religion should be violently persecuted, but early on he could write about religious experiences in positive ways. Stalin tried persecution, yet, according to his daughter, he died shaking his fist at the heavens in a gesture of defiance toward the God who he claimed did not exist. Both examples suggest strong religious experience, although in a very negative way.

For most of those who find religious experience a vibrant or even intriguing aspect of their lives, the call of the Divine is undeniable and inescapable, and it is what gives life its comprehensive meaning. Less religious people often envy those who have this experience and may even try to destroy it in others. But religious experience often catches up with people. It frequently comes into focus when they are apparently far away from any thought of the Divine.

Having grown up in a strongly religious environment—urban America in mid-century—I mistakenly assumed that religious experience was an aspect of life that one learned, and that those who had not learned it were unlikely as adults to be religious people. Nothing could be further from the truth. Our unbelieving times are filled with people raised with little or no religion, or those who have rejected what little there was, and who nevertheless later became the most dedicated religious believers. This fact alone is an affirmation of the idea of grace, the unmerited and unexpected call of God into the life of a totally surprised human being. Professor Gordon Allport, an eminent student of individuals and their religion, points out that it is religion that brings "to the individual a solemn assurance unlike anything else in life, a tranquility, an ever present help in trouble, that makes next steps easier." It is the experience of a "solution found." This experience goes throughout the extremely diverse variety of human beings. From Einstein to Mother Teresa, from Whitehead to Padre Pio, religious experience deeply reflects the profound human experience expressed in the words of Jean-Paul Sartre, an erstwhile atheist, near his death: "I do not feel that I am the product of chance, a speck of dust in the universe, but someone who was expected, prepared, pre-figured; in short, a being whom only a creator could put here, and this idea of a creating hand refers to God."

Those who have read a book such as this are no doubt religious people. We have the responsibility to others who are not yet aware of God to present religious faith in such a way that they would not be repelled. At the same time, we hope that the seriousness and dedication of our own actions will say to them, "If today you hear his voice, harden not your heart" (see Ps. 95:7-8).

For the sake of clarity I have grouped our discussion and selections to look at ordinary and extraordinary religious experience, including the unusual phenomenon of private revelations. Ordinary religious experience refers to the many and varied external incidents and inner insights that may come to a person in the course of life. There is no feeling of the miraculous; there is, however, a heightened awareness of the presence or action of God.

Ordinary Religious Experience

C.S. Lewis
Nothing Satisfies

If I find in myself a desire which no experience in this world can satisfy, the most probable explanation is that I was made for another world. If none of my earthly pleasures satisfy it, that does not prove that the universe is a fraud. Probably earthly pleasures were never *meant* to satisfy it, but only to arouse it, to suggest the real thing.

Christian Behavior

Gordon Allport
The Verification of Experience

Although I have no conclusive evidence on the point, I suspect that the most commonly accepted type of verification is some form of immediate experience, convincing to oneself though not as a rule to others. It is religion's peculiar secret that it brings to the individual a solemn assurance unlike anything else in life, a tranquility, an ever present help in trouble, that makes next steps easier no matter what mesh of circumstances may entangle the life. A person who finds that the practice of faith has brought a genuine solution of conflict is convinced, for to discover order and felicity where there were chaos and distress is to find something extraordinarily real. This experience of a "solution found" is often attended by some degree of mystical perception. One feels that one has reached out a hand and received an answering clasp. One has sent up a cry and heard a response. Whoever verifies his faith in this manner has evidence no less convincing to him than the sensory perception which validates his beliefs in the world about him. Immediacy of this sort persuades him that revelation comes from God to man. In passing, it may be remarked that what has been called "functional revelation" seems to be more common than is "cognitive revelation." That is to say, apparently more people report an access of strength and power than claim clarifying knowledge.

The Individual and His Religion

Eberhard Arnold
The Greatness of God

In every decisive experience, man's insignificance is confronted with God's greatness, man's inadequacy with God's mightiness, man's incapacity with God's power. This experience of God runs through the whole history of mankind as an overpowering of men by God's supremacy. When man stands in reverence before God, his first, intuitive experience of Him is of an almighty Power, before which all human strength is a mere nothing.

Like Elijah, the first prophets veiled their heads in shuddering awe when God was about to draw near to them. The thought of seeing *God* filled all genuine men with terror. In prophetic times, the sight of God cast the beholder to the ground and killed him. For all reverent ages, the mystery of God's greatness is awesome beyond measure. Whenever an overpowering sense of this comes over men, all human powers are conquered, just as once the grim and powerful Beast of Chaos-let-loose was cast down and conquered. Man is bound to shake with terror whenever God draws near.

God's greatness, majesty, and might are beyond all man's powers of imagination. If man were to see God, he would perish, because God is always so far beyond man's capacity to see Him face to face. With whom could he compare God? How could he give a picture of this inconceivable greatness and power? God is unattainably great and glorious. The prophets know very well that beside Him no other power can endure. His divine decree can never be fulfilled by anything human. No human power can stand before Him. The life of God goes far beyond all boundaries of beginning and end. It towers immeasurably above all created things.

The Experience of God and His Peace

Father Reginald Garrigou-Lagrange, O.P.
A Conversation With God

The interior life becomes more and more a conversation with God, in which man gradually frees himself from egoism, self-love, sensuality, and pride, and in which, by frequent prayer, he asks the Lord for the ever new graces that he needs.

As a result, man begins to know experimentally no longer only the inferior part of his being, but also the highest part. Above all, he begins to know God in a vital manner; he begins to have experience of the things of God. Little by little the thought of his own ego, toward which he made everything converge, gives place to the habitual thought of God; and egotistical love of self and of what is less good in him also gives place progressively to the love of God and of souls in God. His interior conversation changes so much that St. Paul can say: "Our conversation is in heaven" (Phil. 3:20). St. Thomas often insisted on this point.

Therefore the interior life is in a soul that is in the state of grace, especially a life of humility, abnegation, faith, hope, and charity, with the peace given by the progressive subordination of our feelings and wishes to the love of God, who will be the object of our beatitude.

The Three Ages of the Interior Life

Extraordinary Religious Experience

I know a man in Christ who fourteen years ago was caught up to the third heaven—whether in the body or out of the body I do not know, God knows. And I know that this man was caught up into Paradise—whether in the body or out of the body I do not know, God knows—and he heard things that cannot be told, which man may not utter (2 Cor. 12:2-4).

Religious experience sometimes has a clarity about it that powerfully raises it above the ordinary perceptions of life. The presence or action of God is so powerful that doubt becomes impossible for the person having the experience. As we shall see, this is not what is properly called a private revelation. Nevertheless, the experience reveals to the individual the presence and power of the divine in such a way as to change the entire perception of reality at the moment. The cause may be external, like the unmistakable observance of direct divine action. The experience of the world-renowned scientist Alexis Carrel, a Nobel prizewinner in medicine, who witnessed a miraculous healing at Lourdes, is an example of a person's extraordinary religious experience that can be shared with others: God's action takes place in the external world, and its results are empirically discernible. In Carrel's case, a young woman on the cusp of death was instantly cured.

Often the experience is internal, completely reversing a person's customary patterns of thinking. The atheist's encounter with the divine described so graphically by André Frossard was internal, and could be shared with others only by a description in words. Nonetheless, this experience completely changed his life—a fact that can be observed by others. The conversion of Saul of Tarsus was just such an extraordinary religious experience. There are extraordinary religious experiences that occur in the lives of believers, putting long-accepted objects of faith in a clear and powerful light. Pascal's famous fragment, a parchment discovered sewn inside his coat after his death, describes such a mystical encounter, as do the narratives of the two women saints Gertrude the Great and Catherine of Genoa.

It is my impression, after working for several decades as a spiritual director, that such experiences are far more common than is assumed. Sadly, many people seem to have the beginnings of a profound experience, but then move away or distrust it, because they fear this experience will require a change in their lifestyle or giving up some cherished pursuit. St. Augustine's warning to "fear Jesus passing by" (see Lk. 18:37) is very pertinent to such cases. On the other hand, some people, having had a powerful experience of the presence of God, proceed to tell everyone that they have had a private revelation. What was meant to be a personal grace for themselves is tooted about to the easily impressed. We can conjure up an image of someone who had witnessed a miracle of Christ or His apostles, then went running back to his Galilean village to boast of his own self-importance. Perhaps this was the very thing that caused Christ to warn His disciples that even those who had cast out demons in His name might not enter the kingdom of heaven.

Extraordinary religious experience is powerful and precious. It is a pearl of great price, and not to be thrown before swine who may trample it and then attack the one who has been so careless with it. The history of religion and of the Church is filled with examples of vivid, extraordinary religious experiences. But like actual acquaintanceship with Jesus in His earthly life, they may bring either a hundredfold blessing or the realization that it might have been better if one had never been born.

Archbishop Anthony Bloom
An Unexpected Presence

One day—it was during Lent, and I was then a member of one of the Russian youth organizations in Paris—one of the leaders came up to me and said, "We have invited a priest to talk to you. Come." I answered with violent indignation that I would not. I had no use for the Church. I did not believe in God. I did not want to waste any of my time....

I sat through the lecture. I didn't intend to listen. But my ears pricked up. I became more and more indignant. I saw a vision of Christ and Christianity that was profoundly repulsive to me. When the lecture was over, I hurried home in order to check the truth of what he had been saying. I asked my mother whether she had a book of the Gospel, because I wanted to know whether the Gospel would support the monstrous impression I had derived from his talk. I expected nothing good from my reading, so I counted the chapters of the four Gospels to be sure I read the shortest, not to waste time unnecessarily. I started to read St. Mark's Gospel.

While I was reading the beginning of St. Mark's Gospel, before I reached the third chapter, I suddenly became aware that on the other side of my desk there was a presence. And the certainty was so strong that it was Christ standing there that it has never left me. This was the real turning point. Because Christ was alive and I had been in his presence I could say with certainty that what the Gospel said about the crucifixion of the prophet of Galilee was true, and the centurion was right when he said, "Truly he is the Son of God." It was in the light of the Resurrection that I could read with certainty the story of the Gospel, knowing that everything was true in it because the impossible event of the Resurrection was to me more certain than any event of history. History I had to believe, the Resurrection I knew for a fact. I did not discover, as you see, the Gospel beginning with its first message of the Annunciation, and it did not unfold for me as a story which one can believe or disbelieve. It began as an event that left all problems of disbelief behind because it was a direct and personal experience.

Beginning to Pray

André Frossard
I Have Seen Him

The end of the chapel was rather brightly lit. The high altar was draped in white and covered with a great many plants and candelabra and a variety of ornaments. Above it hung a large metal cross; at its center there was a white disc, and three others that were slightly different were fixed to the extremities of the cross.

In the interest of art, I had previously visited churches but I had never before seen a host, much less a monstrance with a host in it. I was therefore quite unaware that before me was the Blessed Sacrament, below which many candles were burning. The other discs, the complicated gilt ornaments, all contributed to making identification of this distant sun still more difficult.

I didn't see the point of all this, naturally, since I was not looking for it.

Standing by the door, I looked out for my friend, but I was not able to identify him among the kneeling figures. My glance went from the dimness to the light, fell on the congregation, travelled from the faithful to the nuns, and from the nuns to the altar without any thought consciously crossing my mind. Then, for no particular reason, I fixed my eyes on the second candle on the left-hand side of the cross.

It was at this moment that, suddenly, the series of extraordinary events was set in motion whose extreme violence was about to dismantle the absurd creature that I had been until that moment and give birth to the dazzled child I had never been.

First were the words: *spiritual life.*

They were not said to me nor did I form them in my mind; it was as though they were being spoken by someone close to me who was seeing something which I had not yet seen.

The last syllable had hardly brushed my conscious mind when an avalanche descended upon me. I am not saying that the heavens opened; they didn't open—they were hurled at me, they rose suddenly flashing silently from the depths of this innocent chapel in which they were mysteriously present.

How can I describe what took place in words which refuse to carry the sense, which indeed do worse, for they threaten to intercept what I have to say and, in doing so, to relegate my meaning to the land of fancy? Were a painter to be given the gift of seeing colours that are unknown to man, what would he use to paint them with?

What can I say to describe that which I apprehended?

It was an indestructible crystal, totally transparent, luminous (to such a degree that any further intensity would have destroyed me), with a colour near to blue; a different world, whose brilliance and density made our world seem like the wraith of an unfulfilled dream. What I saw was reality; this was truth and I was seeing it from the dim shore on which I still stood. Now I knew that there is order in the universe and, at its beginning, beyond the shining mists, the manifestation of God: a manifestation which is a presence, which is a person, the person whose existence I should have denied a moment ago, the presence of him whom the Christians call *Our Father.* And I knew that he was gentle, that his gentleness was unparalleled and that his was not the passive quality that is sometimes called by the name of gentleness, but an active shattering gentleness, far outstripping violence, able to smash the hardest stone and to smash something often harder than stone—the human heart.

This surging, overwhelming invasion brought with it a sense of joy comparable to that of a drowning man who is rescued at the last moment, but with this difference, that it was at the moment in which I was being hauled to safety that I became aware of the mud in which, without noticing it, I had till then been stuck; and now I wondered how I had ever been able to breathe and to live in it.

I Have Met Him: God Exists

Alexis Carrel
A Nobel Scientist Meets God

In this report found among Carrel's papers after his death, he refers to himself in the third person, using the name Lerrac, his name spelled backward.

It was now about half-past two. Beneath the rock of Massabielle, the Grotto glittered in the light of its thousand candles. The entrance and the walls were hung with rosaries and crutches. Beyond the high iron grille was a statue of the Virgin, standing in the hollowed rock where Bernadette once saw the glowing vision of the lady in white, the Immaculate Conception.

Before the statue of the Virgin, a large square space was fenced off; it was reserved as the place of honor for the sick. Volunteers of Our Lady of Salvation were on duty to prevent crowding and confusion among the little carts and stretchers.

In front of the iron grille and almost touching it, a stretcher was already lying. Beside it, Lerrac recognized Mlle. d'O.'s slender figure. He and M. made their way toward the Grotto where they could have a close view of the sick and the pilgrims. They stopped near Marie Ferrand's stretcher and leaned against the low wall. She was motionless, her breathing still rapid and shallow; she seemed to be at the point of death. More pilgrims were approaching the Grotto....

Volunteers and stretcher-bearers came crowding in. The little carts were being wheeled from the pools to the Grotto....

Lerrac glanced again at Marie Ferrand. Suddenly he stared. It seemed to him that there had been a change, that the harsh shadows on her face had disappeared, that her skin was somehow less ashen.

Surely, he thought, this was a hallucination. But the hallucination itself was interesting psychologically, and might be worth recording. Hastily he jotted down the time in his notebook. It was twenty minutes before three o'clock.

But if the change in Marie Ferrand was a hallucination, it was the first one Lerrac had ever had. He turned to M.

"Look at our patient again," he said. "Does it seem to you that she has rallied a little?"

"She looks much the same to me," answered M. "All I can see is that she is no worse."

Leaning over the stretcher, Lerrac took her pulse again and listened to her breathing.

"The respiration is less rapid," he told M., after a moment.

"That may mean that she is about to die," said M.

A nonbeliever, the young intern could see nothing miraculous in this change.

Lerrac made no reply. To him it was obvious that there was a sudden improvement of her general condition. Something was taking place. He stiffened to resist a tremor of emotion. Standing against the low wall near the stretcher, he concentrated all his powers of observation on Marie Ferrand. He did not lift his eyes from her face. A priest was preaching to the assembled throngs of pilgrims and patients; hymns and prayers burst out sporadically; and in this atmosphere of fervor, under Lerrac's cool, objective gaze, the face of Marie Ferrand slowly continued to change. Her eyes, so dim before, were now wide with ecstasy as she turned them toward the Grotto. The change was undeniable. Mlle. d'O. leaned over and held her.

Suddenly Lerrac felt himself turning pale. The blanket which covered Marie Ferrand's distended abdomen was gradually flattening out.

"Look at her abdomen!" he exclaimed to M.

M. looked.

"Why yes," he said, "it seems to have gone down. It's probably the folds in the blanket that give that impression."

The bell of the basilica had just struck three. A few minutes later, there was no longer any sign of distension in Marie Ferrand's abdomen.

Lerrac felt as though he were going mad.

Standing beside Marie Ferrand, he watched the intake of her breath and the pulsing at her throat with fascination. The heartbeat, though still very rapid, had become regular.

This time, for sure, something was taking place.

"How do you feel?" he asked her.

"I feel very well," she answered in a low voice. "I am still weak, but I feel I am cured."

There was no longer any doubt: Marie Ferrand's condition was improving so much that she was scarcely recognizable.

Standing beside the stretcher, profoundly troubled, unable to analyze what he beheld, Lerrac looked at M. and Mlle. d'O. to see if they too were aware of this extraordinary change. Mlle. d'O. was watching it as calmly as a doctor watching the setting of a broken bone. She had seen such things before.

Lerrac stood there in silence, his mind a blank. This event, exactly the opposite of what he had expected, must surely be nothing but a dream.

Mlle. d'O. offered Marie Ferrand a cup of milk. She drank it all. In a few minutes she raised her head, looked around, moved her limbs a little, then turned over on her side, without having shown the least sign of pain.

Abruptly Lerrac moved off. Making his way through the crowd of pilgrims whose loud prayers he hardly heard, he left the Grotto. It was now about four o'clock.

A dying girl was recovering.

It was the resurrection of the dead; it was a miracle!

He had not yet examined her; he could not yet know the real condition of her lesions. But he had seen with his own eyes a functional improvement which was in itself a miracle. How simple, how private, it had been! The crowd at the Grotto was not even aware that it had happened.

The Voyage to Lourdes

Blaise Pascal
Pascal's Fragment

MEMORIAL

In the year of grace 1654
Monday, 23 November, the day of St. Clement,
Pope and Martyr, and others in the Roman Martyrology,
the eve of St. Chrysogonus, Martyr, and others, etc....
From about half-past ten in the evening
Till about half an hour after midnight

FIRE

God of Abraham. God of Isaac. God of Jacob
not of the philosophers and the learned.
Certitude joy certitude emotion sight joy
GOD OF JESUS CHRIST
Deum meum et Deum vestrum.
Thy God shall be my God.
Forgetfulness of the world and of everything other than GOD
He can be found only in the ways taught
in the Gospel. *Greatness* of the human soul.
Good Father, the world has not known
Thee, but I have known Thee.
Joy Joy Joy and tears of joy
I have separated myself from Thee
Dereliquerunt me fontem
my God wilt Thou leave me
let me not be eternally separated from Thee
They have life eternal, they that know Thee
Sole true God and He Whom Thou hast sent
JESUS CHRIST
JESUS CHRIST
I have separated myself from Him I have fled renounced crucified Him

St. Gertrude the Great
A Saint at the Passion

The memory of our Lord's Passion was so profoundly engraven on the soul of the Saint that it became as honey to her lips, as music to her ears, and as a transport of joy to her heart. One Good Friday, as she heard the summons to Compline, she felt the same anguish in her heart as if she had been told that her dearest friend was even then about to expire, and she recollected herself to think yet more lovingly of the Passion of her Beloved. Her union with God became so intimate, that on this day and the following she was scarcely able to attend to anything exterior or sensible, unless obliged to do so by charity, of which she always made great account, and this that she might the more surely entertain Him within her who is love; for St. John said, "God is charity. If we love one another, God abideth in us, and His charity is perfected in us" (1 John 4).

She continued in this rapture the remainder of the day, and during the whole of the following day (Holy Saturday). What she experienced therein was such that no human intellect could explain it; for she was so perfectly united to and absorbed in God, by the tenderness of her compassion, that she was entirely dissolved therein; and this was no imperfection, but rather the very height of perfection, as St. Bernard teaches when writing of the words of the Canticles: "'We will make thee chains of gold' (Cant. 1:10): When the soul is wrapt in contemplation, and a flash of heavenly light comes to illuminate it, the Divine infusion accommodates itself to sensible things, either to temper its brilliancy or to instruct in its doctrine, and thus shadows the purity and splendor of its rays, to enable the soul to receive it and to communicate it to others. I believe that these images are produced in us by the holy angels. Therefore, let us attribute to God what is perfectly free from corporal images and to the angels those which are more sensible."

The Life and Revelations of St. Gertrude

St. Catherine of Genoa
The Vision of the Crucified

One day there appeared to her inner vision Jesus Christ incarnate crucified, all bloody from head to foot. It seemed that the body rained blood. From within she heard a voice say, "Do you see this blood? It has been shed for your love, to atone for your sins." With that, she received a wound of love that drew her to Jesus with such trust that it washed away all that previous fright, and she took joy in the Lord.

She was also granted another vision, more striking yet, beyond telling or imagination. God showed her the love with which He had suffered out of love of her. That vision made her turn away from every other love and joy that did not come directly from God.

In that vision, Catherine saw the evil in the soul and the purity of God's love. The two never left her. Had she dwelt on that vision any longer than she did, she would have fainted, become undone.

The Spiritual Dialogue

Private Revelations

I John, your brother, who share with you in Jesus the tribulation and the kingdom and the patient endurance, was on the island called Patmos on account of the word of God and the testimony of Jesus. I was in the Spirit on the Lord's day, and I heard behind me a loud voice like a trumpet saying, "Write what you see in a book and send it to the seven churches" (Rev. 1:9-11).

The piety of innumerable Christians has been deeply affected by reports of private revelations. These are profoundly moving and often complex events that leave those who have experienced them with the conviction that they must do something or teach something that is quite beyond their own manner of acting or thinking. Many who are seriously committed to the spiritual life are repelled by reports of this kind or are at least uninterested in them. Their reservations are very well expressed by the first selection, in which no less an authority than St. John of the Cross, the Mystical Doctor, all but completely dismisses private revelations. He was himself familiar with powerful religious experiences, called intellectual visions, but he did not see them as special messages for others given through himself. Simply put, he thought of these vivid experiences as graces moving his own intellect in an unusually vivid way. John lived in a time of turbulent religious activity, a time filled with visionaries, some of them very much in the public eye. While they excited great interest, John was at the very least skeptical. A number of these popular visionaries were later found to be frauds or at least victims of self-delusion.

While taking John's warnings seriously, we need to recognize that certain visionaries have profoundly affected the course of world history or the religious experience of whole generations of the devout. Who can adequately measure the impact of St. Joan of Arc, whose heavenly voices caused her in a single year to reverse the course of European history and with it the history of the Catholic Church? Many with little or no faith have been intrigued by the saga of this peasant girl, whom Winston Churchill, the leader centuries later of the country she defeated, called the purest figure in European history for a thousand years.

Less spectacular but still having a profound influence are the visionaries who bring a special emphasis to the piety of their times and succeeding generations. Historians often fail to take into account these devout movements in assessing the various factors of Church history or even secular history. For example, the immense popularity of the mystic and stigmatist Blessed Padre Pio may well have been the deciding factor in keeping Italy from becoming the first western European Communist country after World War II.

The recipients of private revelation are easily divided initially into two categories—children and young teenagers on the one hand, and adults, usually devout people, on the other. The latter are then divided into two groups: there are those who very humbly keep the knowledge of the revelation to themselves, divulging it carefully only to spiritual directors and religious authorities, and those who rather dramatically go public and become for a time the center of much attention. It is a fact of Church history that the private revelations that have survived the test of time were given either to the very young and naïve, like St. Joan of Arc or St. Bernadette of Lourdes, who made known what had happened to them, or to very saintly, unworldly adults who went to their graves with only a handful of people knowing of their reports. To this second category belong all the adult visionaries who have had a lasting impact on Catholic piety. We have selected three writings from visionaries who have had such lasting effects. It is clear that Julian, St. Margaret Mary, and Blessed Faustina really add nothing substantial to what we know from the New Testament about the workings of Christ with the soul. In fact, all of these revelations can be considered commentaries on the words of Christ, "Come to me, all who labor and are heavy laden, and I will give you rest. Take my yoke upon you, and learn from me; for I am gentle and lowly in heart, and you will find rest for your souls. For my yoke is easy, and my burden is light" (Mt. 11:28-30).

The experience of visionaries, especially of those to whom the Church has given qualified approval, is always colored by their own knowledge and personality. It is worth noting that unqualified approval equivalent to an article of faith cannot be given to any private revelation.* This is clearly taught by Pope Benedict XIV, who was the great authority on the subject. In dealing with any private revelation, it is important to keep in mind both the subjective element in all human experiences and the possibility and, at times, the likelihood of error. In no way does an approved private revelation have the same authority as Scripture or the teaching of the Church.

Yet when all is said and done, despite the warnings of St. John of the Cross and the popes, there are beautiful and moving messages in some approved revelations. Even the reader who is disinclined to pay attention to such reports or who is not familiar with Catholic devotions at all is likely to come away from reading the following passages with a deeper realization of the love of God and His Son for the struggling individual soul.

---

* See *A Still, Small Voice*, by Father Benedict J. Groeschel, C.F.R., published by Ignatius Press, (1993) for a readable summary of the Church's teaching on private revelations.

St. John of the Cross
All Revelation Is Complete in Christ

Any person questioning God or desiring some vision or revelation would not only be guilty of foolish behavior but also of offending Him, by not fixing his eyes entirely upon Christ and by living with the desire for some other novelty.

God could respond as follows: If I have already told you all things in My Word, My Son, and if I have no other word, what answer or revelation can I now make that would surpass this? Fasten your eyes on Him alone, because in Him I have spoken and revealed all, and in Him you shall discover even more than you ask for and desire. You are making an appeal for locutions and revelations that are incomplete, but if you turn your eyes to Him you will find them complete. For He is My entire locution and response, vision and revelation, which I have already spoken, answered, manifested, and revealed to you by giving Him to you as brother, companion, master, ransom, and reward. Since that day when I descended upon Him with My Spirit on Mount Tabor proclaiming: *Hic est filius meus dilectus in quo mihi bene complacui, ipsum audite* (This is my Beloved Son in Whom I am well pleased, hear Him—Matt. 17:5), I have relinquished these methods of answering and teaching, and presented them to Him. Hear Him, because I have no more faith to reveal nor truths to manifest. If I spoke before, it was to promise Christ; if they questioned Me, their inquiries were related to their petitions and longings for Christ in Whom they were to obtain every good (as is evidenced in all the doctrine of the Evangelists and Apostles). But now anyone asking Me in that way and desiring that I speak and reveal something to him would somehow be requesting Christ again, and more faith, yet he would be failing in faith, because Christ has already been given....

If you desire Me to answer with a word of comfort, behold My Son, subject to Me and to others out of love for Me, and you will see how much He answers. If you desire Me to declare some secret truths or events to you, fix your eyes on Him, and you will discern hidden in Him the most secret mysteries, and wisdom, and the wonders of God, as My Apostle proclaims: *In quo sunt omnes thesauri sapientiae et scientiae Dei absconditi* (In whom are hidden all the treasures of the wisdom and knowledge of God—Col. 2:3).

The Ascent of Mount Carmel, Book 2, Chapter 22

Blessed Faustina Kowalska

Conversation of the Merciful God With a Despairing Soul

Jesus: O soul steeped in darkness, do not despair. All is not yet lost. Come and confide in your God, who is love and mercy.

—But the soul, deaf even to this appeal, wraps itself in darkness.

Jesus calls out again: **My child, listen to the voice of your merciful Father.**

—In the soul arises this reply: "For me there is no mercy," and it falls into greater darkness, a despair which is a foretaste of hell and makes it unable to draw near to God.

Jesus calls to the soul a third time, but the soul remains deaf and blind, hardened and despairing. Then the mercy of God begins to exert itself, and, without any co-operation from the soul, God grants it final grace. If this too is spurned, God will leave the soul in this self-chosen disposition for eternity. This grace emerges from the merciful Heart of Jesus and gives the soul a special light by means of which the soul begins to understand God's effort; but conversion depends on its own will. The soul knows that this, for her, is final grace and, should it show even a flicker of good will, the mercy of God will accomplish the rest.

My omnipotent mercy is active here. Happy the soul that takes advantage of this grace.

Jesus: **What joy fills My Heart when you return to me. Because you are weak, I take you in My arms and carry you to the home of My Father.**

Soul (as if awaking, asks fearfully): Is it possible that there yet is mercy for me?

Jesus: **There is, My child. You have a special claim on My mercy. Let it act in your poor soul; let the rays of grace enter your soul; they bring with them light, warmth, and life.**

Soul: But fear fills me at the thought of my sins, and this terrible fear moves me to doubt Your goodness.

Jesus: **My child, all your sins have not wounded My Heart as painfully as your present lack of trust does— that after so many efforts of My love and mercy, you should still doubt My goodness.**

Soul: O Lord, save me yourself, for I perish. Be my Savior. O Lord, I am unable to say anything more; my pitiful heart is torn asunder; but You, O Lord...

Jesus does not let the soul finish but, raising it from the ground, from the depths of its misery, he leads it into the recesses of His Heart, where all its sins disappear instantly, consumed by the flames of love.

Jesus: **Here, soul, are all the treasures of My Heart. Take everything you need from it.**

Soul: O Lord, I am inundated with Your grace. I sense that a new life has entered into me and, above all, I feel Your love in my heart. That is enough for me. O Lord, I will glorify the omnipotence of Your mercy for all eternity. Encouraged by Your goodness, I will confide to You all the sorrows of my heart.

Jesus: **Tell me all, My child, hide nothing from Me, because My loving Heart, the Heart of your Best Friend, is listening to you.**

Soul: O Lord, now I see all my ingratitude and Your goodness. You were pursuing me with Your grace, while I was frustrating Your benevolence. I see that I deserve the depths of hell for spurning Your graces.

Jesus (interrupting): **Do not be absorbed in your misery—you are still too weak to speak of it—but, rather, gaze on My Heart filled with goodness, and be imbued with My sentiments. Strive for meekness and humility; be merciful to others, as I am to you; and, when you feel your strength failing, if you come to the fountain of mercy to fortify your soul, you will not grow weary on your journey.**

Soul: Now I understand Your mercy, which protects me, and like a brilliant star, leads me into the home of my Father, protecting me from the horrors of hell that I have deserved, not once, but a thousand times. O Lord, eternity will hardly suffice for me to give due praise to Your unfathomable mercy and Your compassion for me.

Divine Mercy in My Soul

St. Margaret Mary Alacoque
The Second Apparition of the Sacred Heart

I saw this divine Heart as on a throne of flames, more brilliant than the sun and transparent as crystal. It had Its adorable wound and was encircled with a crown of thorns, which signified the pricks our sins caused Him. It was surmounted by a cross which signified that, from the first moment of His Incarnation, that is, from the time this Sacred Heart was formed, the cross was planted in It; that It was filled, from the very first moment, with all the bitterness, humiliations, poverty, sorrow, and contempt His sacred humanity would have to suffer during the whole course of His life and during His holy Passion.

He made me understand that the ardent desire He had of being loved by men and of drawing them from the path of perdition into which Satan was hurrying them in great numbers had caused Him to fix upon this plan of manifesting His Heart to men, together with all Its treasures of love, mercy, grace, sanctification, and salvation. This He did in order that those who were willing to do all in their power to render and to procure for Him honor, love, and glory might be enriched abundantly, even profusely, with these divine treasures of the Heart of God, which is their source. It must be honored under the symbol of this Heart of flesh, Whose image He wished to be publicly exposed. He wanted me to carry it on my person, over my heart, that He might imprint His love there, fill my heart with all the gifts with which His own is filled, and destroy all inordinate affection. Wherever this sacred image would be exposed for veneration He would pour forth His graces and blessings. This devotion was as a last effort of His love which wished to favor men in these last centuries with this loving redemption, in order to withdraw them from the empire of Satan, which He intended to destroy, and in order to put us under the sweet liberty of the empire of His love. This He would establish in the hearts of all those who would embrace this devotion.

Letters

Julian of Norwich
All Manner of Things Shall Be Well

One time, our good Lord said: "All things shall be well." And another time, He said: "You shall see for yourself that all manner of thing shall be well." The soul understood several things from these two sayings.

One was this: that it is his will that we should understand that not only does He take care of great and noble things but also of little and humble things, simple and small.... And this is what He means when He says: "All manner of thing shall be well." For he wants us to understand that the smallest thing shall not be forgotten.

Something else I understood was this: that we see such evil deeds done, and such great harm caused by them, that it seems to us that it is impossible that any good deed should come out of them. And we look on them, sorrowing and mourning over them, so that we cannot find rest in the joyful sight of God, as we ought to.

The trouble is this—that the range of our thinking is now so blinkered, so little and small, that we cannot see the high, wonderful wisdom and the power and goodness of the blessed Trinity. And this is what He means when He says: "You shall see for yourself that all manner of thing shall be well." It was as if He said: "Have faith, and have trust, and at the last day you shall see it all transformed into great joy."

Revelations of Divine Love

ELEVEN

Coming Closer to God

Grow in the grace and knowledge of our Lord and Savior
Jesus Christ. To him be the glory both now and to the day
of eternity (2 Pt. 3:18).

G od calls us in a thousand different ways in the course of a short space
of time. This is an aspect of His grace—or the free, unmerited love he
has for His children. One of the secrets of the interior journey is to be sensitive and responsive to the different ways He calls us. *The Imitation of
Christ* gives us this wise insight: "If your heart is pure, every creature will
be to you a mirror of God and a book of holy teaching." The real secret of
the saints is to listen more attentively and to respond ever more faithfully
to the invitations of God encountered in everyday life.

It would be impossible to give even the most succinct list of ways in
which Christ summons the Christian soul in what is called the sacrament of
the present moment. We have included some of the most obvious ways: the
created world, the Bible, the words of the great spiritual writers—in this
case the early Fathers of the Church—the experience of the faithful soul,
and, finally, marriage.

Most of the people who read this book will be married or were once
married. This truly holy way of life, a discipleship all of its own, is much
under attack in our hedonistic and narcissistic time. Several spiritual writers
have been selected by Kevin, the married member of our editorial team, to
illustrate the holy way of marriage. Christian marriage is the best example
of God's way of sanctifying natural good so that it becomes a life in Christ,

a way to holiness. The selections on marriage are mostly addressed to husbands, but should be read as addressing both husbands and wives.

Readers who are not married and not planning to marry can still learn much about discipleship from true Christian marriage, a life of self-giving and sacrifice, a love that in this world is so consecrated by the blood of Christ that, as St. John Chrysostom says, it lasts forever and finds its full expression in the world to come.

The Beauty of Creation

George Macdonald
The Journey Home

It had ceased to be dark; we walked in a dim twilight, breathing through the dimness the breath of the spring. A wondrous change had passed upon the world—or was it not rather that a change more marvelous had taken place in us? Without light enough in the sky or the air to reveal anything, every heather-bush, every small shrub, every blade of grass was perfectly visible, either by light that went out from it, as fire from the bush Moses saw in the desert, or by light that went out of our eyes. Nothing cast a shadow; all things interchanged a little light. Every growing thing showed me, by its shape and color, its indwelling idea—the informing thought, that is, which was its being, and sent it out. My bare feet seemed to love every plant they trod upon. The world and my being, its life and mine, were one. The microcosm and macrocosm were at length atoned, at length in harmony. I lived in everything; everything entered and lived in me. To be aware of a thing, was to know its life at once and mine, to know whence we came, and where we were at home—was to know that we are all what we are, because Another is what he is. Sense after sense, hitherto asleep, awoke in me—sense after sense indescribable, because no correspondent words, no likenesses or imaginations exist, wherewithal to describe them. Full indeed—yet ever expanding, ever making room to receive—was the conscious being where things kept entering by so many open doors. When a little breeze brushing a bush of heather set its purple bells a-ringing, I was myself in the joy of the bells, myself in the joy of the breeze to which responded their sweet *tin-tinning,* myself in the joy of the sense, and of the soul that received all the joys together. To everything glad I lent the hall of my being wherein to revel. I was a peaceful ocean upon which the ground swell of a living joy was continually lifting new waves; yet was the joy ever the same joy, the eternal joy, with tens of thousands of changing forms. Life was a cosmic holiday.

Now I knew that life and truth were one; that life mere and pure is in itself bliss; that where being is not bliss, it is not life, but life-in-death. Every inspiration of the dark wind that blew where it listed, went out a sigh of thanksgiving. At last I was. I lived, and nothing could touch my life. My darling walked beside me, and we were on our way home to the Father.

So much was ours ere ever the first sun rose upon our freedom: what must not the eternal day bring with it.

Lilith

The Voice of Scripture

St. John Chrysostom
The Benefit of Spiritual Reading

I am always encouraging you, and I am not going to stop encouraging you, to pay attention not only to what is said here in church, but also, when you are at home, to continue constantly in the practice of reading the divine Scriptures. And this I never stop always recommending to those who are with us in private conversation. For let not anyone say to me those silly, contemptible words, "I'm stuck at the courthouse all day." "I'm tied up with political affairs." "I'm in an apprentice program." "I've got a wife." "I'm raising kids." "I'm responsible for a household." "I'm a business-man." "Reading the Bible isn't my thing. That's for those who are set apart, for those who have made the mountaintops their home, who have a way of life without interruptions." What are you saying, man? It's not your business to pay attention to the Bible because you are distracted by thousands of concerns? Then Bible reading belongs more to you than to the monks! For they do not make as much use of the help of the divine Scriptures as those who always have a great many things to do…. But you are always standing in the line of battle and are constantly being hit, so you need more medicine. For not only does your wife irritate you, but your son annoys you, and a servant makes you lose your temper. An enemy schemes against you, a friend envies you, a neighbor insults you, a colleague trips you up. Often a lawsuit impends, poverty distresses, loss of possessions brings sorrow. At one moment success puffs you up; at another, failure deflates you. Numerous powerful inducements to anger and anxiety, to discouragement and grief, to vanity and loss of sense surround us on every side. A thousand missiles rain down from every direction. And so we constantly need the whole range of equipment supplied by Scripture....

Since many are the things of this kind besieging our soul, we need the divine medicines, so that we might treat the wounds we already have, and so that we might check beforehand the wounds that are not yet but are going to be, from afar extinguishing the missiles of the devil and repelling them through the constant reading of the divine Scriptures. For it is not possible, not possible for anyone to be saved who does not constantly have the benefit of spiritual reading.

Sermon on Lazarus, 3

The Words of the Fathers

St. Ambrose
The Stray Sheep Prays to Be Found

Ambrose exposes his deep insight into the relationship between the state of his heart and his ability to read Scripture well in the prayer found near the end of his exegesis of Psalm 119:118.... The last verse of the psalm is a prayer for the Lord to seek the psalmist, who has wandered away. "I have strayed like a lost sheep. Seek your servant, for I have not forgotten your commands" (v. 176). Ambrose prays in response:

"Come therefore, Lord Jesus, to look for your servant, to search for the tired sheep. Come, O shepherd, and look for me as Joseph sought his brethren (Gen 37:16). Your sheep has gone astray, while you dwelt in the mountains. Leave there the ninety-nine other sheep, and come after the one which strayed away. Come without the dogs, without the bad workers, without the hirelings too uncouth to enter through the door. Come without seeking help or being announced: long have I awaited your arrival. I know that you will come, "because I have not forgotten your commandments." Come, not with a whip, but with charity and gentleness of heart. Come to me, for I am disturbed by the incursions of the ravening wolves. Come to me, for I have been cast out of Paradise.... I have wandered far from the herd grazing on the heights.... You had placed me there, but the wolf roaming by night drove me away from the fold. Come to look for me, for I too am seeking you. Search for me, find me, gather me to you, carry me. You can find the one you seek: deign to welcome the one you find, and to place him on your shoulders.... Come yourself to look for your sheep, rather than send servants or hirelings to do the searching. Draw me to you in this flesh which failed in Adam; draw me to you, not from Sarah, but from Mary.... Carry me to your cross, which is the salvation of the lost and the only rest of the weary, to your cross by which whoever dies can live again."

Reading Scripture With the Church Fathers

The Obedience of Faith

St. Francis of Assisi
Speaking by Example

How St. Francis gave a true and humble answer to a Doctor of the Order of Preachers who questioned him on a passage of Scripture.

While he was staying in Siena, he was visited by a Doctor of Theology from the Order of Preachers, a man who was both humble and sincerely spiritual. When he had discussed the words of our Lord with blessed Francis for some while, this Doctor asked him about the passage in Ezekiel: "When I threaten the sinner with doom of death, it is for thee to give him word and warn him."

And he said, "Good Father, I know many people who are in mortal sin, and do not warn them of their wickedness. Will their souls be required at my hand?" Blessed Francis humbly answered that he was no scholar, so that it would be more profitable for him to receive instruction from his questioner than to offer his own opinion on Scripture. The humble Doctor then added, "Brother, although I have heard this passage expounded by various learned men, I would be glad to know how you interpret it." So blessed Francis said, "If the passage is to be understood in general terms, I take it to mean that a servant of God should burn and shine in such a way by his own life and holiness that he rebukes all wicked people by the light of his example and the devoutness of his conversation; in this way the brightness of his life and the fragrance of his reputation will make all men aware of their own wickedness."

Greatly edified, the Doctor went away, and said to the companions of blessed Francis, "My brothers, this man's theology is grounded on purity and contemplation, and resembles a flying eagle; but our knowledge crawls along the ground on its belly."

Mirror of Perfection

Oswald Chambers
By the Grace of God I Am What I Am

"His grace which was bestowed upon me was not in vain" (1 Cor. 15:10).

The way we continually talk about our own inability is an insult to the Creator. The deploring of our own incompetence is a slander against God for having overlooked us. Get into the habit of examining in the sight of God the things that sound humble before men, and you will be amazed at how staggeringly impertinent they are. "Oh, I shouldn't like to say I am sanctified; I'm not a saint." Say that before God; and it means—"No, Lord, it is impossible for You to save and sanctify me; there are chances I have not had; so many imperfections in my brain and body; no, Lord, it isn't possible." That may sound wonderfully humble before men, but before God it is an attitude of defiance....

To say, "Thank God, I know I am saved and sanctified," is in the sight of God the acme of humility; it means you have so completely abandoned yourself to God that you know He is true. Never bother your head as to whether what you say sounds humble before men or not, but always be humble before God, and let Him be all in all.

There is only one relationship that matters, and that is your personal relationship to a personal Redeemer and Lord. Let everything else go, but maintain that at all costs, and God will fulfill His purpose through your life. One individual life may be of priceless value to God's purposes, and yours may be that life.

My Utmost for His Highest

Marriage and Family Life

Clement of Alexandria
The Holy Discipleship of Marriage

Both celibacy and marriage have their own different forms of service and ministry to the Lord; I have in mind the caring for one's wife and children. For it seems that the particular characteristic of the married state is that it gives the man who desires a perfect marriage an opportunity to take responsibility for everything in the home which he shares with his wife. The apostle says that one should appoint bishops who by their oversight over their own house have learned to be in charge of the whole church. Let each man therefore fulfill his ministry by the work in which he was called, that he may be free in Christ and receive the proper reward of his ministry....

In general all the epistles of the apostle Paul teach self-control and continence and contain numerous instructions about marriage, begetting children, and domestic life. But they nowhere rule out self-controlled marriage. Rather they preserve the harmony of the law and the gospel and approve both the man who with thanks to God enters upon marriage with sobriety and the man who in accordance with the Lord's will lives as a celibate, even as each individual is called, making his choice without blemish and in perfection....

Paul says that the unmarried cares for the things of the Lord, but he who is married how he can please his wife (see 1 Cor. 7:32-33). What then? Is it not lawful also for those who wish to please their wives according to the will of God to give thanks to God? Is it not allowable for both the married man and his wife to care for things of the Lord together? But just as the unmarried woman cares for the things of the Lord, that she may be holy both in body and spirit (1 Cor. 7:34), so also the married woman cares in the Lord for the things of her husband and the things of the Lord, the one as a wife, the other as a virgin.

Miscellanies

Tertullian
The Unity of Christian Marriage

How shall we ever be able adequately to describe the happiness of that marriage which the Church arranges, the sacrifice strengthens, upon which the blessing sets a seal, at which angels are present as witnesses, and to which the Father gives His consent?...

How beautiful the marriage of two Christians, two who are one in hope, one in desire, one in the way of life they follow, one in the religion they practice. They are as brother and sister, both servants of the same Master. Nothing divides them, either in flesh or in spirit. They are, in very truth, "two in one flesh"; and where there is but one flesh, there is also but one spirit. They pray together, they worship together, they fast together, instructing one another, encouraging one another, strengthening one another. Side by side they visit God's church and partake of God's banquet; side by side they face difficulties and persecution, share their consolations. They have no secrets from one another; they never shun each other's company; they never bring sorrow to each other's hearts. Unembarrassed they visit the sick and assist the needy. They give alms without anxiety, they attend the sacrifice without difficulty, they perform their daily exercises of piety without hindrance. They need not be furtive about making the sign of the cross, nor timorous in greeting the brethren, nor silent in asking a blessing of God. Psalms and hymns they sing to one another, striving to see which one of them will chant more beautifully the praises of their Lord. Hearing and seeing this, Christ rejoices. To such as these He gives His peace. "Where there are two together," there also He is present (Matt. 18:20); and where He is, there evil is not.

To His Wife

St. John Chrysostom
A Love That Lasts Forever

Whenever you give your wife advice, always begin by telling her how much you love her. Nothing will persuade her so well to admit the wisdom of your words as her assurance that you are speaking to her with sincere affection. Tell her that you are convinced that money is not important, that only thieves thirst for it constantly, that you love her more than gold; and indeed an intelligent, discreet, and pious young woman is worth more than all the money in the world. Tell her that you love her more than your own life, because this present life is nothing, and that your only hope is that the two of you pass through this life in such a way that in the world to come you will be united in perfect love. Say to her, "Our time here is brief and fleeting, but if we are pleasing to God, we can exchange this life for the kingdom to come. Then we will be perfectly one both with Christ and each other, and our pleasure will know no bounds. I value your love above all things, and nothing would be so bitter or painful to me as our being at odds with each other. Even if I lose everything, any affliction is tolerable if you will be true to me." Show her that you value her company, and prefer being at home to being out. Esteem her in the presence of your friends and children. Praise and show admiration for her good acts; and if she ever does anything foolish, advise her patiently.

Pray together at home and go to Church; when you come back home, let each ask the other the meaning of the readings and the prayers. If you are overtaken by poverty, remember Peter and Paul, who were more honored than kings or rich men, though they spent their lives in hunger and thirst. Remind one another that nothing in life is to be feared, except offending God. If your marriage is like this, your perfection will rival the holiest of monks.

Sermon on Ephesians

Coventry Patmore
Living in God's Love
　　...Equal and entire,
Therein benevolence, desire,
Elsewhere ill-join'd or found apart,
Become the pulses of one heart,
Which now contracts, and now dilates,
And, both to the height exalting, mates
Self-seeking to self-sacrifice.
Nay, in its subtle paradise
(When purest) this one love unites
All modes of these two opposites,

All balanced in accord so rich
Who may determine which is which?
Chiefly God's Love does in it live,
And nowhere else so sensitive.

Mystical Poems of Nuptial Love

Dietrich von Hildebrand
Transported by Love

Natural conjugal love exposes us to the danger of making the beloved the absolute center of our life. This love can degenerate into idolatry. In supernatural conjugal love, this danger is banished. It consciously builds itself in the love of the rex et centrum omnium cordium [king and center of all hearts]. The ultimate "logos" of this love is participation in that eternal love which Jesus holds for the soul of the beloved. Nor will it be any the less ardent for this, any less directed toward the beloved. On the contrary, it acquires an ardor and ultimateness which the merely natural minded cannot even imagine. For abandonment to a good is deepest and strongest when the good is viewed in the exact order ordained by God. Far from being a superabundance of love, any idolatry is rather a perversion, and therefore a diminution of love....

Conjugal love possesses, as does every authentic love, an intrinsic spiritual fertility which, though mysteriously connected with procreation, is by no means restricted to it. The impulsion to "Lift up your hearts" which characterizes conjugal love does not allow the lovers to become completely absorbed in one another, but generates in both a movement of spiritual ascension; the lovers let themselves be transported upward by their love. A primordial concern for the perfection of the partner arises in their souls....

Christ our Lord has said "For where there are two or three gathered together in My name, there am I in the midst of them" (Matt: 18:20). What sublime value lies in the heart of Christian marriage, where two human beings not only unite themselves in lifting up their eyes to Christ, but also form in Christ an ultimate unity, the very existence of which glorifies the Saviour. What sublime value is inherent in this touching, luminous, chaste conjugal love, which makes both spouses feel, so to speak, in one and the same pulsation of their souls, but one sorrow, one pain, one joy, and one love of Jesus. What beauty is possessed by this tie, a bond which requires of us this conjugal love and implies a task which is an image of our eternal end—the union of the soul with God. Let us think of Saint Elizabeth, who passing the night in prayer, left her hand in the hand of her sleeping husband—a touching expression at once of authentic, ardent conjugal love and of sacred union, fully penetrated by reverence *in conspectu Dei* (before God). Does not a community such as this glorify God in a specifically direct and primary manner?

Marriage

Jacques Leclercq
The Spirit of Poverty in Marriage

Poverty is an essential aspect of Christian perfection. One knows with what entreaties Our Savior invites those who would follow him to become detached from the things of this world. It is difficult for rich men to enter the kingdom of God; those who wish to enter must then fear riches and must love poverty. If husband and wife are eager to achieve that form of Christian perfection in their union, to which they are called by the sacrament which they have received together, they must inevitably face the problem of poverty....

The virtue of poverty is ... the spirit of poverty. It is a form of detachment. If Christ lays such stress on the need for poverty amongst his disciples, it is because they must be detached from the world and its covetousness; their lives must be devoted to the search for the kingdom, to purity of soul, and to the gifts of love. When one covets the riches of this world, one is unable to aspire to the kingdom.

Poverty must be regarded as a function of detachment. If one is not attached to riches, one will not do oneself much harm by possessing them; one will part easily with those which one has. One will remain indifferent to them, and as soon as one ceases to be attached to them, one sees that they are a burden, a check to the liberty of the spirit, for the good things of this world can be our masters more than we are theirs; they take up our time and our thoughts, and however little store we may set by them, they fill us with cares....

The virtue of poverty should be applied to each state according its needs.

Thus the poverty of married people is different from that of religious.... Husbands and wives should live according to the ways of the social milieu in which they find themselves. They should make sure of an existence for themselves and for those belonging to them.... The spirit of poverty consists in not wishing for more and in not making the increase of one's possessions the chief care of one's life....

But as their whole social milieu is impregnated with sensuality and vanity, husband and wife must make positive efforts at detachment, for most of those who live round them attach great importance to the unimportant, and are often only interested in futilities, so that those who treat them with detachment are apt to appear singular. A strong interior life is needed if values are to have their true place restored to them and the ideas which dominate the life of the majority are to be resisted.

We have a natural inclination to exaggerate social requirements and to pretend that these include what are, in fact, merely the results of vanity or of the desire for a comfortable life. There is no simple general solution of these problems, so the only way to achieve a just balance, taking into account what are genuine requirements, while refusing to be submerged by the love of the material and the external, is to be found in an interior life which is concentrated on interior values and tries to avoid being overcrowded with vanities. At this point one has returned to the question of love; the problem which dominates all others is to know where the heart is set. If one is not ready to devote one's time and one's thoughts to material things, one will have no difficulty in finding the just mean.

Marriage: A Great Sacrament

Frank J. Sheed
Union in the Depth of God's Will

Marriage seems to work magic. But it is not all magic. Husband and wife must work hard at it. If one is making no effort, the other must work twice as hard. Love helps, though it is precisely love that is in danger of losing its elan with so much to depress it; prayer helps tremendously. But, in the purely psychological order, nothing helps so much as the reverence that flows from a right vision of what man is—that this loutish man, this emptyheaded woman, is God's image, an immortal spirit, loved by Christ even to the death of the Cross: whatever the surface looks like, this is in the depth of every human being, this in him is what God joined together with this in her. The realization that there is this welding of two into one in the depths of their being, below the level that the eye of the mind can see, is the most powerful incentive to make that union in depth effective through every layer of personality.

Marriage and the Family

TWELVE

Prayer

Pray at all times in the Spirit, with all prayer and supplication. To that end keep alert with all perseverance, making supplication for all the saints (Eph. 6:18).

Prayer is the breathing of the spiritual life. No prayer, no life. Prayer is the way we speak to God, as well as the way He communicates with us. Without a life of prayer, religion becomes merely a set of human convictions, without any inner roots. For this reason our Savior not only gives us an example of personal prayer in His own life and at His death, but He also teaches us how to pray. He tells us to go into our room and close the door so that the Father who hears us in secret may listen to us.

Christian prayer can take several forms. The most important of these are private prayer or meditation, congregational prayer typically including Scripture reading and hymn singing, and, finally, in the lives of most Christians, liturgical or sacramental prayer. Since this anthology is meant for all Christian traditions, the section on liturgical prayer is placed at the end of the chapter. This is not done to suggest that Eucharistic prayer is of less importance to Catholic or Orthodox Christians or to those of Protestant traditions, such as Lutherans and Episcopalians, who come together for liturgical prayer. Protestants who belong to churches without a liturgical tradition may find it interesting to understand what various liturgical Christians are doing on Sunday morning.

We all need to pray, and pray better. A person who does not seek to grow in the life of prayer will, sooner or later, not pray at all. Those who grow in prayer will be sustained by it. A dear old African-American lady, Mother

Moses, named thus because she founded a storefront church, once said to me, "I pray all the time. If I didn't pray, I just could not go on."

I think she said it all.

Meditation

St. Bonaventure
A Guide to Meditation
Whenever you call upon God,
Three ideas
Should guide your act of worship:
First, to humble your heart in reverence and adoration of God;
Second, to expand your heart with good will and thanksgiving;
Third, to lift up your heart in delight,
In that converse between lover and Beloved
Taught by the Holy Spirit in the Canticle of Canticles.
If this be done well,
Such wonderful peace and joy result
That they transport the soul from the realm of the senses,
Causing her to say,
"It is good to be here."
Thus should our prayer end,
Until the soul enters into that wonderful tabernacle,
The very house of God,
Where is heard the voice of one rejoicing in exultation.

To be moved to reverence,
Look upon the divine immensity—
Then consider yourself,
See your own littleness.
To be filled with good will,
Look upon the benevolence of God
And your own unworthiness.
To be raised unto the union of love,
Remember the charity of God
And your own lukewarmness.

Only by such comparisons
Will you go beyond the things of sense.

Once you are moved
To that spirit of reverence for God,
It should be manifested
In three ways:
   First, reverence to the Father—
It is He Who has made you what you are;
   Second, reverence to the Son—
It is He Who has redeemed you
From the dungeon of hell's prison,
Who has journeyed with you
To the vineyard of the Father;
   Third, reverence to the Judge—
For you have been accused before Him,
You have been convicted before Him,
You have confessed your guilt.
Is it not our unquiet conscience that accuses us?
And what convicts us,
If not our very life itself?
Indeed, the sentence due
Is given against us in all justice!

The first type of reverence mentioned above
Should be intense,
The second yet more so,
And the third
Most intense of all.
These stages of reverence may be shown figuratively:
Consider the first an inclination of the head;
The second something more,
Perhaps a genuflection;
And the last—could anything be more fitting?—
A bodily prostration.
In the first act we subject ourselves,
In the second we are made humble,

But the third is the first two
And more—
Complete submission to the Will of God might best explain it.
So, once again, we consider ourselves as little
In the first act of reverence.
In the second
We might look upon ourselves as the very least.
But in the third, we are absolutely nothing.

In order to expand our heart
With good will and thanksgiving,
In other words, with benevolence to God,
Three things are necessary:
  We must consider our unworthiness,
  We must consider the greatness of His grace,
  We must consider the vastness of His mercy.
Observe the things which God has given to us;
Think of the many times He has forgiven our sins;
How very much He has promised us.
In the first place our heart has been expanded
Almost to capacity;
Second, it has been torn apart with love
For Him Who rends it,
And third, it has poured forth its precious oil of love
According to the words of Lamentations:
"Pour out thy heart like water
Before the face of the Lord."
To continue:
We must raise our hearts in quietude,
We must attain a certain complacency of spirit;
And this, too, is done in three steps:
First, that our love be so conformed
With that of our Creator
That we are enraptured by the very fact
That only God is pleasing to us;
Second, that our heart be joyful
Because we ourselves are pleasing only to God;

And lastly, that we be happy to see others
Sharing and partaking in this same complacency.

Do we not see here a love which is gratuitous;
A love which is due in justice;
A love which is a combination of both?
In the first, the world is crucified
To man;
In the second, man is crucified
To the world;
In the third, man is crucified
For the world,
So that he wishes to hang upon the wood
Of the world,
To die for all —
But for one reason:
That they, too,
May be pleasing to God.
This, my dear soul,
Is the ascent and the state of purest charity —
Unless you have attained it,
Never consider yourself perfect!
You are closest to the attainment of this perfection
When the heart is not only willing but even eager
To die for salvation —
The salvation of fellow men!
Was it not St. Paul who said:
"I will most gladly spend
And be spent myself
For your souls"?
But one does not reach this perfect love of neighbor
Unless he first has attained a perfect love of God:
This follows from reason.
For who can love the creature
Without loving the Creator more?

The Enkindling of Love

Thomas Merton

A Modern Spiritual Writer Gives an Outline of Interior Prayer

Meditation is really very simple, and there is not much need of elaborate techniques to teach us how to go about it. But that does not mean that mental prayer can be practiced without constant and strict interior discipline. This is especially true in our own time, when the intellectual and moral flabbiness of a materialistic society has robbed man's nature of its spiritual energy and tone. Nevertheless, the necessity for discipline does not imply the obligation for all men to follow one identical and rigid system. There is a difference between being strict and being rigid. The well-disciplined soul, like a well-disciplined body, is agile, supple, and adaptable. A soul that is not pliable and free is incapable of progress in the ways of prayer. An unwise rigidity may seem to produce results at first, but it only ends by paralyzing the interior life.

There are, however, certain universal requirements for the sane practice of mental prayer. They cannot be neglected.

Recollection

In order to meditate, I have to withdraw my mind from all that prevents me from attending to God present in my heart. This is impossible unless I recollect my senses. But it is almost useless to try to recollect myself at the moment of prayer if I have allowed my senses and imagination to run wild all the rest of the day. Consequently, the desire to practice meditation implies the effort to preserve moderate recollection throughout the day. It means living in an atmosphere of faith and with occasional moments of prayer and attention to God. The world in which we live today presents a tantalizing problem to anyone who wants to acquire habits of recollection.

The price of true recollection is a firm resolve to take no willful interest in anything that is not useful or necessary to our interior life. The world we live in assails us on every side with useless appeals to emotion and to sense appetite. Radios, newspapers, movies, television, billboards, neon-signs surround us with a perpetual incitement to pour out our money and our vital energies in futile transitory satisfactions. The more we buy, the more they urge us to buy. But the more they advertise, the less we get. And yet, the more they advertise, the more we buy. Eventually all will consist in the noise that is made, and there will be no satisfaction left in the world except that of vain hopes and anticipations that can never be fulfilled.

The Sense of Indigence

In order to make a serious and fruitful meditation, we must enter into our prayer with a real sense of our need for these fruits. It is not enough to apply our minds to spiritual things in the same way as we might observe some natural phenomenon or conduct a scientific experiment. In mental prayer we enter a realm of which we are no longer the masters and we propose to ourselves the consideration of truths which exceed our natural comprehension and which, nevertheless, contain the secret of our destiny. We seek to enter more deeply into the life of God. But God is infinitely above us, although He is within us and is the principle of our being. The grace of close union with Him, although it is something we can obtain by prayer and good works, remains nevertheless His gift to us.

One who begs an alms must adopt a different attitude from one who demands what is due to him by his own right. A meditation that is no more than a dispassionate study of spiritual truths indicates no desire on our part to share more fully in the spiritual benefits which are the fruit of prayer. We have to enter into our meditation with a realization of our spiritual poverty, our complete lack of the things we seek, and of our abject nothingness in the sight of the infinite God.

Sincerity

The desires and sorrows of our heart in prayer rise to the heavenly Father as the desires and sorrows of His Son, by virtue of the Holy Spirit who teaches us to pray and who, though we do not always know how to pray as we ought, prays in us, and cries out to the Father in us....

"Likewise the Spirit also helpeth our infirmity. For we know not what we should pray for as we ought; but the Spirit Himself asketh for us with unspeakable groanings. And He that searcheth the hearts knoweth what the Spirit desireth; because He asketh for the saints according to God" (Romans 8:15-17, 26, 27).

It can therefore be said that the aim of mental prayer is to awaken the Holy Spirit within us and to bring our hearts into harmony with His voice, so that we allow the Holy Spirit to speak and pray within us, and lend Him our voices and our affections that we may become, as far as possible, conscious of His prayer in our hearts.

This implies a difficult and constant attention to the sincerity of our own hearts. We should never say anything in mental prayer that we do not really mean, or at least sincerely desire to mean. One of the reasons why our mental prayer easily grows cold and indifferent is that we begin with aspirations that we do not feel or cannot really mean at the moment. For instance, we fall on our knees out of habit, and without directing our attention to God we begin to tell Him that we love Him, in a more or less exterior and mechanical fashion, hardly even aware of what we are saying. It is true, that we have a more or less habitual desire to love God, and if we attend to what we are doing we are capable of "purifying our intention" more or less as if we were using a mental windshield-wiper, wiping away juridical specks of self-love. We don't really *want* things that go contrary to God and to His will.

Concentration and Unity

We have already seen that progress in the life of prayer means the emergence of one dominant attraction — a concentration of the interior life on one objective, union with God. We have remarked that this objective is usually obscure to our experience. The desire for God becomes more intense and more continual, and at the same time our knowledge of Him, rising above precise and definite concepts, becomes "dark" and even confused. Hence the anguish of the mystic who seeks God in the night of pure faith, above the level of human ideas, knowing Him not by light but by darkness. Contemplative prayer apprehends God by love rather than by positive knowledge. But this union of love, which gives the soul an "experience" of God, is effected in the soul by the action of the Holy Spirit, not by the soul's own efforts.

Simple Steps

Here it might be worthwhile to outline the simple essentials of meditative prayer, in schematic form.

1. *Preliminary:* a sincere effort of recollection, a realization of what you are about to do, and a prayer of petition for grace. If this beginning is well made, the rest ought to follow easily.

2. *Vision:* the attempt to see, to focus, to grasp what you are meditating on. This implies an effort of *faith.* Keep working until faith is clear and firm in your heart (not merely in your head).

3. *Aspiration:* From what you "see" there follow certain practical consequences. Desires, resolutions to act in accordance with one's faith, to live
one's faith. Here, an effort of *hope* is required — one must believe in the
possibility of these good acts, one must hope in the fulfillment of good
desires, with the help of God. Above all, one must have a sincere hope in
the possibility of divine union.

4. *Communion:* here the prayer becomes simple and uncomplicated. The
realization of faith is solid, hope is firm, one can rest in the presence of
God. This is more a matter of simple repose and intuition, an embrace of
simple *love.* But if activity is required, let love have an active character, in
which case the prayer is more like the last level (3). Or love may take rather
the form of *listening* to the Beloved. Or the form of *praise.* More often
than not, we can be content to simply rest, and float peacefully with the
deep current of love, doing nothing of ourselves, but allowing the Holy
Spirit to act in the secret depths of our souls. If the prayer becomes confused or weak, we can return to one of the earlier stages, and renew our
vigilance, our faith, our love.

We can end with a brief and sincere prayer of thanksgiving.

Spiritual Direction and Meditation

William of St. Thierry
The Prayer of Love for Christ

Among these souls my spirit also, Lord, will be taught sometimes to worship you, who are Spirit, in spirit and in truth, nor will the flesh oppose my
doing so when its desires have ceased or grown less keen.

But in the meantime, since [my spirit] cannot move as freely as it ought
among things divine, you will dispose its own concerns for it as sweetly
as befits it. For, since I have not yet progressed beyond the elementary
stage of sensory imagination, you will allow and will be pleased if my still-
undeveloped soul dwells naturally on your lowliness by means of some
mental picturing. You will allow her, for example, to embrace the manger
of the newborn babe, to venerate the sacred infancy, to caress the feet of
the crucified, to hold and kiss those feet when he is risen, and to put her
hand in the print of the nails and cry: "My Lord and my God!" And in all
these things ... I worship and adore what I see and hear in my imagination,

and what my hands handle of the Word of life.

Therefore, although we know you now no longer according to the flesh, but as you now sit glorified at the Father's right hand in heaven, being made so much better than the angels as you have by inheritance obtained a more excellent name than they—therefore, I say, we make our prayer, present our worship, and offer our petitions to that same flesh of ours, which you have not cast off but glorified. O blessed is that temple of the Holy Spirit, in which the memory of Christ uplifted on the cross is ever green, where his blood flows ever fresh to save the faithful, loving soul, in whom the Prophet's prayer, "O deliver me and be merciful unto me," is ever being answered!

For the effect of our redemption is repeated in us as often as we recall it in affective prayer. And, since we cannot do even this as we would, with even greater daring we make a mental picture of your passion for ourselves, so that our bodily eyes may possess something on which to gaze, something to which to cleave, worshiping not the pictured likeness only, but the truth the picture of your passion represents.

For when we look more closely at the picture of your passion, although it does not speak, we seem to hear you say: "When I loved you, I loved you to the end. Let death and hell lay hold on me, that I may die their death; eat, friends, and drink abundantly, beloved, unto life eternal."...

For though this picturing of your passion, O Christ, our pondering on the good that you have wrought for us leads us forthwith to love the highest good. That good you make us see in the work of salvation, not by an understanding arising from human effort nor by the eyes of our mind that tremble and shrink from your light, but by the peaceful experience of love, and by the good use of our sight and enjoyment of your sweetness, while your wisdom sweetly orders our affairs. For he labors who would go up some other way, but he who enters by you, O Door, walks on the smooth ground and comes to the Father, to whom no one may come, except by you. And he no longer labors to understand knowledge beyond his reach, for the bliss of a well-disposed conscience absorbs him utterly. And as the river of joy floods that soul more completely, she seems to see you as you are. In sweet meditation on the wonderful sacrament of your passion she muses on the good that you have wrought on our behalf, the good that is as great as you yourself are great, the good that is yourself. She seems to herself to see you face to face when you thus show her, in the cross and in the work of your salvation, the face of the ultimate Good. The cross itself becomes for her the face of a mind that is well-disposed toward God....

This, Lord, is your face towards us and our face towards you, full of good hope. Deck me with this in your salvation, conform me to this face of your Anointed, for you cannot turn that face away whenever it appears before you in your holy place. Go, man, whoever you are who find this treasure hidden in the field of your own heart! Sell all that you have, sell yourself as a slave forever, that you may gain this treasure for your own! For then you will be blest and all will be well with you. Christ in your conscience is the treasure that you will possess.

Meditation 10

Contemplative Meditation

The Work of Contemplation

This is what you are to do: lift your heart up to the Lord, with a gentle stirring of love desiring him for his own sake and not for his gifts. Center all your attention and desire on him, and let this be the sole concern of your mind and heart. Do all in your power to forget everything else, keeping your thoughts and desires free from involvement with any of God's creatures or their affairs whether in general or in particular. Perhaps this will seem like an irresponsible attitude, but I tell you, let them all be; pay no attention to them.

What I am describing here is the contemplative work of the spirit. It is this which gives God the greatest delight. For when you fix your love on him, forgetting all else, the saints and angels rejoice and hasten to assist you in every way—though the devils will rage and ceaselessly conspire to thwart you. Your fellow men are marvelously enriched by this work of yours, even if you may not fully understand how; the souls in purgatory are touched, for their suffering is eased by the effects of this work; and, of course, your own spirit is purified and strengthened by this contemplative work more than by all others put together. Yet for all this, when God's grace arouses you to enthusiasm, it becomes the lightest sort of work there is and one most willingly done. Without his grace, however, it is very difficult and almost, I should say, quite beyond you.

And so diligently persevere until you feel joy in it. For in the beginning it is usual to feel nothing but a kind of darkness about your mind, or as it were, a *cloud of unknowing.* You will seem to know nothing and to feel nothing except a naked intent toward God in the depths of your being. Try as you might, this darkness and this cloud will remain between you and your God. You will feel frustrated, for your mind will be unable to grasp him, and your heart will not relish the delight of his love. But learn to be at home in this darkness. Return to it as often as you can, letting your spirit cry out to him whom you love. For if, in this life, you hope to feel and see God as he is in himself, it must be within this darkness and this cloud. But if you strive to fix your love on him, forgetting all else, which is the work of contemplation I have urged you to begin, I am confident that God in his goodness will bring you to a deep experience of himself.

The Cloud of Unknowing

Archbishop Alban Goodier, S.J.
The Prayer of Friendship With Christ

First, prayer of the Illuminative Way draws the soul to think less about itself, and more about "God and His Christ." There is now a totally new orientation, a totally new interest, from prayer of the Purgative Way; the soul has its eyes turned, henceforth, on a Person far more attractive, and far more worth contemplating, than its miserable little self. It realizes itself less and God and Jesus more, studies itself less and them more, cares for itself less and them more; in the end puts off self altogether and puts on Jesus Christ, judging itself and all things in His light alone.

Hence, second, its purpose is less to correct itself of its faults or vices—these are now left to the examination of conscience—but more to acquire what is good. And by good is meant, not so much this or that explicit virtue, for that is still in some sense a consideration of self, but what will help the soul better to serve its Beloved, what will make it more pleasing in the sight of its Beloved, what will draw its Beloved nearer to it, and it to Him. So far as itself is concerned, its one aim is to become more like to Him, to be perfect as its heavenly Father is perfect, to seek first the kingdom of God and His justice, almost ignoring the rest, knowing well that all other things will be added unto it, scarcely caring whether they are or not.

Thirdly, since love is the beginning and end of such prayer, and since knowledge is sought, not for its own sake, but only to feed and increase this love, the soul by this kind of prayer will inevitably be drawn to do something to prove its love, to a spontaneous desire for sacrifice, to manifest its love by somehow paying and even suffering for it. And this produces a new kind of happiness, a new satisfaction, a new delight, totally transcending that of perfect contrition, however great that may have been. It is the happiness of perfect friendship, of devotedness to one who has won our hearts, and is the beginning of heroism.

An Introduction to the Study of Ascetical and Mystical Theology

Brother Lawrence of the Resurrection
A Wise and Simple Friar Talks of Prayer
Dear Friend:
I write because you want to hear from me so badly
about how I arrived at the
habitual sense of God's presence.
This *sense* is God's gift,
But I write with great difficulty
and only because you insist.
Moreover, I write
only under the condition that you
show this letter to no one.
If I knew you would let others see it,
all the desire I have
for your spiritual formation
would leave me powerless to make me write.

Now to answering your question:
I found many books that give
lots of ways to come to God.
They suggest any number of
spiritual exercises.

But I concluded that the books would puzzle me
more than help me.
After all,
I sought for no more than
how to be God's
and God's alone.
My goal made me resolve
to give my all for *The All.*
So, after giving myself wholly to God,
to take care of my sins,
I renounced—
because I loved Him so much—
everything not of God.
Now I began to live
as if He and I were the only ones
alive in the world.
Sometimes I thought of myself as
a poor criminal, and
He as my Judge.
At other times,
I thought of Him as my Father.
Always I worshipped Him as often as I could,
keeping my mind in His holy presence.
When I wandered
I brought Him back to my mind.
This was a painful exercise
but I persisted,
even through all difficulties.
But never did I trouble or
disquiet my mind
when my thoughts wandered involuntarily.
I made practicing His presence
my business
as much right through
the day
as at the appointed times of prayer.

At all times—
every hour,
every minute,
even at the height of business—
I drove away from my mind
everything interrupting the
sense of the presence of God.

That, in a nutshell, gives you
my everyday practice
ever since I took up religion in earnest.
Though I have practiced His presence
very imperfectly,
I have greatly benefited from
what I have done.
The benefits, I know very well, all come
from God
—His mercy and goodness—
because we can do nothing without Him,
and I can do fewer good things
than anyone!

But when we stand firm
to keep ourselves in His holy presence
and to make Him absolutely
central in our lives;
This not only hinders us from
offending Him
or doing anything that displeases Him
(at least willfully),
it also gives rise to freedom
—a divine freedom—
and, if you will not misunderstand me,
a familiarity with God
that makes possible
asking and receiving
the graces we need.

To summarize:
Repeating these acts often
translates them into habit,
then the presence of God
becomes, so to speak,
natural to us.
Please join me in giving Him thanks
for His great goodness to me;
I can never wonder enough at
the many favors
He has done for so miserable a sinner as I!
I want the whole world,
material things included,
to praise Him.
Amen.

The Practice of the Presence of God

Prayer of an English Puritan
In Prayer I Am Lifted Up
O LORD,
In prayer I launch far out into the eternal world,
and on that broad ocean my soul triumphs
over all evils on the shores of mortality.
Time, with its gay amusements and cruel disappointments
never appears so inconsiderate as then.
In prayer I see myself as nothing;
I find my heart going after thee with intensity,
and long with vehement thirst to live to thee.
Blessed be the strong gales of the Spirit
that speed me on my way to the New Jerusalem.
In prayer all things here below vanish,
and nothing seems important
but holiness of heart and the salvation of others.
In prayer all my worldly cares, fears, anxieties disappear,
and are of as little significance as a puff of wind.

In prayer my soul inwardly exults with lively thoughts
at what thou art doing for thy church,
and I long that thou shouldest get thyself a great name
from sinners returning to Zion.
In prayer I am lifted above the frowns and flatteries of life,
and taste heavenly joys;
entering into the eternal world
I can give myself to thee with all my heart,
to be thine for ever.
In prayer I can place all my concerns in thy hands
to be entirely at thy disposal,
having no will or interest of my own.
In prayer I can intercede for my friends, ministers,
sinners, the church, thy kingdom to come,
with greatest freedom, ardent hopes,
as a son to his father,
as a lover to the beloved.
Help me to be all prayer and never to cease praying.

The Valley of Vision

Liturgical Prayer

Evelyn Underhill
An Anglican Looks at the Liturgy

The Liturgy recapitulates all the essentials in this life of sanctification—to repent, to pray, to listen, to learn; and then to offer upon the altar of God, to intercede, to be transformed to the purposes of God, to be fed and maintained by the very life of God. And though it is the voice of the Church, nonetheless in it is to be recognized the voice of each separate soul, and the care of the Praying Church for each separate soul. "Holy Things for the Holy!" cries the celebrant in the earliest liturgies, as he lifts up the consecrated gifts. Not "Good Things for the Good"; but supernatural things for those imperfect creatures who have been baptized into the Supernatural, translated to another order—those looking towards God the Perfect and beginning to conceive of life as a response to God the Perfect;

but unable without the "rich bread of Christ" to actualize the state to which they are called.

> I will go up to the Altar of God;
> Of God, who giveth joy to my youth!

The spirit of adventure, courage, vitality, zest, are among the qualities of the good communicant. He is there because he has accepted his mysterious vocation; is prepared to embrace his great opportunity, respond to the awful invitation of God, whatever it may involve for him, with reverence, courage and delight. "Blessed be the Kingdom of the Father, the Son, and the Holy Spirit!" exclaims the Orthodox priest at the beginning of the rite. It is to this Kingdom and its interests that the worshipper looks. Each of these specks of consciousness is pressed from within, drawn from without, to the altar at which it is offered for the purposes of Love.

All the great petitions of the Lord's Prayer are here to be carried through into action. The Liturgy declares and expresses the filial dependence of man upon God the Transcendent; it could not exist save in virtue of that link with the Transcendent. It is, from first to last, a hallowing of the Name of God. It calls man, the head of creation, to join with angels and archangels in adoring God. It opens the doors of the natural world to the coming of His consecrating and saving power. In it the creature offers itself under tokens and without reserve for the purposes of His Will, is fed with heavenly food, reconciled and established in the Kingdom of Love, and subdued to the guidance and fostering care of the Unseen. Step by step, conduct, feeling, will, and thought are quieted and transformed to this great purpose. By serial acts of penitence, self-offering, adoration, and communion, the transition is made from the ever-changing world of use and wont to the world that is insusceptible of change.

The Mystery of Sacrifice

Father Louis Bouyer
A Catholic Understanding of the Eucharist

Christian contemplation, inasmuch as it is contemplation of the Mystery, tends to the realizing, in the strongest sense of the word, of that which the Mystery is according to the phrase of St. Paul, "Christ in us, hope of glory" (Col. 1: 27).

Word and Sacrament.

But this is possible only on the basis of the sacramental life. The divine Word presents the Mystery to us as the substance of our faith. But it is in the sacraments that it causes us effectively to participate in it and that faith can make our own the Mystery here proclaimed.

Faith, indeed, is only the opening of the soul, to be achieved in prayer, to the Word of God coming to us in and by the Church. The Word of God illuminated by the tradition of the Church is concentrated in the Mystery: Christ and His cross. But, in the Church, the Mystery is not merely proclaimed. Rather, with the very authority of God, it is proclaimed as present. It is then represented, rendered present for us, in us. It is for the sacraments to apply to us this permanent presence and actuality of the Mystery....

The Word of God is not, therefore, simply verbal expressions nor even ideas: it is always an act, in which Someone reveals Himself in giving Himself. Finally, it is this Someone Himself. This Someone, Christ, the living Word of the Father, remains present in the Church to continue to speak to us here. He is present, in fact, and He speaks to us now by the ministry of the hierarchical apostolate which He instituted, the hierarchy, that is, of which the principle is given us in the words of the Gospel: "As the Father has sent me, I also send you.... He who hears you, hears me, and he who hears me, hears Him who sent me" (John 20:21 and Luke 10: 16).

Thus in the Church established on the foundation of the apostolate understood in this way, Christ continues to speak, and His Word, which remains His own in the very act of its being spoken, retains on the lips of His ministers the creative power proper to the divine Word. This is what happens in the sacraments.

It is in them, again, that the Mystery, the object of the Word, is carried out in the Church as "Christ in us, the hope of glory." Christ, who died *for us* once for all and thereafter rose, here continues to die and to rise again *in us* so that we may rise with Him forever at the end of time.

The Mass, Focus of the Sacramental Life.

In the Mass, we go quite naturally from the Mystery *proclaimed* by the word of the Gospel to the Mystery *made present* by the words of consecration. These two "words" are indeed closely related, as we have already said:

the first tends to the second. The word of consecration is but the Gospel word in the fullness of its meaning and actuality: giving us, *hic et nunc*, according to its own design, what it has begun by revealing to us, and revealing to us as that which is to become our own.

This is also why, conversely, we perceive the whole meaning of the proclaimed word only in the sacramental celebration. As St. Paul says: "Whenever you eat this bread and drink this cup, you *proclaim* the death of the Lord, until He comes" (1 Cor. 11:26).

The Word that proclaims the love of the Father became act in the death of Christ. And the word that proclaims the death of Christ in turn becomes act in the Eucharistic consecration. This, in return, is "the proclamation" of that death, in the fullness of its meaning and its actuality, not only by us but in us....

The body of Christ present in the sacrament and the body of Christ which is the Church are not merely two different bodies. The body of Christ which is the Church is called so because in it we are all united in one single body by the fact of being all nourished by the body of Christ which once died on the cross and today nourishes the life of the Mystery in us.

We see at the same time what is the nature of the reality proper to the sacramental order, the reality which faith immediately has in view. The reality of the sacraments is not a reality which somehow can subsist by itself. It is the reality of signs, but of signs which communicate, in the strongest sense of the word, that which they signify. They are, as it were, the meeting-place of the encounter between the reality of Christ, of His saving work, and the reality of ourselves, of our individual lives, which are to be, as it were, plunged into His death and into His new life in order to be brought to the fullness of His resurrection. By the sacramental mystery, the sacrifice of Christ is to penetrate our entire life, in such a way as to make of it, according to the formula of St. Paul, "a holy and living sacrifice, acceptable to God: the offering of our own bodies, which is our reasonable worship" (Rom. 12:1). In this light, our sacrifices are not to be added to the cross of Christ as if from without, which would be nonsense: they can take their reality only from His. It is we who are to be, not added to, but incorporated in Christ, in such a way that it can be said, "It is no longer we who live, but Christ Who lives in us" (cf. Gal. 2: 20).

According to Catholic tradition, all Christians actually take part in the sacrifice of the Mass. Here the relationship between the ministerial priesthood of the hierarchy and the royal priesthood of the whole body of Christ is clarified, in the economy of the participation of all in the unique sacrifice of the Savior.

In the document in which we see the word "liturgy" (the original meaning of which is "a public service rendered by an individual to the community") first applied to Christian worship, St. Clement of Rome tells us that the celebration of the Eucharist is carried out by the cooperation of the "liturgies" proper to the different members of the Church.

The "liturgy" of "the high-priest," as he says — that is, of the Bishop or the priest of the second rank who takes his place —is to proclaim the divine Word with apostolic authority and then to "make the eucharist," by pronouncing over the bread and cup the great prayer of consecration. These two functions, as we see them in Christ Himself Whom the "high-priest" represents in the assembly of His own, are closely connected. The one calls to the other, and, we might even say, gives rise to it.

For is Christ not the Word of God made man? In other words, the Divine Word addressed in all its fullness to mankind here evokes the perfect response in His own person.

Introduction to Spirituality

Father Alexander Schmemann,
distinguished scholar of the Orthodox Church in America
An Orthodox Appreciation of the Liturgy
The time has come now to offer to God the totality of all our lives, of ourselves, of the world in which we live. This is the first meaning of our bringing to the altar the elements of our food. For we already know that food is life, that it is the very principle of life and that the whole world has been created as food for man. We also know that to offer this food, this world, this life to God is the initial "eucharistic" function of man, his very fulfillment as man. We know that we were created as *celebrants* of the sacrament of life, of its transformation into life in God, communion with God. We know that real life is "eucharist," a movement of love and adoration toward God, the movement in which alone the meaning and the value of all that exists can be revealed and fulfilled. We know that we have lost this eucharis-

tic life, and finally we know that in Christ, the new Adam, the perfect man, this eucharistic life was restored to man. For He Himself was the perfect Eucharist; He offered Himself in total obedience, love and thanksgiving to God. God was His very life. And He gave this perfect and eucharistic life to us. In Him God became our life.

And thus this offering to God of bread and wine, of the food that we must eat in order to live, is our offering to Him of ourselves, of our life and of the whole world. "To take in our hands the whole world as if it were an apple!" said a Russian poet. It is our Eucharist, it is the movement that Adam failed to perform, and that in Christ has become the very life of man: a movement of adoration and praise in which all joy and suffering, all beauty and all frustration, all hunger and all satisfaction are referred to their ultimate End and become finally *meaningful*. Yes, to be sure, it is a *sacrifice:* but sacrifice is the most natural act of man, the very essence of his life. Man is a sacrificial being, because he finds his life in love, and love is sacrificial: it puts the value, the very meaning of life in the other and gives life to the other, and in this giving, in this sacrifice, finds the meaning and joy of life.

We offer the world and ourselves to God. But we do it *in Christ* and *in remembrance of Him*. We do it in Christ because He has already offered all that is to be offered to God. He has performed once and for all this Eucharist and nothing has been left unoffered. In him was *Life—and* this Life of all of us, He gave to God. The Church is all those who have been accepted into the eucharistic life of Christ. And we do it *in remembrance of Him* because, as we offer again and again our life and our world to God, we discover each time that there is nothing else to be offered but Christ Himself—the Life of the world, the fullness of all that exists. It is His Eucharist, and He is the Eucharist. As the prayer of offering says—"it is He who offers and it is He who is offered." The liturgy has led us into the all-embracing Eucharist of Christ, and has revealed to us that the only Eucharist, the only offering of the world is Christ. We come again and again with our lives to offer; we bring and "sacrifice"—that is, give to God—what He has given us; and each time we come to the *End* of all sacrifices, of all offerings, of all eucharists, because each time it is revealed to us that Christ has *offered* all that exists, and that He and all that exists has been offered in His offering of Himself. We are included in the Eucharist of Christ and Christ is our Eucharist.

For the Life of the World

John and Charles Wesley
Hymns on the Lord's Supper in the Methodist Tradition

1

In that sad memorable night,
When Jesus was for us betray'd,
He left His death-recording rite,
He took, and bless'd, and brake the bread,
And gave His own their last bequest,
And this His love's intent express:

Take, eat, this is My body, given
To purchase life and peace for you,
Pardon and holiness and heaven;
Do this My dying love to show,
Accept your precious legacy,
And thus, My friends, remember Me.

He took into His hands the cup,
To crown the sacramental feast,
And full of kind concern look'd up,
And gave what He to them had blest;
And drink ye all of this, He said,
In Solemn memory of the deed.

This is My blood which seals the new
Eternal covenant of My grace,
My blood so freely shed for you
For you and all the sinful race;
My blood that speaks your sins forgiven,
And justifies your claim to heaven.

The grace which I to all bequeath
In this Divine memorial take,
And, mindful of your Savior's death,
Do this My followers, for My sake,
Whose dying love hath left behind
Eternal life for all mankind.

2

Then let us go, and take, and eat
The heavenly, everlasting meat,
For fainting souls prepared;
Fed with the living Bread Divine,
Discern we in the sacred sign
The body of the Lord.

The oblation sends as sweet a smell,
Even now it pleases God as well
As when it first was made;
The blood doth now as freely flow,
As when His side received the blow
That show'd Him newly dead.

Then let our faith adore the Lamb
Today as yesterday the same,
In Thy great offering join,
Partake the sacrificial food,
And eat Thy flesh and drink Thy blood,
And live for ever Thine.

3

Let all who truly bear
The bleeding Savior's name,
Their faithful hearts with us prepare,
And eat the Paschal Lamb.
Our Passover was slain
At Salem's hallow'd place,
Yet we who in our tents remain
Shall gain His largest grace.

The eucharistic feast
Our every want supplies,
And still we by His death are blest
And share His sacrifice:
By faith His flesh we eat,

Who here His passion show,
And God out of His holy seat
Shall all His gifts bestow.

4
O Thou, eternal Victim, slain
A sacrifice for guilty man,
By the eternal Spirit made
An offering in the sinner's stead,
Our everlasting Priest art Thou,
And plead'st Thy death for sinners now.

Thy offering still continues new,
Thy vesture keeps its bloody hue,
Thou stand'st the ever-slaughter'd Lamb,
Thy priesthood still remains the same,
Thy years, O God, can never fail,
Thy goodness is unchangeable.

O that our faith may never move,
But stand unshaken as Thy love!
Sure evidence of things unseen,
Now let it pass the years between,
And view Thee bleeding on the tree,
My God, who dies for me, for me!

THIRTEEN

Devotion

Teach me thy way, O Lord, that I may walk in thy truth; unite my heart to fear thy name. I give thanks to thee, O Lord my God, with my whole heart, and I will glorify thy name for ever. For great is thy steadfast love toward me; thou hast delivered my soul from the depths of Sheol (Ps. 86:11-13).

Devotion properly understood means a deep personal surrender to God in thanksgiving and repentance. In this sense devotion is a response to the command to love the Lord with all our heart, soul, strength, and mind (see Lk. 10:27). In recent decades the word devotion has taken on a pejorative meaning among some Christians. It has been seen as a purely emotional or subjective phenomenon related to histrionic or emotionally dependent personalities. Indeed, we do occasionally meet such people in the Gospels—Mary of Magdala seems to be one. It is worth noting that Christ treats these souls with compassion and responds to their devotion in a gracious and accepting way.

Devotion, however, should not be restricted to highly emotional kinds of people. Persons of great intelligence and ability, often illustrious preachers and theologians like John Wesley and Cardinal Newman, are capable of deep devotion. It may well be that what is needed in contemporary Christianity is a sincere devotion to Christ expressed in many ways for many different kinds of people. Ruth Jones, the daughter of the eminent Quaker writer Rufus Jones, described to me once how the silence of a Quaker meeting could be deeply devotional. On the other hand, Eastern Churches usually join the devotional with the liturgy itself rather than having separate devotional services. Religion without devotion is a very dry piece of toast indeed.

For Orthodox and Catholic Christians, devotion to the Mother of Christ, the angels, and the saints is also a secondary but significant part of the expression of faith. Such devotion goes back at least to the end of the second century. We have again included a few selections on these devotions. While the sixteenth-century reformers generally frowned on the invocation of the saints, they often spoke of their admiration for these great followers of Christ and of the place they had already assumed in the kingdom of heaven.

In whatever way devotion expresses itself, it must be sincere and integrated with a person's life and behavior. Otherwise the statement of Jesus, "Not everyone who says to me, 'Lord, Lord,' shall enter the kingdom of heaven" (Mt. 7:21) will apply to them. Devotion should be the fruit of a true love of God and should not be self-deception.

Devotion is for many the greatest encouragement of their life of faith and their expression of prayer and love of God. Those who feel that they are too intellectual to have a devotional life might consider the image of the Russian Orthodox spiritual writer Bishop Ignatius Brianchaninov that we ought to burn the thoughts of our minds on the altars of our hearts with the fire of love. I think this is a perfect description of intelligent devotion which, in the words of *The Imitation of Christ*, is a "loud cry in the ears of God."

Oswald Chambers
The Holy Spirit Prays Within Us
"We know not what we should pray for as we ought: but the Spirit itself maketh intercession for us with groanings which cannot be uttered" (Rom. 8:26).

We realize that we are energized by the Holy Spirit for prayer; we know what it is to pray in the Spirit; but we do not so often realize that the Holy Spirit Himself prays in us prayers which we cannot utter. When we are born again of God and are indwelt by the Spirit of God, He expresses for us the unutterable.

"He," the Spirit in you, "maketh intercession for the saints according to the will of God" (Rom. 8:27), and God searches your heart not to know what your conscious prayers are, but to find out what is the prayer of the Holy Spirit.

The Spirit of God needs the nature of the believer as a shrine in which to offer His intercession. "Your body is the temple of the Holy Ghost" (1 Cor. 6:19). When Jesus Christ cleansed the temple, He "would not suffer that any man should carry any vessel through the temple." The Spirit of God will not allow you to use your body for your own convenience. Jesus ruthlessly cast out all them that sold and bought in the temple, and said—"My house shall be called the house of prayer; but ye have made it a den of thieves" (Luke 19:46).

Have we recognized that our body is the temple of the Holy Ghost? If so, we must be careful to keep it undefiled for Him. We have to remember that our conscious life, though it is only a tiny bit of our personality, is to be regarded by us as a shrine of the Holy Ghost. He will look after the unconscious part that we know nothing of; but we must see that we guard the conscious part for which we are responsible.

My Utmost for His Highest

Devotion to the Father

St. Augustine
How Much God Has Loved Us

How much Thou hast loved us, O good Father, Who hast spared not even Thine own Son, but delivered Him up for us wicked men! (see Rom. 8:31-32). How Thou hast loved us, for whom he who thought it not robbery to be equal with Thee became obedient even unto the death of the Cross (see Phil. 2:6,8). He who alone was free among the dead, having power to lay down His life and power to take it up again (John 10:18); for us He was to Thee both Victor and Victim, and Victor became Victim: for us He was to Thee both Priest and Sacrifice, and Priest because Sacrifice; turning us from slaves into Thy sons, by being Thy Son and becoming a slave. Rightly is my hope strong in Him, who sits at Thy right hand and intercedes for us; otherwise I should despair. For many and great are my infirmities, many and great; but Thy medicine is of more power. We might well have thought Thy Word remote from union with man and so have despaired of ourselves, if It had not been "made flesh and dwelt among us" (John 1:14).

Terrified by my sins and the mass of my misery, I had pondered in my heart and thought of flight to the desert; but Thou didst forbid me and strengthen me, saying: And Christ died for all: that they also who live, may now not live to themselves but with Him who died for them (see 2 Cor. 5:15). See, Lord, I cast my care upon Thee, that I may live: and I will consider the wondrous things of Thy law (see Ps. 119:18). Thou knowest my unskillfulness and my infirmity: teach me and heal me. He Thy only One, in whom are hidden all the treasures of wisdom and knowledge, has redeemed me with His blood. Let not the proud speak evil of me (see Ps. 119:22), for I think upon the price of my redemption, I eat it and drink it and give it to others to eat and drink; and being poor I desire to be filled with it among those that eat and are filled: "and they shall praise the Lord that seek Him" (Ps. 22:26).

Confessions, Book 10

Devotion to Jesus

William of St. Thierry
The End of Prayer Is Love

Lord, you have led me astray, and I have followed your leading; you were the stronger, and you have prevailed. I heard you say: "Come unto me, all you who labor and are heavy laden, and I will refresh you" (Matt. 11:28). I came to you, I trusted in your word, and in what way have you refreshed me? I was not laboring before, but I am laboring now and ready to drop with the toil! I was not burdened formerly, but now I am worn out beneath my load. You also said: "My yoke is pleasant and my burden light" (Matt. 11:30). Where is that pleasantness? Where is that lightness? Already I grow weary of the yoke, already I am fainting beneath the burden. I have looked all round, and there is no one to help me; and I have sought, but there is nobody to give me aid. Lord, what does this mean? Have mercy on me, for I am weak. Where are your mercies of old? Our fathers, who preceded us along this road, did they possess the earth by their own sword? Was it their own arm that saved them? Most surely it was not; it was your arm and the light of your countenance. Why was that so? Because they were found pleasing in your sight. O you who command the saving of Jacob, you are my king and God. What, then, is it in me that has displeased you, Lord? Why do you not judge your servant? You said, with reference to the homage of the sinful woman: "She has done what she could" (Mark 14:8). Have I not also done all that I could? Indeed it seems to me that I have done more than I thought I had the power to do!

The Lord: My son, do not despise your father's chastening; do not grow weary when you are reproved by him; for "whom the Lord loves he chastens and scourges every son whom he receives" (Heb. 12:6). Indeed what son is there whom his father does not correct? If you are beyond chastening, you are not a son. I have not led you astray, my son; I have led you sweetly on until now. That which was said to you, that which was cried to you: "Come unto me," has been cried aloud to all; but all do not receive the grace to come. To you it has been given so to do in preference to many great ones who are rich in their own eyes. Have I committed sin in doing good to you? You complain that I do not refresh you. If I had not refreshed you, you would have fainted away. You groan beneath my yoke and are weary of my burden. The thing that makes the sweetness of my yoke, the lightness of my burden, is charity. If you had charity, then you would feel that sweetness. Your flesh would not labor, if it loved you; or, if it did, charity would mitigate the toil. You cannot bear my burden and my yoke alone; but if you have charity along with you to share the yoke and the burden you will be surprised to find how sweet they are.

Response. Lord, that is what I said. I have done what I could. The thing that seems to have been given into my own power, namely, my wretched body and feeble limbs, I have handed over to your service. Had it been also in my power to have charity, I should have reached perfection long ago. If you do not bestow it then I have not got it; and if I may not have it, I cannot go on. You know, you see how little I can do. Take of that little whatever you will, and give me that full and perfect charity.

The Lord: Am I then to supply your deficiencies and also give you the charity for which you ask? But, my son, you must accept my chastening. There is no going except by the Way. If you do not forsake this road, then you will reach your goal. I myself go before you, and you must follow as you see me go before. I endured and labored and you must labor too. I suffered many things, it behooves you too to suffer some. Obedience is the way to charity, and you will get there if you keep to it. But you must recognize how great a thing is charity, and worthy to be bought at a high price. For God is charity; when you reach that you will labor no more....

Response.... As to my body, Lord, I do not know what to ask; you know what is good for me concerning it. If it so please you, let it be strong and healthy; and equally, if you so will, let it be weak and sick. And when it is your will that it should die, then let it die, provided only that the spirit finds salvation in your day. For this one thing only do I implore your mercy in regard to my body—namely, that you would teach me how to rule and guard it, while I remain alive, that I may yield to none of its irrational desires, and yet refuse it nothing that it really needs.

The end of the law is charity, and that is the end of my prayer. O you who have willed to be called charity, give me charity, that I may love you more than I love myself; not caring at all what I do with myself, so long as I am doing what is pleasing in your sight. Grant me, O Father—though I dare not always call myself your child—grant me at least to be your faithful little servant and the sheep of your pasture. Speak to your servant's heart sometimes, O Lord, so that your consolations may give joy to my soul. And teach me to speak to you often in prayer. Take to yourself all my poverty and need, O Lord, my God and Father. Have pity on my weakness, you who are my strength. And may it be to your great glory that my feebleness continues to serve you. Amen.

Meditation 13

Devotion to the Holy Spirit

Cardinal Stephen Langton,
Archbishop of Canterbury
Come, Holy Spirit, come!
And from your celestial home
Shed a ray of light divine!

Come, Father of the poor!
Come, source of all our store!
Come, within our bosoms shine!

You, of comforters the best;
You, the soul's most welcome guest;
Sweet refreshment here below;

In our labor, rest most sweet;
Grateful coolness in the heat;
Solace in the midst of woe.

O most blessed Light divine,
Shine within these hearts of yours,
And our inmost being fill!

Where you are not, man has naught,
Nothing good in deed or thought,
Nothing free from taint of ill.

Heal our wounds, our strength renew;
On our dryness pour your dew;
Wash the stains of guilt away:

Bend the stubborn heart and will;
Melt the frozen, warm the chill;
Guide the steps that go astray.

On the faithful, who adore
And confess you, evermore
In your sev'nfold gift descend;

Give them virtue's sure reward;
Give them your salvation, Lord;
Give them joys that never end. Amen. Alleluia.

Veni Sancte Spiritus

Devotion to the Saints

St. Augustine
Being Perfected in Martyrdom

Perfection of some kind is to be found in this life, and the martyrs achieved it. That's why, as the faithful know, Church custom has it that at the place where the names of the martyrs are recited at God's altar, we don't pray for them, while we do pray for the other departed brothers and sisters who are remembered there. It is insulting, I mean, to pray for martyrs, to whose prayers we ought rather to commend ourselves. They have tackled sin, after all, to the point of shedding their blood. To people on the other hand, who were still imperfect and yet partly justified, the apostle says in his letter to the Hebrews, "For you have not yet fought to the point of shedding your blood, as you struggle against sin" (Heb 12:4). So if they hadn't yet shed their blood, there can be no doubt that others had. Who had got to the point of shedding their blood? The holy martyrs, of course.

Sermon 159

St. John of Damascus
The Army of Christ

We depict Christ as our King and Lord, then, and do not strip Him of His army. For the saints are the Lord's army. If the earthly emperor wishes to deprive the Lord of His army, let him also dismiss his own troops. If he wishes in his tyranny to refuse due honor to these valiant conquerors of evil, let him also cast aside his own purple. For if the saints are heirs of God and co-heirs with Christ, they will also share in the divine glory and dominion. If they have partaken of Christ's sufferings and are His friends, shall they not receive a share of glory from the Church on earth? "No longer do I call you servants," God says, "but I have called you friends" (John 15:15). Shall we strip them of the glory given them by the Church?... I bow before the images of Christ, the incarnate God; of our Lady, the Theotokos and Mother of the Son of God; and of the saints, who are God's friends. In struggling against evil, they have shed their blood; they have imitated Christ who shed His Blood for them by shedding their blood for Him. I make a written record of the prowess and sufferings of those who have walked in His footsteps, that I may be sanctified, and be set on fire to imitate them zealously. St. Basil says, "The honor given to the image is transferred to its prototype."...

God, who alone is holy, rests in holy places: that is, the Theotokos (the Mother of God), and all the saints. These are they who have become likenesses of God as far as is possible, since they have chosen to cooperate with divine election. Therefore God dwells in them. They are truly called gods, not by nature, but by adoption, just as red-hot iron is called fiery, not by its nature, but because it participates in the action of the fire. He says, "You shall be holy, for I the Lord your God am holy" (Lev. 19:2). First, then, is the election to holiness. Then, once the right choice has been made, God helps those who make it to increase in goodness, for He says, "I will make my abode among you" (Lev. 26:11). We are God's temple and the Spirit of God dwells in us (1 Cor. 3:16). "He gave them authority over unclean spirits, to cast them out, and to heal every disease and infirmity," (Mt. 10:1) and, "he who believes in Me will also do the works that I do: and greater works than these will he do" (John 14:12). And again, "'As I live,' says the Lord, 'those who honor Me, I will honor'" (see 1 Sam. 2:30) and, "provided we suffer with Him in order that we may also be glorified with Him" (Rom. 8:17) and, "God has taken His place in the divine council; in the midst of the gods He holds judgment" (Ps. 82:1).

Therefore, since they are truly gods, not by nature, but because they partake of the divine nature, they are to be venerated, not because they deserve it on their own account, but because they bear in themselves Him who is by nature worshipful. We do not back away and refuse to touch red-hot iron because of the nature of iron, but because it has partaken of what is hot by nature. The saints are to be venerated because God has glorified them, and through Him they have become fearful to the enemy, and are benefactors for the faithful. They are not gods and benefactors by their own nature, but because they were loving servants and ministers of God, they have been endowed with boldness before Him. Therefore we venerate them, because the king is given honor through the worship given to his beloved servants. They are obedient servants and favored friends, but they are not the King Himself. When someone prays with faith, offering his petition in the name of such a favored friend, the King receives it, through the intercession of the faithful servant, because He accepts the honor and faith which the petitioner has shown to His servant. Thus, those who approach God through the apostles enjoyed healing, for the shadow of the apostles, or even handkerchiefs and aprons touched to them, gushed with cures (Acts 5:15).

On the Divine Images

Devotion Leads to a Christian Life

Christoph Blumhardt
We Too Are Called to Be Saints
This is the Lord's proclamation to earth's farthest bounds: "Tell the people of Zion that their salvation is coming. The Lord brings his reward with him, and his recompense accompanies him" (Isa. 62:11).

Lord our God, we thank you that we may go to meet you with open hearts, with jubilant faith, and with this joyful shout, "God's salvation is coming! Through Jesus Christ day is dawning on earth for all nations." Stay with us and help us. Send us your Spirit to strengthen us, especially in times of trouble. Let all nations come before you. Let us tell all peoples, "Be comforted. The salvation of our God, who is also your God, is coming. In this salvation we will rejoice together forevermore to the glory of our God." Amen.

Lift Thine Eyes

Prayer of an English Puritan
Teach Me to Live a Holy Life
O God of the open ear,
Teach me to live by prayer as well as by providence,
for myself; soul, body, children, family, church;
Give me a heart frameable to thy will;
so might I live in prayer,
and honor thee,
being kept from evil, known and unknown.
Help me to see the sin that accompanies all I do,
and the good I can distil from everything.

Let me know that the work of prayer is to bring my will to thine,
and that without this it is folly to pray;
When I try to bring thy will to mine it is to command Christ,
to be above him, and wiser than he:
this is my sin and pride.
I can only succeed when I pray
according to thy precept and promise,
and to be done with as it pleases thee,
according to thy sovereign will.
When thou commandest me to pray for pardon, peace, brokenness,
it is because thou wilt give me the thing promised,
for thy glory, as well as for my good.
Help me not only to desire small things
but with holy boldness to desire great things
for thy people, for myself,
that they and I might live to show thy glory.
Teach me that it is wisdom for me to pray for all I have,
out of love, willingly, not of necessity;
that I may come to thee at any time,
to lay open my needs acceptably to thee;
that my great sin lies in my not keeping the savor of thy ways;
that the remembrance of this truth is one way
to the sense of thy presence;
that there is no wrath like the wrath of being governed
by my own lusts for my own ends.

The Valley of Vision

Thomas Merton
With Fear and Trembling
Let us frankly recognize the true import and the true challenge of the
Christian message. The whole Gospel kerygma becomes impertinent and
laughable if there is an easy answer to everything in a few external gestures
and pious intentions. Christianity is a religion for men who are aware that
there is a deep wound, a fissure of sin that strikes down to the very heart
of man's being. They have tasted the sickness that is present in the inmost

heart of man estranged from his God by guilt, suspicion and covert hatred. If that sickness is an illusion, then there is no need for the Cross, the sacraments and the Church. If the Marxists are right in diagnosing this human dread as the expression of guilt and inner dishonesty of an alienated class, then there is no need to preach Christ anymore, and there is no need either of liturgy or of meditation. History has yet to show the Marxists are right in this matter however, since by advancing on their own crudely optimistic assumptions they have unleashed a greater evil and a more deadly falsity in man's murderous heart than anyone except the Nazis. And the Nazis, in their turn, borrowed from Nietzsche a similar false diagnosis of the Christian's "fear of the Lord." It is nevertheless true that the spirit of individualism, associated with the culture and economy of the West in the Modern Age, has had a disastrous effect on the validity of Christian prayer. But what is meant by individualism in the life of prayer?

The interior life of the individualist is precisely the kind of life that closes in on itself without dread, and rests in itself with more or less permanent satisfaction. It is to some extent immune to dread, and is able to take the inevitable constrictions and lesions of an inner life complacently enough, spiriting them away with devotional formulas. Individualism in prayer is content precisely with the petty consolations of devotionalism and sentimentality. But more than that, individualism resists the summons to communal witness and collective human response to God. It shuts itself up and hardens itself against everything that would draw it out of itself. It refuses to participate in what is not immediately pleasing to its limited devotional tastes here and now. It remains centered and fixed upon a particular form of consolation which is either totally intimate or at best semi-private, and prefers this to everything else precisely because it need not and cannot be shared.

The purpose of this fixation (which can be maintained with a stubborn will and a minimum of faith) is to produce reassurance, a sense of spiritual identity, an imaginary fulfillment, and perhaps even an excuse for evading the realities of life.

It is unfortunately all too true that bogus interiority has saved face for pious men and women who were thus preserved from admitting their total nonentity. They have imagined that they were capable of love just because they were capable of devout sentiment. One aspect of this convenient spiritual disease is its total insistence on ideals and intentions, in complete divorce from reality, from act, and from social commitment. Whatever one interiorly desires, whatever one dreams, whatever one imagines: that is the beautiful, the godly and the true. Pretty thoughts are enough. They substitute for everything else, including charity, including life itself.

It is precisely the function of dread to break down this glass house of false interiority and to deliver man from it. It is dread, and dread alone, that drives a man out of this private sanctuary in which his solitude becomes horrible to himself without God. But without dread, without the disquieting capacity to see and to repudiate the idolatry of devout ideas and imaginings, man would remain content with himself and with his "inner life" in meditation, in liturgy or in both. Without dread the Christian cannot be delivered from the smug self-assurance of the devout ones who know all the answers in advance, who possess all the clichés of the inner life and can defend themselves with infallible ritual forms against every risk and every demand of dialogue with human need and human desperation.

Contemplative Prayer

EPILOGUE

Our sample of experiences of many travelers on the road to what St. Augustine calls "the interior Sinai" comes to an end. There is a sense of incompleteness because already dozens of other selections come to mind, and, if these were included, they would lead to thousands more. We hope that you have found most of the passages enlightening and that some have resonated with you at your present stage on the spiritual journey. Don't be surprised if some of what you passed over as curious or uninteresting may in the future express what you will be experiencing then.

We all take the same journey and must pass through the same stages and ways. But like travelers across a continent, we have different experiences of the same reality. Some find the Great Plains exhilarating; others find them dull and dreary. Some find mountain climbing a great adventure; others are frightened and can't wait to get back to the plains. Mishaps, wrong turns, dangers, and even fatal mistakes can occur at almost any phase of the journey. Some are doing quite well at the beginning; others who have traveled for a long time are in trouble and may even turn back.

Having reviewed the bits and pieces of the adventures of so many different people along the way, from cloistered nuns to a repentant murderer awaiting execution, we ask the question: Are there some general rules or guiding principles that emerge? There must be something to be learned. Here are a few that occur to us.

Be led by God and His Providence. In no aspect of human endeavor is it more necessary to grasp the meaning of the psalmist, "The Lord is my shepherd" (Ps. 23:1).

Model your life on Christ. There is a way in your own individual life to be a follower of Christ. Usually we pick and choose some aspect of the life of Christ to guide us, and then we leave out other things that we find frightening or too demanding. Most of us avoid the Cross, and yet it is the central mystery and message of Jesus of Nazareth. By love He transformed the worst sin ever committed into the act that redeemed the world.

Learn from failure and keep going. On this journey we all stumble and fall. But like the apostles, we must put our pride in our pocket and get up, ask forgiveness, and move right along.

Realize more and more that the spiritual life is essentially the work of the Holy Spirit. Our participation, although it may appear to be a very active struggle to do good—to "press on," in the words of St. Paul—is ultimately a cooperation with the Holy Spirit. Our essential task is not to do things for God, but rather not to resist God's trying to do good things for us. Holiness is His work. Our task is to avoid resisting Him. Many people waste a great deal of time and effort doing what they want on the spiritual road instead of letting the Holy Spirit lead: they must do this, they must be there, they must learn some other things. This is not really following Christ; it is walking beside Him and making suggestions.

Avoid as much as possible spiritual self-indulgence. Human beings have a natural religious sense, often linked with an appreciation of inner beauty or good works. This natural religiosity is as necessary as eating and drinking, and without it our spiritual lives can become anemic. But natural religion is not faith, hope, and charity. The Gospels are very clear that we "will weep and lament, but the world rejoice" (Jn. 16:20) and that "there will not be left one stone upon another" (Mk. 13:2). Without a natural sense of religion we become dark and inhuman fanatics, like the inquisitors or the witch-hunters. But if this religious sense is overindulged, we become gnostics and religious dilettantes. This is the great danger of the so-called New Age. The spiritual life is a work of God's grace, and although grace uses nature, it is only by God's mercy and unmerited love that we grow at all.

Work for humility. The ultimate enemy to be defeated on the spiritual journey is pride. This negative element is so pervasive that the spiritual life can be accurately described simply as the process of overcoming pride and self-love. There is such a thing as legitimate pride and self-regard, but these often conceal a self-love that says, "I will not serve."

Imitate God in His mercy, forgiveness, and compassion. Along with the fact that, in the Sermon on the Mount, Christ makes mercy, forgiveness, and generosity the essential criteria of discipleship (see Mt. 5-7; see also Lk. 6:20-49), these qualities are the best and most rewarding ways to overcome self. The admonitions of St. Francis cited in his famous prayer—"Make me an instrument of your peace..."—are an excellent reminder of what we really need to be doing on our spiritual journey.

Remember that the road to God begins right here and now. The saying that the medieval mystics placed in the mouth of God is very helpful to keep in mind: "Where I find you is where I will call you." There is no moment in any human life, even a moment of abominable sin, when God cannot call the individual. Remember the centurion at Calvary who supervised the Crucifixion and afterwards said, "Truly this man was the Son of God!" (Mk. 15:39).

Use the spiritual gifts God gives you. This book has been directed to Christians of all denominations. Christ has given us all His Baptism. Some have additional sacraments, which have proved to be immensely helpful. Some have a special love for and familiarity with Sacred Scripture. All have traditions of prayer, devotion, and charity, enriched by the efforts of saintly and very dedicated Christians of the past. All have the example of holy people who have gone before us. Some may have found the invocation of the saints, beginning with the Mother of Christ, very helpful; others may have no experience with this at all. Whatever we have been given, we should make use of it with thankfulness to God.

Listen every day to the call to holiness. The spiritual writers tell us that God calls all to holiness. We cannot know or judge how He calls others, but we are obliged to help them by encouragement and good example as best and as often as we can. But individually we are called, and at the end of our lives we shall certainly render an account of our response. "You will seek me and find me; when you seek me with all your heart, I will be found by you, says the Lord" (Jer. 29:13-14). Settle for nothing less. And when you have done all you can, when you have surrendered everything that has been asked of you, when you have gone on in darkness and fear, when you have used up every drop of energy, join the saints in their prayer at the end of the journey, "Lamb of God, who takes away the sins of the world, have mercy on us."

ACKNOWLEDGMENTS

Excerpts from the following books are gratefully acknowledged. An effort has been made to contact holders of copyright. In any case in which this effort has not succeeded, the copyright holder is asked to contact the publisher.

Excerpt from Sir Arthur Eddington, *The Nature of the Physical World* (New York: Macmillan Co., 1928, 1935).

Excerpt from Abraham Isaac Kook in Herbert Weiner, *9-1/2 Mystics: The Kabbala Today* (New York: Holt, Rinehart and Winston, 1969).

Excerpt from William Law, *An Appeal to All Who Doubt,* in Robert Llewelyn and Edward Moss, editors, *Fire from the Heart: Daily Readings with William Law* (London: Darton, Longman and Todd, 1986).

Excerpts from the writings of Theophan the Recluse from Igumen Chariton of Valamo, compiler, *The Art of Prayer,* E. Kadloubovsky and Elizabeth M. Palmer, translators (London: Faber & Faber Ltd., 1966); used with permission.

Excerpt from Nicholas of Cusa from *The Vision of God,* Emma Gurney Salter, translator, © E.P. Dutton & Co, 1928; used by permission of J.M. Dent & Sons Ltd.; all rights reserved.

Excerpts from Augustine, *The Confessions,* Frank J. Sheed, translator (Sheed and Ward, 1943); reprint by permission of Hackett Publishing Company, Inc.; all rights reserved.

Excerpt from *The Three Ages of the Interior Life* by Reginald Garrigou-Lagrange, M. Timothea Doyle, O.P., translator, Rockford, IL: Tan Books and Publishers. Reprinted with permission; all rights reserved.

Excerpts from *Markings,* by Dag Hammarskjöld, translated by Leif Sjöberg and W.H. Auden. Translation copyright © 1994 by Alfred A. Knopf Inc. and Faber & Faber Ltd. Reprinted by permission of Alfred A. Knopf Inc., and Faber & Faber Ltd.

Excerpts from Franca Zamboni, *Teresa of Calcutta: A Pencil in God's Hand,* translated by Jordan Aumann, O.P., Staten Island: Alba House. Reprinted by permission of Alba House; all rights reserved.

Excerpts from Gerald Heard, *The Creed of Christ* (New York: Harper and Row, 1940); © Gerald Heard; all rights reserved.

Excerpt from Rudolph Schnackenburg, *The Moral Teaching of the New Testament,* J. Holland-Smith and W.J. O'Hara, translators, (London: Burns & Oates, 1965). Reprinted by permission of Burns & Oates; all rights reserved.

Excerpts from John Henry Newman from Erich Przywara, S.J., editor, *The Heart of Newman* (London: Sheed and Ward, 1930; reprinted by Ignatius Press, San Francisco 1997).

Excerpts from Cajetan Mary da Bergamo, *Humility of Heart,* Cardinal Herbert Vaughan, translator, (Westminster, MD: Newman Bookshop, 1944; England, 1903); reprinted by Tan Books, Rockford, IL, 1978.

Excerpt from St. Francis de Sales, *The Introduction to the Devout Life,* from *The Liturgy of the Hours* © 1974, International Committee on English in the Liturgy, Inc.; all rights reserved.

Gabriel of St. Mary Magdalen, O.C.D., *Divine Intimacy: Meditations on the Interior Life for Every Day of the Liturgical Year,* Discalced Carmelite Nuns of Boston, translators (Rockford, Ill.: Tan Books and Publishers, Inc.). All rights reserved.

Excerpt from Saint Ephrem, *Hymns on Paradise*, Sebastian Brock, translator, © Sebastian Brock (Crestwood, N.Y.: St. Vladimir's Seminary Press, 1990), page 90.

Excerpts from Christoph Blumhardt, *Lift Thine Eyes: Evening Prayers for Every Day of the Year* (Ulster Park, N.Y.: The Plough Publishing Co., 1998).

Excerpt from *Enfolded in Love*, edited by Robert Llewelyn, published and © 1980, 1994, and 1999 by Darton, Longman and Todd Ltd, and used by permission of the publishers. Excerpts from *Enfolded in Love: Daily Readings with Julian of Norwich*, members of the Julian shrine, translators. Reprinted with permission of Templegate Publishers; all rights reserved.

Excerpts from Dietrich von Hildebrand, *Transformation in Christ*, © 1948, 1976 Dietrich von Hildebrand; 1990 Alice von Hildebrand. Reprinted with the permission of Sophia Institute Press, Box 5284, Manchester, NH 03108; 1-800-888-9344.

Excerpt from C.S. Lewis, *The Problem of Pain*, © C.S. Lewis. Reprinted by permission of Harper-Collins Publishers Ltd, London. All rights reserved.

Excerpt from Fulton J. Sheen, *The Eternal Galilean* (Staten Island, N.Y.: Alba House, 1997 [1934]). Reprinted by permission of Alba House; all rights reserved.

Excerpt from *The Royal Way of the Cross* by François de Salignac de la Mothe-Fénelon, © 1982. Edited by Hal M. Helms. Used by permission of Paraclete Press.

Excerpt from *Abandonment to Divine Providence* by Jean-Pierre de Caussade. © 1975 by John Beevers. Used by permission of Doubleday, a division of Random House, Inc.

Benedict J. Groeschel, C.F.R., *A Priest Forever: The Life of Father Eugene Hamilton* (Huntington, Ind.: Our Sunday Visitor Press, 1998).

Excerpts from *The Heart of Compassion: Daily Readings with St. Isaac of Syria,* Sebastian Brock, translator, A.M. Allchin, editor. Reprinted with permission of Templegate Publishers; all rights reserved.

Excerpt from Romano Guardini, *Prayers from Theology,* Richard Newnham, translator (New York: Herder & Herder, 1959).

Excerpts from Fyodor Dostoyevsky, *The Brothers Karamazov,* Constance Garnett, translator (New York: Random House, 1950 [1919]).

Excerpt from Søren Kierkegaard from Robert van de Weyer, editor, *Daily Readings with Søren Kierkegaard* (Springfield, Ill.: Templegate Publishers).

Excerpts from Catherine de Hueck Doherty, *O Jesus: Prayers from the Diaries of Catherine de Hueck Doherty* (Combermere, Ontario: Madonna House Publications, 1996).

Excerpt from James Monti, *The King's Good Servant but God's First* (San Francisco: Ignatius Press, 1997).

Excerpt from Terence Cooke from John J. Reardon, editor, *This Grace Filled Moment* (New York: Rosemont Press, 1984).

Excerpt from Christoph Blumhardt, *Christoph Blumhardt and His Message,* R. Lejeune, editor (Rifton, N.Y.: The Plough Publishing House, 1963); used with permission of the Plough Publishing House

Dom Jean-Baptiste Chautard, O.C.S.O., *The Soul of the Apostolate,* Thomas Merton, translator and editor (Trappist, KY: The Abbey of Gethsemani, 1946); reprinted with permission of the Merton Legacy Trust.

Excerpt from *The Sermons of St. Francis de Sales for Lent,* volume 3, Nuns of the Visitation, translators, Lewis S. Fiorelli, O.S.F.S., editor (Rockford, Ill.: Tan Books and Publishers, 1987); reprinted with permission; all rights reserved.

Excerpts from Maximilian Kolbe from Patricia Treece, *A Man for Others: Maximilian Kolbe, Saint of Auschwitz* (Huntington, Indiana: Our Sunday Visitor, 1982).

Excerpt from Dom Helder Camara, *The Conversions of a Bishop: An Interview with José de Broucker,* Hilary Davies, translator (London: Collins, 1979); *Les Conversions d'un Evéque* (Paris: Editions du Seuil, 1977).

Excerpt from John Henry Newman, in Meriol Trevor, editor, *Meditations and Devotions* (Wheathampstead, England: Anthony Clarke Books, 1964).

Excerpt from *Francis de Sales, Jane de Chantal: Letters of Spiritual Direction,* translated by Péronne Marie Thibert, V.H.M. © 1988 by Péronne Marie Thibert, V.H.M., Wendy M. Wright, and Joseph F. Power, O.S.F.S. Used by permission of Paulist Press, Inc.

Excerpt from Evelyn Underhill, *The Essentials of Mysticism and Other Essays* (New York: E.P. Dutton and Co., 1960 [1920]).

Excerpt from Josef Pieper, *The Silence of St. Thomas,* Daniel O'Connor, translator (London: Faber & Faber Ltd., 1957); Kosel Verlag, Munich, Germany.

Excerpt from *Sit, Walk, Stand* by Watchman Nee, © 1957 by Angus I. Kinnear. First published by Gospel Literature Service, India. American edition published in 1977 by Tyndale House Publishers, Inc. Used by permission of Kingsway Publications, Ltd., Sussex, England, and Tyndale House Publishers; all rights reserved.

Excerpts from Alban Goodier, S.J., *An Introduction to the Study of Ascetical and Mystical Theology: The Substance of Seventeen Lectures Given at Heythrop College, Chipping Norton, Oxfordshire* (Milwaukee: The Bruce Publishing Co., 1938).

José de Vinck, *Revelations of the Women Mystics* (Staten Island, N.Y.: Alba House, 1985).

Excerpts from *Bonaventure: The Soul's Journey into God; The Tree of Life; The Life of St. Francis,* translation and introduction by Ewert Cousins © 1978 Paulist Press, Inc. Used by permission of Paulist Press, Inc.

Excerpt from Jacques Fesch, *Light over the Scaffold and Cell 18,* edited and presented by Augustin-Michel Lemonnier and translated by Sister Mary Thomas Noble, O.P., Staten Island: Alba House, 1996, pages 107–09. Reprinted by permission of Alba House; all rights reserved.

Excerpt from C.S. Lewis, *Christian Behaviour* (New York: Macmillan Co., 1943).

Excerpt from Gordon Allport, *The Individual and His Religion: A Psychological Interpretation* (New York: Macmillan Co., 1950).

Eberhard Arnold, *The Experience of God and His Peace: Volume 3 of Inner Land* (Rifton, N.Y.: The Plough Publishing House, 1975) used with permission of the Plough Publishing House.

Excerpt from *Beginning to Pray* by Anthony Bloom © Archbishop Anthony Bloom. Used by permission of Paulist Press, Inc.

André Frossard, *I Have Met Him: God Exists,* Marjorie Villiers, translator (New York: Herder & Herder, 1971); *Dieu existe, je l'ai rencontré* (Paris: Libraire Arthème Fayard, 1969).

Excerpts from *My Utmost for His Highest* by Oswald Chambers. © 1935 by Dodd Mead & Co., renewed © 1963 by the Oswald Chambers Publications Assn. Ltd., used by permission of Discovery House Publishers, Box 3566, Grand Rapids, MI 49501, and of the Oswald Chambers Publications Association Ltd., United Kingdom. All rights reserved.

Excerpt from Clement of Alexandria in *Alexandrian Christianity,* The Library of Christian Classics, Volume II, J.E.L. Oulton and Henry Chadwick, translators (Philadelphia: The Westminster Press, 1954, and London: SCM Press, 1954).

Excerpt from Tertullian from *Tertullian: Treatises on Marriage and Remarriage,* translated and annotated by William P. LeSaint, S.J., S.T.D. © 1951 by the Rev. Johannes Quasten and the Rev. Joseph C. Plumpe. Used by permission of Paulist Press, Inc.

Excerpt from John Chrysostom, *On Marriage and Family Life,* Catharine P. Roth, translator, © St. Vladimir's Seminary Press, 1986, pages 61-62; reprinted with permission of St. Vladimir's Seminary Press, 575 Scarsdale Road, Crestwood, NY 10707; all rights reserved.

Excerpt from Dietrich von Hildebrand, *Marriage,* © 1984, 1991 Alice von Hildebrand. Reprinted with the permission of Sophia Institute Press, Box 5284, Manchester, NH 03108; 1-800-888-9344.

Excerpt from Jacques LeClercq, *Marriage: A Great Sacrament,* The Earl of Wicklow, translator (London: Burns Oates and Washbourne Ltd, 1951); reprinted by permission of Burns & Oates; all rights reserved.

Excerpt from Frank J. Sheed, *Marriage and the Family* (New York: Sheed and Ward).

Excerpt from Alexander Schmemann, *For the Life of the World,* © St. Vladimir's Seminary Press, 1973, pages 34–35. Reprinted with permission of St. Vladimir's Seminary Press, 575 Scarsdale Road, Crestwood, NY 10707; all rights reserved.

Excerpt from *The Works of Saint Augustine: A Translation for the 21st Century,* III/5, Edmund Hill, O.P., translator (New Rochelle, N.Y.: New City Press, 1992). Reprinted with permission of the Augustinian Heritage Institute; all rights reserved.

Excerpts from John of Damascus, *On the Divine Images,* David Anderson, translator, © St. Vladimir's Seminary Press, 1980, pages 28–29, 84–85. Reprinted with permission of St. Vladimir's Seminary Press, 575 Scarsdale Road, Crestwood, NY 10707; all rights reserved.

Excerpt from Thomas Merton, *The Climate of Monastic Prayer* (Spencer, MA: Cistercian Publications, 1969), pp. 144-46. Also published as *Contemplative Prayer* (Garden City, N.Y.: Doubleday, 1968) reprinted by permission of Cistercian Publications, Western Michigan University, Kalamazoo, MI 49008; all rights reserved.